DISCARDED

JOHN COLET AND MARSILIO FICINO

Oxford University Press, Amen House, London E.C.4
GLASGOW NEW YORK TORONTO MELBOURNE WELLINGTON
BOMBAY CALCUTTA MADRAS KARACHI LAHORE DACCA
CAPE TOWN SALISBURY NAIROBI IBADAN ACCRA
KUALA LUMPUR HONG KONG

JOHN COLET
From the bust in St. Paul's School, London

MARSILIO FICINO
From the bust by Antonio de Piero Ferrucci in the
Cathedral at Florence, 1521–2

JOHN COLET
AND MARSILIO FICINO

BY

SEARS JAYNE

OXFORD UNIVERSITY PRESS
1963

© *Oxford University Press* 1963

PRINTED IN GREAT BRITAIN AT
THE UNIVERSITY PRESS
ABERDEEN

FOR

NEIL KER

PREFACE

The existence of the manuscript materials which are the subject of this study was first pointed out to me by Mr. Neil Ker, Librarian of Magdalen College, and Reader in Palaeography at Oxford; in gratitude for this and many other intellectual debts to Mr. Ker over a period of ten years I have dedicated the work to him. The materials themselves are now in the keeping of the Warden and Fellows of All Souls College, Oxford, who have generously given me permission to publish this part of their treasure. In preparing the materials for publication I have been much assisted by Mr. J. B. Trapp, of the Warburg Institute, and Mr. A. E. Wardman, of the University of Reading. The details of their assistance are explained in the Introduction, but I should like to express here my gratitude for their essentially collaborative assistance with the text and translation.

Although the project began and ended in England, it owes its existence mainly to American agencies for the encouragement of research. The work was begun during a year's study in England in 1954–5, under the auspices of the Fulbright Program and the Guggenheim Foundation. It was sustained for three years by generous assistance from the Research Committees of the University of Virginia and the Claremont Graduate School. Arrangements for publication were made by The Renaissance Society of America; to the editorial committee and officers of that Society, especially Mr. W. G. Constable, President, and Professor Josephine W. Bennett, Secretary, I am indebted for generous encouragement as well as searching criticism. Mr. John Zeigel and Dennis Higgins have assisted greatly with the index.

Like all students of Ficino, but much more than most, I am indebted to the amazing philosophical, linguistic, and palaeographical achievements of Professor Paul O. Kristeller. Prodigal of his time, and untouched by professional pettiness, Professor Kristeller is no less impressive in his generosity than in his scholarly gifts. His selfless devotion to the advancement of learning is an inspiration to all who have called upon him for help.

S. J.

Claremont, California

CONTENTS

FRONTISPIECE:

ABOVE. John Colet, from the bust in St. Paul's School, London. *Photograph by courtesy of the Warburg Institute, London*

BELOW. Marsilio Ficino, from the bust in the Cathedral at Florence. *Photograph by Alinari*

INTRODUCTION

I.	GENERAL BACKGROUND	3
II.	BIOGRAPHICAL RELATIONS	14
III.	INTELLECTUAL RELATIONS IN GENERAL	38
IV.	THE INTELLECT-WILL PROBLEM	56
V.	CONCLUSION	77

LIST OF ABBREVIATIONS 80

TEXT AND TRANSLATION

I.	CORRESPONDENCE	81
II.	MARGINALIA	84

APPENDIXES

A.	THE IDENTIFICATION OF COLET'S HAND	135
B.	PASSAGES MARKED FOR READING IN FICINO'S TABLE OF CONTENTS	138
C.	PASSAGES UNDERLINED IN FICINO'S TEXT	139
D.	COLET AND FICINO'S 'DE RAPTU PAULI'	146

BIBLIOGRAPHY 149

INDEX 161

INTRODUCTION

I: GENERAL BACKGROUND

(A) *The Circumstances*

LIKE many other figures of the English Renaissance, the Dean of St. Paul's, John Colet (?1467–1519) is a man of whom we write much more than we know. There are eight major biographies of Colet; twentieth-century scholarship alone has produced two critical monographs, a dozen essays, and at least four dissertations.[1] Yet all of these studies use essentially the same materials: the meagre information provided by Erasmus, and the scanty writings of Colet himself.[2]

The testimony of Erasmus, which is limited to his correspondence,[3] has been asked to bear burdens of proof far beyond its slender virtues. As for Colet's own writings, they are notoriously few. At his death in 1519, Colet left one published work,[4] but his contemporaries thought of him as having left nothing at all. 'As for John Colet', said Thomas Harding (1516–72), 'he hath never a worde to shew, for he wrote no workes.'[5] Even in 1876, the industrious biographer, J. H. Lupton, with the considerable help of John Pits, had found only a dozen or so Latin theological tracts in manuscript to add to the few works of Colet then in print.[6]

One wishes that Colet had paid more heed to the shadow of oblivion as it fell across his page one winter night in 1496, when he added to a letter he was

---

[1] See the Bibliography, pp. 149–59.

[2] The only major biographical discoveries about Colet which have been made since 1521 are the following:

(a) A number of biographical details from English records, transcribed by Bishop White Kennett (1660–1728) in B.M. MS. Lansdowne 1030, and first published by Samuel Knight in his biography of Colet in 1724.

(b) A record of Colet's presence in Rome in 1493, first published by W. K. Ferguson in 1934, and since verified by other records in Rome. See p. 17.

(c) A resignation of Colet, first published by William Nelson in 1948. See Bibliography.

[3] The letters of Erasmus which are addressed to, or mention, Colet are listed in section IV of the Bibliography, pp. 149–59.

[4] His convocation sermon of 1511. See Bibliography.

[5] Quoted by John Jewel (1522–71), Bishop of Salisbury; see *DNB* life of Colet.

[6] Lupton prints a list of twenty-eight known works of Colet, including letters, in an appendix to his translation of Colet's *Letters to Radulphus*, trans. J. H. Lupton (London, 1876), pp. 307–14. Lupton's list is based on an earlier list by John Pits in *Relationum historicarum de rebus anglicis tomus unus* (Paris, 1619), i. 692. For known extant works see section I of the Bibliography.

writing the following melancholy postscript: 'When you have read this sheet, please return it to me as I do not keep copies of my letters. Not that they are worth preservation; still, if they are left behind me, they might help to keep alive some recollection of me.'[1]

Fortunately, at All Souls College, Oxford, there has recently been discovered a book which Colet owned and which does 'keep alive some recollection' not only of Colet, but also of Marsilio Ficino. The volume concerned is a copy of the first edition of the *Epistolae* of Ficino, published at Venice in 1495.[2] In addition to the printed text of Ficino, the volume contains, in Colet's own hand, two letters from Ficino to Colet, one letter from Colet to Ficino, and some 5,000 words of Colet's marginal commentary. The All Souls volume thus presents us with one of the few extant detailed commentaries by a Tudor scholar on the work of an Italian humanist, and adds a good deal to the available primary material about John Colet.

The fact that Colet knew the *Epistolae* of Ficino was known as early as 1869, when Lupton discovered a quotation from that book embedded in one of Colet's works.[3] Colet's own copy of the *Epistolae* was known to the Hon. A. F. Egerton in the early years of this century, but was recently 'rediscovered' by Mr. N. R. Ker, who pointed it out in 1952 to Abbé Raymond Marcel of Paris. Abbé Marcel was in Oxford at the time looking for materials in connection with his projected seven-volume edition of the works of Ficino. He was interested in the All Souls volume primarily from the point of view of Ficino scholarship. Since I learned about the volume independently, again from Mr. Ker, in connexion with my work on Colet, Abbé Marcel and I have agreed to divide the spoils, he publishing the Ficino part of the material, and I the Colet part. Abbé Marcel has already published the Latin text of one of the two letters of Ficino in the volume,[4] and will publish the other letter in due time. Meanwhile he has kindly given me permission to publish English translations of the two Ficino letters along with my translations of all the Colet material in the volume. In the following discussion of these materials I shall examine them from the point of view of Colet scholarship only, since Abbé Marcel is dealing with their significance in the work of Ficino.

---

[1] Letter to Richard Kidderminster, Abbot of Winchcombe (in Gloucestershire), trans. in part by J. H. Lupton, *Life of John Colet* (London, 1887), p. 93.
[2] The shelf-mark of the Colet copy at All Souls is h. infra 1.5. For the bibliographical history of the *Epistolae* see P. O. Kristeller, *Supplementum Ficinianum* (Florence, 1937), i, pp. lxvii–lxviii.
[3] Colet's abstract of the *Ecclesiastical Hierarchy* [of the Pseudo-Dionysius], trans. J. H. Lupton (London, 1869), pp. 36–38.
[4] Raymond Marcel, 'Les découvertes d'Erasme en Angleterre', *Humanisme et Renaissance*, xiv (1952), 122.

(B) The Contents of the Volume

Although Ficino's book is entitled *Epistolae*, it is not merely a collection of letters.[1] In its 394 folio pages are included more than a dozen long theological treatises; and most of the hundreds of letters in the volume are actually philosophical and theological essays, with titles, written with publication in mind. Most of the materials in the volume date from the period 1473 to 1494; throughout that period Ficino was the head of the Platonic Academy at Florence,[2] and his letters were characteristically written *ex cathedra*, often in multiple copies to multiple addressees. Many of the letters were, in effect, form letters, giving the 'official' Platonic answers to the questions which Ficino was asked most often; copies of such letters were kept on file and sent as occasion demanded. Many, perhaps most, of the letters in the *Epistolae* volume elaborate upon, explain, or defend passages in Ficino's earlier published works.

The letters and treatises are arranged in twelve books, in roughly chronological order except that Book II consists primarily of theological treatises, grouped together because Ficino thought that works which concerned God should be separated from those which concerned man.[3]

Ficino's *Epistolae* were relatively popular in sixteenth-century England, not only for their subject matter, but also for their form. English library catalogues of the period often list copies of the *Epistolae*.[4] Gabriel Harvey, in his own marginalia,[5] cites from the *Epistolae* the long treatise on the divine madness, a treatise which Colet annotates extensively. William Fulwood also cites Ficino's book as an example of good epistolary form in his own work on the art of letter-writing, *The Enimie of Idlenesse* (1568).[6]

That the All Souls copy of the *Epistolae* was Colet's may be guessed from the fact that one of the letters copied on the flyleaves is addressed to Colet from Ficino, but the palaeographical evidence, reviewed in Appendix A below, makes it clear that all of the manuscript additions to the volume, letters as well

---

[1] For a full account of the composition of the *Epistolae*, see Kristeller, *Supplementum*, i, pp. lxxxvii–cx. On some philosophical aspects of the *Epistolae* see Ettore Galli, *La Morale nelle Lettere di Marsilio Ficino* (Pavia, 1897).

[2] The fullest modern biography of Ficino is Abbé Raymond Marcel's *Marsile Ficin* (Paris, 1958). See also Arnaldo Della Torre, *Storia dell'Accademia Platonica di Firenze* (Florence, 1902). In English see Nesca A. Robb, *Neoplatonism of the Italian Renaissance* (London, 1935) and the brief discussion of the Academy in H. L. Stewart, 'The Platonic Academy of Florence', *Hibbert Journal*, xliii (1945), 226–36.

[3] Kristeller, *Supplementum*, i. xciv.

[4] e.g. J. R. Liddell, 'The Library of Corpus Christi College, Oxford', *Library*, 4th ser., xviii (1938), 385–416.

[5] Ed. G. C. Moore Smith (Stratford-on-Avon, 1913), p. 105.

[6] *STC* 11476.

as marginalia, were written there by Colet, with the following exceptions:
1. Marginal notes transcribed here as items **2–4**,[1] and the first part of **5**.
2. Items **71** and **75**, in a seventeenth-century hand.
3. Item **76**, a short list of logic books, written on a back flyleaf, in a different seventeenth-century hand.

The fact that the letters in the volume are in Colet's own hand is of special interest. Ficino frequently sent presentation copies of his works to his admirers, inscribing in the front a letter to the person addressed; one's first guess about the All Souls volume would have been that it was such a book sent by Ficino to Colet, but that is apparently not the case; all three of the letters on the flyleaves seem to have been copied there by Colet himself, two of them apparently from originals sent him by Ficino, and the third his own draft of a letter sent by him to Ficino. Colet thus seems to have acquired the book independently and to have himself initiated the correspondence, possibly because the published correspondence of Ficino showed him how many relatively unknown people like himself had written to the great scholar and had been given the courtesy of serious replies (cf. especially underlined passages **34** and **35**, App. C below). Once Colet had heard from Ficino, he would naturally have regarded the volume containing Ficino's published correspondence as the proper place to keep the additional Ficino 'letters'. Thus the correspondence itself represents one of Colet's interests in the All Souls volume, but he had other interests in it as well.

These interests were theological; they are shown in three different ways. He has checked on the first page of Ficino's long table of contents the titles of seventeen tracts. He has underlined or marked with marginal brackets thirty-five passages of Ficino's text, scattered throughout the volume. And, finally, he has written extensive marginal comments on at least sixty-eight of Ficino's 'letters', also scattered from beginning to end of the volume. Except for one brief passage in **5** and a short poem in **35**, all of the letters and marginalia in the volume are in Latin.

The titles checked in Ficino's table of contents (see Appendix B) suggest that Colet read the book at least partly for homiletic purposes. For example, he has checked the following chapter titles:

The dignity of the priesthood. (**8**)

Prayers are not to be scorned. (**11**)

---

[1] In order to avoid repeating the word *item* with each reference to a passage in the marginalia, I have adopted the convention of using hereafter the item number alone, in bold face type; by convention also, I refer to the marginalia by item number instead of by page number.

Man without religion is further from salvation than the brute creation. (**14**)

Passages underlined by Colet (see Appendix C) are also characteristically homiletic and moral. For example:

No pleasure really means anything unless one has someone to share it with. (**10**)

Nero was not a human being, but some kind of monster in human skin. (**13**)

We work in order to have leisure, and we wage war in order to live in peace. (**17**)

If you wonder, Dear Cosimo, why Lorenzo should speak at such length when Solomon spoke so briefly, I should reply that Lorenzo was forced to speak at such length *because* Solomon spoke so briefly. The more tightly Solomon tied the knot, the more work it took to untie it. . . . But do not let me be guilty of prolixity myself in the very process of excusing proxility. (**9**)

It is possible, of course, that some of the underlining in the volume may be by hands other than Colet's, but most of the underlining occurs in conjunction with marginalia in Colet's hand and in all likelihood is his own. Thus we are probably justified in seeing as Colet's own the Christian and Platonic interests reflected in underlined passages such as the following:

Paul and Dionysius, the wisest of Christian theologians, say that things invisible, which belong to God, are known through those things which have been done and which are seen in this world. . . . (**8**)

Evils are a necessary part of life. Moreover, as the Platonists say, it is impossible to root out evil altogether. . . . For in combating evil one is not combating flesh and blood, says the apostle Paul, but certain tyrant spirits of the dark air. (**27**)

Colet's marginal notes on the text vary from a mere 'nota' (**18**) to long passages of independent speculation. Many are single words or short phrases designed merely to serve as guides to the contents of the text:

Nature (**38**)

Aristotle (**34**)

Morning dreams (**24**)

The margins are filled with long strings of such key words, names, and phrases picked out of the gray mass of Ficino's text. Colet's characteristic technique of annotation, however, is to reduce Ficino's text to a table or diagram; the scholastic background of both Ficino [1] and Colet lent itself to this technique, and Colet seems to have been particularly addicted to the habit of working everything into a set of triplets, after the manner of the Pseudo-Dionysius. Thus we see Colet writing:

>   supernatural forms: without matter or quantity
>   celestial forms: with quantity, but without matter, and subject to motion
>   natural forms: with quantity and matter. (**42**)

and again:

>   the soul   law
>   the spirit   medicine
>   the body   business (**6**)

or again:

>   reverent to God
>   The righteous man is beautiful in himself
>   kind to others (**25**)

In some places Colet's tables become rather extended. For example, at one place (**41**) he copies out not once but twice Ficino's list of the nine ranks of the angels, and in another (**59**) he copies out, again twice, Ficino's list of the colours of the chromatic scale. Most of the longer paraphrases are written in complete sentences, but everywhere Colet's instinct for tabular parallelism and correspondence is extremely strong. For example, on folio lxx^v of the text Ficino says:

I am bringing with me, when I come, five short theological tracts which I have written during this last stay in the country. One is on Divine providence, the names of God, and the joy of contemplating God. Another is on the ascent from material elements first to an immaterial heaven, then to the world soul, which is without quantity, then to the angelic mind, which is not subject to change, then to God, who is substance without accident. . . .[2]

---

[1] cf. P. O. Kristeller, 'Humanism and Scholasticism in the Italian Renaissance', *Byzantion*, xvii (1945), 346–74; reprinted in P. O. Kristeller, *Studies in Renaissance Thought and Letters* (Rome, 1956), pp. 553–83.

[2] Ficino, *Epistolae*, fol. lxx^v:
Fero mecum theologica opuscula quinque hoc ultimo nostrae rusticationis tempore a nobis composita de divina providentia nominibusque dei et gaudio contemplantis. De ascensu a materia elementorum ad coelum sine materia. Ad animam sine quantitate. Ad angelum mutationis expertem. Ad deum sine accidente substantiam. . . .

GENERAL BACKGROUND

Colet annotates the passage as follows:

    heaven, without matter
    the elements, with matter
    without accident   God
    without change   Angel
    without quantity   soul
    without matter   heaven (47)

One other example of Colet's paraphrasing technique will illustrate the large number of passages which are annotated in complete sentences. In a letter on folio xcvi[v] Ficino begins:

I have written a book against the worthless pronouncements of astrologers. I send you herewith the preface; I shall send the rest as soon as my scribe has finished copying it. Those who claim that every event is determined by the stars are not only themselves involved in three dangerous errors, but also involve the masses in those errors. For, insofar as they can, they take away from the supreme and omnipotent God [His] providence and absolute rule over the world.[1]

Colet's comment in the margin reads:

The pronouncements of astrologers, based on the influence of the stars, are false and worthless and are the cause of pernicious error. For they take away the providence and omnipotence of God when they say that all events occur necessarily as a result of the compulsion of the stars. Where is the providence of the supreme God and where is His absolute and free authority if everything is caused by the inferior stars? (51)

Like his paraphrases, Colet's more independent comments vary in form. For example, in one of his letters Ficino sketches a satirical portrait of the typical pseudo-intellectuals of his day,[2] whom he calls 'not *philosophi* but *philopompi*'. In the margin at that point Colet, has written 'philopompi' and four lines below, 'Cantabrigienses'. (28)

Others of Colet's independent comments are glosses on the meaning of Ficino's text. For example, in a short letter on folio lxx[r] Ficino happens to use

---

[1] Ficino, *Epistolae*, fol. xcvi[v]:
Scripsi librum contra vana astrologorum judicia. Mitto ad te prohemium. Reliquum mittam cum primum scriba noster excripserit. Qui singula necessario fieri a stellis affirmant tribus potissimum pernitiosis erroribus et involvuntur ipsi et vulgus involvunt. Nam summo et omnipotenti deo quantum in eis est propriam rerum auferunt providentiam absolutumque mundi totius imperium.
Ficino, *Epistolae*, fol. xxvii[r]:

[2] Sunt multi nostris saeculis non philosophi sed philopompi qui sensum Aristotelicum se tenere superbe nimium profitentur: cum tamen Aristotelem ipsum raro admodum atque parumper loquentem: et tunc quidem non graece propria exprimentem immo barbare aliena balbutientem audiverint: immoque minime intellexerint. Hi cum in foro inter pueros garriunt scire non nihil vulgo videntur. Si domi eos prudenter interroges, pauca in physicis, pauciora in mathematicis, paucissima in methaphysicis scire deprehendes.

the term 'palinode'. In the margin at that point Colet supplies the following etymological definition of the term:

palinode, that is, a recantation, from *palyn*, which means *again*, and *odos*, which means *singing*. [The word] is used when we write wrongly on a subject and then, by rewriting, change our tune and treat the same subject rightly. (**45**)

In still other notes Colet's thought abandons altogether the main highway of Ficino's text, and strikes off on its own side roads. For example, in the margin of a tract entitled 'A Theological Prayer to God', (fol. xxxiii^v) Colet has written in English an apostrophe to the Virgin Mary:

> O Virgin chosen unto the great and wondrous miracle
>   to be the Mother of Christ, both God and Man!
> O marvellous mother and bearer and bringer forth of
>   Him that brought forth all others,
> And made thee also from nought that thou
>   shouldest conceive him from somewhat.
> O dear daughter of Goode [God], which wert made
>   the mother of Jesus Christ by the Holy Ghost!
> O clear ground of life! O house of Christ's godhead!
> O comfortable root of health, from thee sprang the great
>   Physician, restorer and healer of mankind. (**35**)

This apostrophe shows more interest in the tradition represented by the early Tudor prayer-book called *Fifteen Oes* than in the text of Ficino, but this note is exceptional. Most of Colet's marginalia reflect a close and critical examination of Ficino's ideas, with the result that the All Souls volume illuminates not only Colet's life but also his opinions. We shall examine the volume from the biographical and intellectual points of view in turn; but first a few words should be said about the form in which the materials are presented here.

(C) *Editorial Policy*

The first draft of my transcription of the materials in the All Souls volume was made mainly from a microfilm copy of the original. This draft was checked with the original by Mr. C. D. Jack, now of Sebright School. A second draft was checked with the original by J. B. Trapp and A. E. Wardman, who made a great many radically important changes in transcription and translation. The resulting version I was able to check with the original, and J. B. Trapp and A. E. Wardman have read the proofs of this book.

When I first undertook to edit the All Souls volume, I planned to publish only the longer marginal comments (along with the letters) and to translate only those which represented independent observations of Colet rather than mere paraphrases of Ficino's text. As I worked with the materials, however, I discovered that many of the shorter notes illuminated Colet's thought quite as significantly as the longer ones, and moreover, that most of Colet's long paraphrases of Ficino's text involved some degree of independence or shift in point of view on Colet's part. In the end, therefore, I decided to transcribe and translate all of the manuscript additions in the volume, regardless of length, character, and origin. The only exception to this principle of complete inclusion is that where Colet repeats in the outer margin for the sake of legibility single word comments which he had first written in the inner margin, I have recorded such repeated words only once. With this exception I have intended to transcribe and translate all manuscript material in the volume. I have also recorded, in Appendix B, the passages marked for reading in Ficino's table of contents, and, in Appendix C, all passages in Ficino's text which Colet has underlined or marked with brackets.

Since Ficino regarded his *Epistolae* as essays, I have grouped the marginalia according to the specific letter to which they apply. Several longer ones are divided into separately titled sections; rather than give the titles of these sections, I have grouped the marginalia in order under the title of the treatise as a whole. Thus **7,** for example, includes many marginalia, from several successive pages, but they all belong to one long treatise. For convenience of reference I have translated Ficino's titles, but it will be recognized immediately that they are often not a very useful guide to the contents. In most cases the marginalia apply to the letter in the margin of which they are written. In one exceptional case, Ficino's letter on 'The Definition...of Virtue', Colet filled up the margins (see **31**) on the leaf where the letter appears (fol. xxviii^r) and then turned back to the previous leaf to record the rest of his comments. Thus **29,** which is written on folio xxvii^r, applies to a letter on folio xxviii^r.

In order to make it possible for the scholar to use Colet's marginalia in conjunction with any copy of the 1495 *Epistolae* of Ficino, I have indicated where in Ficino's text each marginal note occurs. At the beginning of each group of notes I give the folio on which it appears, and in the left margin of the Latin text of the note I give the location on the page; if the note is in the top margin on the page, I have labelled it 'head'; if it is in the bottom margin, I have labelled it 'foot'; if it is in either of the two side margins, I have given the number of the line opposite which the note occurs, counting from the first line of the text on each page.

Many of the shorter marginal notes, if translated simply word for word out of context, would have meant very little to the modern reader; for example, it would have been of little value to transcribe Colet's two words 'sacerdotes Deum' (fol. v^v) and translate them simply 'priests God'; what I have tried to do is to give enough context in translating short phrases to make their significance reasonably clear to the reader; thus I have translated the passage cited: '[See that the] priests [pray to] God [for me]' (9) and amplified it further with a note.

At the point in his commentary on *Romans* where Colet paraphrases a long passage from Ficino's *Theologia Platonica*, he excuses himself as follows for not quoting verbatim:

Thus much have I related, after Marsilius, touching the excellence of love; using, however, my own words for the most part as I pleased, and my own manner of writing; not that I dream of being able to express it more fittingly or clearly than Marsilius (than whose language nothing can be finer in philosophy), but because in the use of our freedom of speech, I have taken the liberty of inserting what I would in the course of writing.[1]

In the All Souls volume Colet takes even greater liberties with Ficino's language, giving us ample opportunity in passage after passage of parallel statement to understand Erasmus's criticism:

For though eloquent both by nature and training, and though he had at his command a singularly copious flow of words while speaking, yet when writing, [Colet] would now and then trip in such points as critics are given to mark, and it was on that account, if I mistake not, that he refrained from writing books.[2]

What Erasmus states thus charitably, Lupton also suggests, with a kindly British litotes: 'Colet's style is not the easiest that can be imagined for translation. . . .'[3]

As is obvious in Colet's revisions and corrections in the drafts of letter C, a vast abyss separated Colet from Ficino in the use of the Latin language. Ficino's highly sophisticated rhetoric is delivered with the self-assured tone of

---

[1] Colet, *Lectures on Romans*, trans. J. H. Lupton (London, 1873), p. 32:

Haec tradidimus de amoris excellencia, Marcilium secuti, sed nostris verbis nostroque scribendi modo maxime pro nostro arbitrio usi; non quod putamus nos aut aptius aut lucidius quam Marcilium (quo nihil in philosophia potest esse eloquencius) ea exprimere posse; sed quod libertate loquendi usi, habuimus facultatem inter scribendum inserendi quae voluimus et dirigendi sermonis eo quo nostro proposito maxime conveniret (p. 157).

Except for the materials in the All Souls volume, all works of Colet quoted in translation in this introduction are quoted in the translation of J. H. Lupton unless otherwise specified.

[2] Erasmus, *Epistolae*, IV, p. 523.

Cum enim esset et natura et eruditione facundus, ac dicenti mira suppeteret orationis hubertas, tamen scribens subinde labebatur in his quae solent notare critici. Atque hac, ni fallor, gratia a libris scribendis abstinebat. (trans. is Lupton's, *Life of Jehan Vitrier* . . ., p. 39).

[3] Colet, *Commentary on First Corinthians*, trans. J. H. Lupton (London, 1874), p. viii.

a recognized master. By contrast, Colet's Latin notes appear, not surprisingly, awkward and obscure. But in general, his Latin is that of the ordinary educated Englishman of the later Middle Ages. In such matters as orthography (e.g. doubling consonants, as *diffinitio* for *definitio*, *concilliavit* for *conciliavit*, *legittima* for *legitima*) or vernacular word order (e.g. *aliqua composita sunt media inter animam serenam et crassum corpus*) he follows the common practice of his day, not yet affected by humanist reforms.

In transcribing the manuscript materials in the volume (and also the passages from the printed text in the appendixes) I have silently expanded all abbreviations. I have tried to reproduce exactly the spelling of Colet's text, with three exceptions: I have changed u before a vowel to v throughout; I have changed spacing between letters to indicate word-division in a few cases where the crowded spacing of the margin has left the issue unclear; and I have modernized his capitalization. I have used [sic] to call attention to all obvious errors which cannot be explained as matters of normal fifteenth-century practice; if the correct form is perhaps not obvious, I have used [i.e. . . .] instead of [sic]. Colet uses only two forms of punctuation, the full stop and the colon; in order to make his meaning clear, I have occasionally, without comment, modernized his punctuation.

The printed text of the Venice, 1495 edition of the *Epistolae* is itself very crude in punctuation and spelling. I have corrected this text by the Basle, 1576 edition of Ficino's *Opera*.

In editing a classical Latin text one normally indicates editorial additions and exclusions by means of angular and square brackets. Since the material here consists mainly of marginalia, and since I wanted to preserve Colet's own aberrations as fully as possible, I have made no editorial exclusions. Such additions, of letters or words, as were necessary to make the meaning clear I have entered within square brackets.

II: BIOGRAPHICAL RELATIONS

JOHN COLET lived for fifty-three years, from about 1466[1] to 1519. His simple bachelor life[2] had only three chapters. During his first seventeen years he lived mainly in London, as a schoolboy. The last period, of fourteen years, he also spent in London, as Dean of St. Paul's. The locus of the middle period of his life was not London but Oxford, and it is this Oxford period of twenty-two years with which we are concerned here, for the relation between Colet and Ficino may best be understood in the context of Colet's relation to Oxford.

The traditional account of Colet's first seven years at Oxford is that of Anthony à Wood, who says that Colet was sent to Oxford 'about 1483 (at which time one or more of his sirname [sic] were of S. Mary Magdalen College) where, after he had spent seven years in logicals and philosophicals, [he] was licensed to proceed in arts'.[3] This account is mainly right, but Colet's association with Magdalen College has never been confirmed. The registers of the college for that period contain no reference to any person named Colet.[4] There were ten colleges at Oxford in Colet's day,[5] but only two can show any documentary claim to him; one is Exeter, where he is known to have dined twice in 1516,[6] and the other is All Souls, where his book was recently discovered.

As a matter of fact, however, it is extremely unlikely that Colet was ever officially a member of any college at all. Most of the colleges prescribed poverty as a condition of holding a fellowship;[7] whereas Colet was supported by independent means and while still an undergraduate had accepted several ecclesiastical preferments, any one of which would have disqualified him for a fellowship. If he had merely rented a room in some college, as Grocyn did at

---

[1] Colet's original monument in St. Paul's gave his age at his death as fifty-three. See Samuel Knight, *The Life of Dr. John Colet* (London, 1724), p. 261, from William Dugdale's *History of St. Paul's Cathedral* (London, 1657). Dugdale's engraving (p. 64) is reproduced opposite p. 206 of the article cited in the note to my frontispiece.

[2] The most up to date account of the bare facts of Colet's life, with documentation, is that of A. B. Emden, in *A Biographical Register of the University of Oxford to 1500* (Oxford, 1957), i. 462–4.

[3] Anthony à Wood, *Athenae Oxonienses*, ed. Philip Bliss (London, 1813), i, col. 22.

[4] *Magdalen College Register*, ed. by J. R. Bloxham (Oxford, 1853–85), 8 vols., and *Magdalen College Register*, ed. W. D. Macray (London, 1894–1915), 8 vols.

[5] Merton, University, Balliol, Exeter, Oriel, Queen's, New, Lincoln, All Souls, and Magdalen.

[6] Register of Exeter College, ed. C. W. Boase, *OHS*, xxvii (1894), p. lxxi: 'xxiiid. . . . pro vino dato Doctori Collett 2bus vicibus.'   [7] e.g. see the statutes of New College, All Souls, Magdalen, etc.

Exeter,[1] the fact should have appeared in the bursar or battel books of one of the colleges, but so far no such record has been found. Since the University required all students to live either in college or in one of the halls,[2] we should probably conclude that Colet lived in one of the halls.

If Colet was born in 1466, he probably entered Oxford, as Wood says, in 1483, at the age of seventeen.[3] Wood says, and Erasmus confirms,[4] that Colet received the M.A. degree, but the University has no record of either his B.A. or his M.A. degree. The University Register for the period 1464 to 1504 is missing,[5] but we can probably see his progress at the University reflected in his external preferments. Entering in 1483, he would have proceeded at the end of two years to his sponsorial; just at this point (6 August 1485), and perhaps in recognition of Colet's achievement, his cousin, Sir William Knevet, presented Colet to his first ecclesiastical living, the rectory of Dennington, Suffolk.[6] In July of 1487, Colet would have finished his first four years and received the B.A. degree. After three more years, in July 1490, he would have commenced M.A. The following October he received another living, this time the rectory of Thurning, Hampshire, given him by his father.[7]

If we accept Wood's conjecture that Colet received the M.A. degree in 1490, we may then conclude that he spent the next two years, 1490–1 and 1491–2, lecturing at Oxford on the arts and philosophies, for all new Masters were required to remain at the university for two years after receiving their degrees, to lecture as 'necessary regents' before they could go on to other faculties, or leave altogether.[8]

At the end of his regency, in the summer of 1492, Colet could have entered active ecclesiastical service, but the more usual course was to remain in the university. As Gibson says, 'After regency, masters of Arts were expected to proceed to one of the higher faculties. It was taken for granted that masters would enter the theological faculty unless the statutes of their colleges required them to enter some other faculty.'[9] Since Colet was not ordained until several years later, we may presume that at the end of his regency he intended to follow the usual course and enter the faculty of theology.

[1] Montagu Burrows, 'Memoir of William Grocyn', *Collectanea* II, *OHS*, xvi (1890), 337.
[2] See Strickland Gibson, *Statuta Antiqua Oxonienses* (Oxford, 1931), 226.
[3] The normal age for matriculation was sixteen or seventeen. See C. E. Mallet, *A History of the University of Oxford* (London, 1924–1927), ii, 141.   [4] See below, note 5, p. 16.
[5] *Register of the University of Oxford*, 1449–63, 1505–71, ed. C. W. Boase, *OHS*, i (1885), pp. v–vii.
[6] Reg. Norw. xii fol. 116; cited by Emden.
[7] Reg. Russell, Lincs. xxii, fols. 259ᵛ, 263: cited by Emden. On 20 July 1486, at the end of his third year at Oxford, Colet had also received the Rectory of Hilberworth, Norfolk; see Wm. Campbell, ed., *Materials for History of Henry VII* (R.S.) i. 513.
[8] Gibson, *Statuta*, pp. c–ci and 54.   [9] Gibson, *Statuta*, pp. cii and 347.

In that faculty the next degree before him was the Bachelor of Divinity. The requirements for this degree were four more years of reading and listening to lectures, followed by an additional three years of opposing, responding, and preaching.[1] What Colet evidently planned was to do his four years of reading on the continent, from the fall of 1492 to the fall of 1496, and then to return to Oxford for his three years of opposing and responding, from 1496 to 1499.

Why should Colet have decided to do his four years of theological reading on the continent? The best general answer is that it was being done. During the nine years Colet had been at Oxford, many other Oxford scholars had travelled to Italy,[2] and two of them would have had a special interest for Colet; these were Thomas Linacre (1460?–1524) and William Grocyn (1446?–1519). Linacre, a fellow of All Souls, left Oxford in 1487,[3] the year of Colet's B.A., and stayed in Italy until 1492, returning to Oxford shortly before Colet left. Colet and Linacre were close friends, at least until 1512, and Linacre doubtless had some influence on Colet's decision to go to Italy.

Grocyn's influence was probably greater still; he was Reader in Divinity at Magdalen College from 1481 to 1487,[4] including the first four years of Colet's stay at Oxford. In 1488 Grocyn resigned his Readership and went to Italy for three years. He returned to Oxford in the spring of 1491, while Colet was lecturing as an M.A., and was still living in Oxford when Colet left for Italy. Colet and Grocyn were extremely close in later years, when Colet invited Grocyn to lecture at St. Paul's and named Grocyn's godson, William Lily, to be the first headmaster of St. Paul's school; it seems very likely that Grocyn, a theologian just back from three stimulating years with some of the outstanding Hellenists on the continent, including Poliziano in Florence, and Hermolao Barbaro in Rome, must have played an important part in Colet's decision to spend the first four years of his Bachelor of Divinity training on the continent.

Until recently all we knew about Colet's studies on the continent was the statement of Erasmus that Colet studied in Italy, in Paris, and at Orléans, and that he studied mainly the Church Fathers.[5] In spite of this, most of Colet's

---

[1] Gibson, *Statuta*, pp. cix–cx and 48, 50.

[2] See G. B. Parks, *The English Traveler to Italy* (Stanford, 1954), i, 423–94, and Appendix, pp. 621–40. The large number of degrees in canon law given to Englishmen in Italy (especially at Bologna, Padua, and Florence) and at Oxford as well suggests that the degree in canon law may have been used as a popular short-cut substitute for the longer degree in theology proper.

[3] On Linacre's trip to Italy see especially G. B. Parks, *The English Traveler*, i. 455–61; P. S. Allen, 'Linacre and Latimer in Italy', *EHR*, xviii (1903), 514–17; and R. J. Mitchell, 'Thomas Linacre in Italy', *EHR*, l (1935), 669–78.

[4] Montagu Burrows, 'Memoir of William Grocyn', pp. 336–7.

[5] Erasmus, *Epistolae*, iv. 515.

biographers have tried very hard to explain the Italian part of the journey on the basis of Colet's interests in Platonism, suggesting, for example, that Colet must have visited Florence and met Ficino.[1] But we now have evidence which confirms Erasmus's statement that Colet's interests on the continent were primarily theological, and which also tells us that Colet never did meet Ficino.

We now know that in March 1493, Colet was admitted to the English hospice in Rome. Colet registered as a contributor to the hospital of Santo Spirito in Rome on 14 March 1493,[2] and as a member of the confraternity of the English Hospice in Rome on 3 May 1493.[3] (On the earlier date Colet is listed with his parents, but they need not have been and probably were not present.)

We know that Colet had ecclesiastical matters on his mind while he was in Rome because on 1 April 1493, he wrote a letter to the Dean of York, Christopher Urswick (1448–1522), sending him a copy of Aeneas Sylvius's history of the Bohemian heretics during the Hussite wars; in the letter he indicates that he had met Urswick in Rome during Urswick's embassy there on behalf of Henry VII sometime between November 1492, and April 1493.[4] Less than a year after Colet sent this gift to Urswick, and while Colet himself was still on the continent, Urswick turned over to Colet his own prebend of Botevant at York.[5] The implication is that even while Colet was still on the continent he was making arrangements for his clerical future in England.

Our final information about Colet's activities in Italy comes from the correspondence between Colet and Ficino in the All Souls volume. As background for this evidence we should remind ourselves of a few facts about the relations between the two men before 1493.

At Colet's birth, in 1467, Ficino was already an active scholar of thirty-four, the head of the Platonic Academy at Florence.[6] From 1467 to 1492

---

[1] Seebohm, Lupton, Marriott, and even W. K. Ferguson repeat this suggestion.

[2] See the *Liber Fraternitatis* of the Hospital, edited by Pietro Egidi in *Fonti per la Storia d'Italia* (Istituto Storico Italiano), xlv (1914), 107–446.

[3] Liber 17 among the archives of the Venerable English College in Rome, first reported by V. J. Flynn in 'Englishmen in Rome during the Renaissance', *MP*, xxxvi (1938), 121–38. My citations of this and the preceding records of Colet's stay in Rome are based upon Parks, *The English Traveller*, i. 357–82 and 466–7. See also Cardinal F. A. Gasquet, *History of the Venerable English College, Rome* (London, 1920), p. 24.

[4] The letter was first published by W. K. Ferguson in 'An Unpublished Letter of John Colet', *AHR*, xxxix (1934), 696–9; the volume containing Colet's letter is now Princeton University Library MS. 89.

[5] Colet resigned the rectory of Thurning at the same time; see Reg. Russell, Lincs, xxii, fol. 263, cited by Emden. Colet's assignment to the Prebend of Botevant at York is dated 5 March 1494 by John Le Neve, *Fasti Ecclesiae Anglicanae*, ed. T. D. Hardy (Oxford, 1854), iii. 176. Le Neve names the previous holder as Edward Cheiney, appointed 24 December 1490, but Le Neve appears to have missed the intervening short tenure of Urswick, dated by *DNB* as beginning 21 March 1493.

[6] See Table I, p. 36.

neither man left his own country. Thus up to the time he was twenty-five years old Colet could not possibly have met Ficino and probably did not correspond with him, but he probably did know some of Ficino's published works. By the end of 1492 Ficino had published seven works. Of these seven, Colet later shows a knowledge of three or four;[1] he probably knew at least two of them before he left England in 1492.

During the period of Colet's stay on the continent Ficino was a world-renowned scholar in his sixties, conducting an enormous correspondence and holding court among his 'lovers', as he called them, in the extremely esoteric society of the Careggian Academy. Colet, on the other hand, was an unknown English theological student in his twenties who had never published a word. If Colet had managed to obtain an audience with the great man at Careggi, Erasmus would probably have mentioned the fact in his biography of Colet.

In any case the All Souls volume now makes it virtually certain that Colet did not in fact meet Ficino, though he did correspond with him after returning to England. The deciding evidence is Colet's own statement in a letter to Ficino that he still hoped to be able to meet him some day.

We may reconstruct the facts of the correspondence between Colet and Ficino as follows. The correspondence probably did not take place before 1494; if it had, Ficino's own letter to Colet would probably have been included in the published volume.[2] Ficino's *Epistolae* were published in March 1495. Colet was still on the continent at the time, since we hear of him in Paris toward the end of that year, but we do not know when he acquired his copy of the book, whether in Italy, France, or England. It seems likely that the appearance of Ficino's correspondence in print may itself have suggested to Colet that he, too, might write to the great Platonist. At any rate, Colet seems to have initiated the correspondence, with a flattering letter which I have called Letter A.

Letter A is not known to exist, perhaps because of Colet's habit of not keeping copies of his letters, but Ficino's reply to Letter A does exist, copied in Colet's own hand, on a back flyleaf of the All Souls volume. This reply is Letter B in the correspondence edited here (see p. 81).

This letter suggests that neither man knew very much about the other. Ficino addresses Colet in the letter as 'beloved', but this fact tells us little about their true relation, since Ficino addressed all of his admirers as 'beloved'.

[1] In addition to Ficino's Plato and Plotinus, Colet knew the *Theologia Platonica* and possibly the *De ta*.

[2] Letters much shorter and less substantial in content than that to Colet were published in the collec-on; cf. *Epistolae*, fol. cxc[r].

Moreover, when Ficino says, with pretended deprecation, that his works have doubtless given Colet a false picture of him, the observation carries a double irony. Since Colet seems to have addressed Ficino in Letter A in the metaphor of the sun, one might infer that among other 'works' of Ficino upon which Colet's view of him was based was the *De sole et lumine* (1493).[1] It is equally likely, however, that Colet derived his idea of addressing Ficino as the sun from the *Epistolae* themselves, for that volume contains not only several statements [2] of the sunlight analogy for God, but also a letter in which Ficino himself identifies himself with the sun,[3] and in the same language which he later used for his letter to Colet: 'Utinam nostrum hoc lumen non Lunam videatur proferre sed Solem.' In the margin of the *Epistolae* at this point Colet has written 'non lunam sed solem'. Thus Ficino's works, in one sense, gave Colet a quite accurate picture of Ficino's true egocentric nature. By a deeper irony, however, Ficino's statement is perfectly true, for the devout and ascetic Colet, who is said to have deplored the relic-kissing of the Canterbury pilgrimage,[4] probably would have been shocked to realize that the great theologian-philosopher whom he thought he saw in Ficino's books was actually, by Colet's standards, a conjurer and astrologer, the high priest of a cult of pagan idolatory.[5]

Deceived or not, however, Colet did not allow Ficino's reply to go unacknowledged. On the back of the flyleaf on which he had copied Ficino's letter, Colet scribbled off two drafts of a reply. That reply, which I have called Letter C, is a tortured effort to match Ficino's rhetoric; though brief, it tells us a great deal about Colet. In its choice of rhetorical figures[6] it shows us how familiar Colet was with Ficino's own writings as well as with Paul's letter

---

[1] The *De sole et lumine* was published in February 1493; see especially the Preface, addressed to Piero de'Medici:

Itaque cum nuper ad mysterium illud Platonicum pervenissem, ubi Solem ad ipsum Deum artificiosissime comparat, placuit rem tantam aliquanto latius explicare praesertim quia Dionysius noster Areopagita Platonicorum primus, cuius interpretationem in manibus habeo, similem Solis ad Deum comparationem libenter amplectitur. . . . Idque de Sole mysterium quasi Phoebeum munus, ad te potissimum et Phoebi Musarum ducis alumnum et Musarum patronum mittere, cui etiam universa haec nova Platonis interpretatio dedicatur ut hac interim luce quasi Luna quadam, quale futurum sit Platonicum opus totum tanquam Sol ad Lunam, augureris, . . . (Ficino, *Opera*, p. 965).

[2] See especially *Epistolae*, fols. xliii^r, lvv, and lxii^{r-v}; see also Colet's marginalia 44.

[3] *Epistolae*, fol. cxc^r, a letter to Lorenzo de'Medici dated 18 February 1493, and entitled 'In librum de Sole dono missum'.

[4] The person described in Erasmus' account of the pilgrimage as 'Gratianus Pullus' is usually identified as Colet. See Lupton, *Life*, p. 208.

[5] For this side of Ficino's activities at Careggi see especially D. P. Walker, 'Ficino's *Spiritus* and Music', *Annales Musicologiques*, i (1953), 131–50; 'Orpheus the Theologian and Renaissance Platonists', *Journal of the Warburg Institute*, xvi (1953), 100–20 and *Spiritual and Demonic Magic from Ficino to Campanella* (London, 1958).

[6] See Latin text of the letter, p. 82, where I have preserved all of Colet's original readings along with his corrections.

to the Romans;[1] and in its own subject matter, it tells us something which we have not heretofore known about Colet's personal relations with Ficino, namely that the two men had never met: 'If I can only look upon you and see you in person, I shall be truly blessed. I live in expectation of [seeing you], and I [also] die from expectation, having waited too long, as it seems, for a glimpse of you.' (Letter C)

Colet here says specifically that he would like to meet Ficino. If Colet wrote this after he returned to England, then he could never have met Ficino at all, since Colet never again left England, and Ficino died in 1499, having never left Italy in all his life. That Colet did write Letter C after he returned to England is not absolutely certain, but it is highly probable, for, at the bottom of the page on which he has copied Letter B from Ficino, and in the same ink and hand, Colet has written the following note: 'Next Monday, *at the usual time and place*, John Colet will try to expound as best he can, with God's help, St. Paul's first Epistle to the Corinthians'[2] [italics mine]. The position of this note on the page below Ficino's letter suggests that the letter may have had something to do with Colet's decision to announce his lectures on 1 Corinthians. The reference to 'the usual time and place' shows that this note was written in England after Colet had already given some of his Oxford lectures on the works of Paul; Colet appears to have written the note immediately after copying Ficino's Letter B. After scribbling the note, Colet seems then to have turned the page and to have written at the top of the verso, the two drafts which constitute Letter C.[3] The note announcing his lectures on Corinthians was written in England, after Colet had received Letter B. Letter C seems to have been written after the note, as a reply to Letter B; therefore Letter C must have been written in England. Since Letter C implies that Colet had not met Ficino, and since the two men could not have met after the writing of Letter C, the All Souls volume all but proves that although Colet corresponded with Ficino, he never met him personally.

---

[1] The distinction which Colet makes between 'living' and 'living well' is anticipated in the *Epistolae* fols. 1ʳ and xviiiʳ. Colet's rhetorical play with the words *video* and *vivo* seems shallow beside Ficino's similar effort:

> Mens autem quaelibet volendo facit opera potius quam videndo. Videndo enim replicat formas intus, volendo eas explicat extra, videndo respicit verum, cui propria est diffusio. *Theologia Platonica* ii, p. xi (*Opera*, p. 108).

The key conceit of the letter is drawn from Rom. viii. 24–5:

> For we are saved by hope: but hope that is seen is not hope: for what a man seeth, why doth he yet hope for?
> But if we hope for that we see not, then do we with patience wait for it.

[2] Marginalia **73**.

[3] The only alternative is that Colet first copied Letter B where it appears on the recto, leaving a large space vacant at the bottom of the page, then immediately drafted his reply on the verso, and finally later returned to jot down the note about the Corinthians lectures in the vacant space below Letter B. This alternative seems unlikely because the ink and hurried hand are so uniform in all three pieces.

On a front flyleaf of the All Souls volume Colet has written a third prose passage, longer than either of the two letters already described. Although it has no heading, it addresses itself in the text to 'dear John', and appears in style and subject to be a second letter from Ficino to Colet. It is a long and sophistic discussion of a theological question and sounds as though it had been written in answer to a specific question from Colet, a question which he had perhaps posed in the lost remainder of Letter C. I have called this theological passage Letter D, but since it is not dated and does not otherwise contribute to our knowledge of the biographical relations between the two men, I shall discuss its significance later, in connexion with their philosophical relations.

The effect, then, of the correspondence in the All Souls volume is to confirm Erasmus' statement that Colet's primary interest during his stay in Italy was theological. The same may probably be said of his stay in France, though about this part of his continental tour we know virtually nothing because the archives at Orléans and Paris have not so far yielded any trace of his work at at those two centres.[1] There is, however, a hint of his stay in Paris, as we shall see, in his activities after he returned to England.

The date of Colet's return to England, like most other details of his life, must be inferred from other evidence. We know that he was in Paris in December 1495,[2] and had been at Oxford for three years in the autumn of 1499;[3] thus we may infer that he returned to England in the spring of 1496. After a short visit with his parents, Colet went directly to Oxford, presumably to resume his academic work in theology. At that point in his progress towards the B.D. degree, having completed his four years of reading, he should have begun his three years of opponency. But according to Erasmus Colet spent these three years not in opponency, but in lecturing on the Bible.[4]

There are two difficulties here. The first is that the university statutes expressly prohibited anyone from lecturing on the Bible until he had acquired

---

[1] In the register of the 'German' nation at Paris for this period (Sorbonne Arch. 91 (85)), there are two references to a Joannes Coletus (fols. 189ᵛ and 190ʳ), dated 1519, but this is a different Colet, of the diocese of Toul in France. In the register of the 'German' nation at Orleans (Archives du Loiret D 213), there is no record of any Colet. The Paris register I have examined myself in microfilm. The Orleans register was examined for me by M. L. Monnier, Director of Archives. The Paris microfilm was lent to me by Professor A. L. Gabriel, Director of the Medieval Institute at Notre Dame University, U.S.A. Professor Gabriel's study of the English-German nation at Paris is summarized in the *Resumés des Communications* of the XIᵉ Congrès International des Sciences Historiques (Uppsala, 1960), 220-2.

[2] In a letter to Erasmus Colet mentions Erasmus' review of a new book by Robert Gaguin, *De originibus et gestis Francorum*. The date of the earliest known copy of this book is 1497, but the advertisement in the Lyons, 1497 edn. cites a '1ᵉ ed. 1495' (see J. C. Brunet, *Manuel du Libraire*, col. 1438). Colet's letter is in Erasmus, *Epistolae*, i. 242-3.

[3] Erasmus, *Epistolae*, i. 248.   [4] Erasmus, *Epistolae*, iv. 515.

the B.D. degree,[1] and Colet did not have the B.D. degree, as Erasmus himself points out. The second difficulty is that even if Colet had had a B.D. degree, he would have had to lecture on the *Sentences* before he could lecture on the Bible.[2]

Either Erasmus is wrong, or Colet was given permission to lecture on the Bible as an exception to the statutes. We should look into this situation in a little more detail. Erasmus says that Colet lectured on the Bible without any degree in theology, and without any intention of seeking such a degree. Erasmus may very well be wrong, and probably is, about Colet's intentions in 1496, since he did not even meet Colet until three years later, but Erasmus is surely not wrong about the striking fact that Colet was allowed to lecture on the Bible without a B.D. degree. What I suggest happened is that Colet supplicated for permission to present lectures on the Bible in satisfaction of the usual requirement of three years of opponency for the B.D. degree, and that he was granted that permission. The likelihood of this procedure seems to me to be borne out by the fact that the revised statutes of 1565 provide that henceforth lectures on the Bible shall be accepted as satisfying the B.D. requirement in oppositions and responsions.[3]

We may well ask, however, if Colet actually intended to get the B.D. degree, why would he have thought of requesting permission to go about it in this way? Three possible motives suggest themselves. One is Colet's well-known hostility to scholasticism; he would have been eager to avoid the conventional regimen of oppositions and responsions. Another is the fact that at Paris it was customary to lecture on the Bible before lecturing on the *Sentences*;[4] the B.D. at Oxford was technically only a permission to lecture on the *Sentences*, and Colet may very well have reasoned that if lectures on the Bible could precede those on the *Sentences* at Paris, they could at Oxford as well. Finally, Colet may have been moved to want to lecture on the Bible by the inauguration of a new series of public lectures in the autumn of 1497. A priest named Edmund Wylford, the chaplain of Lady Margaret Beaufort, came to Oxford in that year as the first Lady Margaret Professor of Divinity.[5] His lectures on the *Quodlibeta* of Duns Scotus are said to have attracted large audiences, and may have spurred Colet to impatience with the ordinary process of opponency and inspired him to request permission to give similar public lectures on the Bible.

[1] Gibson, *Statuta*, p. 52. The neglect of the Bible at Oxford described by Knight in *The Life of Dr. John Colet*, pp. 50–51, is not confirmed by the statutes.
[2] Gibson, *Statuta*, pp. cx and 50–51.   [3] Gibson, *Statuta*, pp. cxi and 381.
[4] See Hastings Rashdall, *The Universities of Europe in the Middle Ages*, ed. F. M. Powicke and A. B. Emden (Oxford, 1936), iii. 26.
[5] H. C. M. Lyte, *A History of the University of Oxford* (London, 1886), p. 373.

But whatever his motives, he probably made his request to the university within the usual framework of candidacy for the B.D. degree. It seems likely that if, as we have presumed, Colet returned to England in the spring of 1496, he may have spent one school year, 1496–7, in the normal programme of opponency for the B.D. before supplicating to begin his lectures on the Bible the following autumn, for he was in his third year of the lectures when Erasmus arrived in Oxford in the fall of 1499.[1] Thus we may assign his lectures on the Bible to the academic years 1497–8, 1498–9, and 1499–1500.

Colet's activities during these three years have until recently been obscure; we have had only a few pieces of evidence to go on. In a letter to Richard Kidderminster, Abbot of Winchcombe, presumably written in the winter of 1497,[2] Colet describes an evening in which he discussed the Epistle to the Romans with a man who had been an 'attentive listener' at his lectures of the previous [i.e. Michaelmas] term. That same winter (17 December 1497) Colet was ordained Deacon in St. Martin's Le Grand in London; and in March 1498, he was ordained priest in the same church.[3]

It is possibly significant of Colet's being at the end of his series that he suggested to Erasmus, in the winter of 1499–1500, that Erasmus stay at Oxford and give a series of lectures on the Pentateuch or the book of Isaiah,[4]—books of the Old Testament which Colet himself felt inadequate to speak on, but so far as Erasmus's letters reflect Colet's activities at Oxford during this period, they show us a man engaged more in disputation than in lecturing. Erasmus gives us at least three relatively detailed views of Colet engaged in disputation with Erasmus and other theologians,[5] but not one description of a specific lecture.

We do learn something, however, about Colet's Oxford lectures from the All Souls volume, and we must now digress at some length from our chronological narrative to examine that subject.

Certain things about the lectures we may infer from the University customs of the period. There were theoretically four terms in the University year in Colet's time:

---

[1] Seebohm created a good deal of confusion by supposing that Erasmus came to Oxford in 1498. For the correct date, see A. Hyma, 'Erasmus and the Oxford Reformers', *Nederlandsch Archief voor Kerkgeschiedenis*, N.S., xxv (1932), 97.

[2] Letter to the Abbot of Winchcombe, translated in part from Cambridge Univ. MS. Gg. IV. 26 by Lupton in *Life*, pp. 90–93.

[3] He had shortly before (apparently) been made canon of St. Martin's and Prebendary of Goodeaster; see Henry Wharton, *Historia de Episcopis et Decanis Londinensibus* (London, 1695), p. 234. His ordination as deacon is recorded in Reg. Savage, London; cited by Emden. His ordination as priest, dated 25 March 1498, is recorded in Reg. Smith, Linc. xxiv, fol. 7v; also cited by Emden.

[4] Erasmus, *Epistolae*, i. 248.

[5] See Seebohm, *Oxford Reformers*, pp. 97–125, and Erasmus, *Epistolae*, i. 245–60.

Michaelmas term: from 10 October to 17 December.
Hilary term: from 14 January to Palm Sunday Eve.
Easter term: from the Wednesday after Easter to the Thursday before Whitsun.
Trinity term: from the Wednesday after Trinity to 14 September.

In practice there were only three terms, Michaelmas, Hilary, and a third term beginning the Wednesday after Easter and ending 7 July.[1] Each day of the term had a set function in the University calendar. It was either an 'ordinary' lecture day (a *le* day), a limited lecture day (a *le fe* day), a disputation day (a *dis* day), or a holiday.[2] At least thirty days in each term had to be 'ordinary' lecture days. 'Ordinary' lectures were delivered by the regular University faculty, that is to say, M.A.s in regency, in the mornings, between 7 a.m. and noon, on 'ordinary' lecture days.

'Ordinary' lectures were given in one of the 'schools' or lecture halls in Schools Street, rented by the lecturer for that purpose for an entire term, and students normally paid a fee directly to the lecturer.[3]

There was another kind of lecture, called the 'cursory' lecture, which was given in the afternoons by candidates for the M.A. degree, but Colet's lectures on the Bible can hardly have been of this kind, for he was not an M.A. candidate and had already given 'ordinary' lectures in the University for two years.

Colet's lectures belong to still a third kind, the 'free public' lecture. In earlier times no one had been allowed to give his lectures free of charge unless he was the son of an Earl or a Baron; but in 1433 the University authorized all M.A.s to give their lectures free to the general public if they wished.[4] Unfortunately the University had made no provision to endow such lectures, and the lecturer had to have independent means if he wished to give them. The 'free public' lectures were like 'ordinary' lectures except that no admission was charged. Among other Oxford scholars who had given 'free public' lectures before Colet, the most interesting to us is Grocyn, who had lectured on Greek in 1491–2, after he returned from Italy.[5] It was in an effort to make up for the lack of University endowment of such public lectures that Lady Margaret Beaufort instituted the Lady Margaret Professorships at Oxford and Cam-

---

[1] See Gibson, *Statuta*, pp. lxxx–lxxxi and Christopher Wordsworth, *The Ancient Kalendar of Oxford*, OHS, xlv (1904), 24.
[2] See Gibson, *Statuta*, p. lxxxi, and Wordsworth, *Ancient Kalendar*, 26–27; for the full University calendar, marked to show on which days lectures were given, see Wordsworth, pp. 231 ff.
[3] Gibson, *Statuta*, p. ci. [4] See Lyte, *History of Oxford*, p. 218.
[5] See Montagu Burrows, 'Memoir of Grocyn', p. 347.

bridge in 1497.¹ It was the unendowed 'free public' lecture of the kind given by Grocyn and the 'Lady Margaret Professor', Wylford, that Colet undertook to give.

The subject of Colet's lectures, according to Erasmus, was the Epistles of Paul. Since Erasmus, in a letter later to Colet, chides him for not having yet published his lectures on Paul's Epistles,² we may presume that Erasmus, at least, thought that Colet intended to publish his lectures, but he did not do so in his own lifetime. The only extant records of the lectures are some notes of lectures on Romans, and notes of lectures on 1 Corinthians.³ If, as Erasmus says, Colet discussed *all* the Epistles,⁴ he must also have lectured on at least a dozen other Epistles as well,⁵ but of those lectures we have no known record.⁶ I should like to suggest that the reason for this is that the early lectures (those before the first series on Romans) were in the old fashioned mode and so were deliberately not saved. The first series on Romans were also in that mode, but were kept, possibly in order to keep the commentary on the whole of Romans intact.

There is also no record which tells us certainly in what order Colet's lectures were given, but with the help of the All Souls volume I think we can now reconstruct that order with some accuracy.

First, we may be sure, I think, that neither of the two extant sets of lectures was the first to be given. As for the lectures on 1 Corinthians, the note in the All Souls volume announces those lectures for the 'same time and place' as his earlier lectures.⁷ As for the lectures on Romans, Colet tells us in the letter

---

[1] See C. E. Mallet, *History of the University of Oxford* (London, 1924), i. 414, citing Wood, *Athenae Oxonienses*, i. 654.

[2] Erasmus, *Epistolae*, i. 404.

[3] In the volume containing Colet's *Letters to Radulphus*, Lupton prints a fragment of a commentary on Peter (pp. 285-303), from Trinity College Cambridge MS. O.4.44. Thomas Gale, the owner of the manuscript, attributed the commentary on Peter to Colet, but there is no solid evidence for the attribution.

[4] Erasmus, *Epistolae*, iv. 515.

[5] The Pauline canon in Renaissance times included fourteen books. See R. M. Hawkins, *The Recovery of the Historical Paul* (Nashville, 1943). For medieval conceptions of Paul see A. Souter, *Earliest Latin Commentaries on the Epistles of Paul* (Oxford, 1927) and Friedrich Stegmüller, *Repertorium Biblicum Medii Aevi* (Madrid, 1950 ff.); modern commentaries are summarized in Albert Schweitzer, *Paul and His Interpreters* (London, 1912); there is no full study of Renaissance conceptions of Paul.

[6] The *De compositione sancti corporis Christi mystico*, edited and translated by Lupton in the volume containing *Letters to Radulphus* (London, 1876), pp. 31-45 (English) and 185-95 (Latin), may be part of another series of lectures on Paul; part of the fragment deals with Gal. iii and vi in that order. I have omitted this work from my account of the chronology of Colet's major works not only because it is not major, but also because I cannot assign it a place with any conviction. I rather think that it is later than any of those works; for example, in it Colet discusses the concept of goodness of character as a necessity to good action, a concept dealt with not only in the marginalia to the *Epistolae* of Ficino, but also in the third commentary on Romans (cf. *De corpore*, p. 34; marginalia **50**; and *Lectures on Romans*, p. 93).

[7] See marginalia **73**. We know that Colet believed First Corinthians to have been written before Romans (see *Lectures on Romans*, p. 94); in the light of Colet's emphasis on historical exegesis, he might

to Abbot Kidderminster that a visitor who had been an 'attentive listener' at his lectures during the previous term had called on him at home to ask him for further suggestions about reading St. Paul; for this person, Colet reports, he explicated the first chapter of Romans 'without premeditation'; the event reported in this letter would hardly have taken place if Colet had already discussed Romans in his public lectures.

On the other hand, if Colet's lectures on Romans were not the first to be given, they must certainly have been among the earliest, for in them we see Colet's transition from the old-fashioned scholastic technique[1] of Biblical exegesis to the revolutionary technique for which he is now famous. Colet worked on Paul's letter to the Romans in three separate stages.[2] The first is a line by line exposition of the text of Romans i–v only. Colet says he began this *Exposition* for a young man named Edmund,[3] but it may have been delivered as a series of lectures.[4] Perhaps Edmund was the 'visitor' mentioned by Colet to the Abbot of Winchcombe, in which case the *Exposition* must include some of the material sent to the Abbot with the request that it be returned. In any case, the *Exposition* of Romans i–v seems to have been Colet's first commentary on

---

have been presumed to have lectured on the epistles in the order of their composition, but he obviously did not do so.

[1] An example of this older method may be seen in Ficino's own commentary on Romans (*Opera*, pp. 425–72), discussed below. Here is a typical passage:

'Invisibilia enim Dei a creatura mundi per ea quae facta sunt, intellecta conspiciuntur.' Si forte quaeras quomodo Deus Philosophis, perque Philosophos Gentilibus suam aperuerit veritatem, respondet Paulus duobus praecipue modis, per intelligibile lumen atque sensibile. . . . (*Opera*, p. 436).

It should be noted that both of the first two editions of Ficino's *Opera* (Basle, 1561) and (Basle, 1576) have the same pagination; this is the pagination to which Professor P. O. Kristeller refers in his *Philosophy of Marsilio Ficino* (New York, 1943, and Florence, 1953), and to which I refer throughout this essay.

[2] Colet used the Vulgate Bible for all his exegetical work (see Lupton, *Hierarchies*, p. 23). In editing Colet's works Lupton distinguished only two works on Romans (see *Life*, pp. 63–64). One he calls an *Exposition of Romans* published with Colet's *Letters to Radulphus* (London, 1876); the *Exposition of Romans* is the first of the three commentaries in my account. The second and third are both included in what Lupton calls *Lectures on Romans* (London, 1873).

[3] . . . my well-mannered young friend Edmund, for whose instruction I undertook this literal exposition . . . (*Exposition of Romans*, p. 67):

meo Edmundo eximia verecundia adolescenti, ad cuius instructionem hanc litteralem expositionem, aggressus sum . . . (p. 212).

Lupton conjectures that Edmund was Edmund Knevet, a distant relative who was one of Colet's legatees. (*Exposition of Romans*, pp. xxxv–xxxvi.) Colet himself tells us nothing about the boy except that he was too young to understand Rom. i. 25.

[4] The structure of the *Exposition* is very loose; inserted in the comments on Romans are miscellaneous aphorisms (e.g. p. 51) and prayers (e.g. p. 113). Since Colet twice refers to Edmund in the third person, the work seems to imply some other audience:

Although an interpreter of Scripture is not called upon to play the part of a Grammarian . . . yet, since my young friend Edmund, for whom I am composing this, is studying literature along with his theological reading, I am willing to be a Grammarian for him on this occasion, by explaining the meaning of the word 'prevaricator' [in Rom. i. 27]. *Exposition of Romans*, p. 81.

Romans;[1] its exegetical method is the old method of quotation and explication, and it shows little if any interest in Platonism.[2]

For what reasons Colet dropped this first commentary on Romans after chapter v, we do not know. When, after an interval, he returned to Romans, his exegetical method had changed fundamentally. This second stage of his work on Romans is recorded for us in a series of lecture notes covering Romans vi–xi.[3] The notes reflect a fully developed form of the method with which Colet is commonly associated: the method of examining the historical and grammatical meaning of the text as a whole, relating it to the historical circumstances in which it was written, and explaining Paul's meaning in terms of analogous doctrines from the theology of Platonism. Throughout the second series of lectures on Romans Colet's language is strongly Platonic, paraphrasing Pico[4] and two early works by Ficino.[5] Since Colet's first commentary on Romans shows no interest at all in Platonism, this ostentatious parade of Platonism in the second commentary raises the question, 'What happened between the first two stages of Colet's work on Romans to produce this astonishing alteration in approach?' I suggest that what intervened between the two stages was the writing of the commentary on Genesis. This work, done independently of the public lectures on the Epistles of Paul, was written as a series of letters to a private person identified only as Ralph.[6] In order to understand Genesis Colet had apparently studied Pico's commentary on that work, called the *Heptaplus*. Like Pico Colet discusses only the hexameral section of Genesis, and like Pico, Colet discusses it as a poetic accommodation to the human intellect of the divine mystery of the creation, a mystery revealed in the creation story of the Platonists.

---

[1] The title at the head of chap. 1 in the manuscript dates from a much later time: Commentaria in Divum Paulum Ioannis Colet Decani Sancti Pauli (*Exposition of Romans*, p. 204), but it is clear from mistakes in the manuscript (e.g. p. 91 English, p. 229 Latin) that it is only a copy of an earlier manuscript. That the *Exposition of Romans* i–v preceded Colet's work on the rest of Romans is obvious from the nature of that later work. The only reason for saying that it 'seems' to be Colet's first commentary on Romans is that there may conceivably be some earlier work of which we have no knowledge.

[2] An instructive example is the contrast between Colet's and Ficino's exegesis of the same Biblical passage, Rom. i. 20, where Paul discusses the relation between *visibilia* and *invisibilia*. Colet discusses the passage in *Exposition of Romans*, pp. 65–66; Ficino discusses the same passage in *Opera*, p. 436.

[3] *Lectures on Romans*, pp. 1–57 (Latin pp. 135–74). At the beginning of this commentary (Lupton, pp. 1–2) Colet repeats an epitome of the entire book of Romans which he had written for his first commentary (see *Exposition of Romans*, pp. 49–50), and he gives a short summary of what he had said in that earlier commentary on each of the first five chapters of Romans; then with chapter 6 he begins the second commentary proper.   [4] Pico's *Heptaplus*, Proem to Lib. VII, at *Lectures on Romans*, p. 27.

[5] Ficino's *Plotinus* (*Enneads*, I, i) (*Opera*, pp. 1548–9) at *Lectures on Romans*, pp. 16–17; and Ficino's *Theologia Platonica* (*Opera*, pp. 324–5) at *Lectures on Romans*, pp. 29–32.

[6] Edited and translated by Lupton as Colet's *Letters to Radulphus* (London, 1876). Efforts to identify the Ralph addressed in these letters have so far produced nothing but conjecture. The most plausible candidate is Ralph Collingwood, later Dean of Lichfield, suggested by Lupton, *Life*, pp. 89, n. and 114.

There are two reasons for thinking that the commentary on Genesis was written between the first two commentaries on Romans; one reason is that Colet seems to be carrying over into the Romans commentary a thorough familiarity with both Ficino and Pico, who were his major authorities in the Genesis commentary. Moreover, the Genesis commentary seems to serve as a transitional work in terms of method: in the first Romans commentary Colet is still using the old method; in the Genesis commentary he is trying a new method but a method not his own—he slavishly follows what Pico had done with the Biblical text because he has not himself had enough experience in applying Platonism to Biblical exegesis to depart freely from Pico's model; finally, in the second Romans commentary, Colet launches into Paul's letter to the Romans on his own, applying Platonism as best he can independently, though still somewhat awkwardly, as the large and undigested chunk of the *Theologia Platonica* shows.

For these reasons I suggest that among Colet's surviving works the first three in order were:

1. First commentary on Romans (i–v only).
2. Commentary on Genesis.
3. Second commentary on Romans (vi–xi only).

For some unexplained reason Colet's second commentary on Romans was completed only through Romans xi, at which point he dropped Romans for a second time[1] and turned, as I believe, to further study of the Platonists. There were actually two works involved, I think, in this second period of Platonic study: one was the *Epistolae* of Ficino and the other the *Hierarchies* of Dionysius. Both were read about the same time, and the relation between them requires further explanation. For the present I shall take up the *Epistolae* and give my reasons for thinking that the reading of the *Epistolae* came after the second commentary on Romans.

The first reason is this. Although in the second commentary on Romans Colet cites or uses some of the other early works of Ficino, he shows no knowledge of the *Epistolae*. It seems likely that if he had read the *Epistolae* at the time, he would have cited that, too, for the reason that at one place in the commentary he makes a particular point of a long paraphrase from Ficino's *Theologia Platonica*;[2] the idea discussed in this passage, the idea of the superiority of love to intellect in the soul's search for God, is discussed at length by Ficino in the *Epistolae* in a passage which Colet has annotated copiously in the

---

[1] At the end of this commentary (*Lectures on Romans*, p. 57; Latin, p. 174) is the word *Finis*.
[2] See note 5, p. 27.

All Souls copy.[1] If Colet had read the *Epistolae* before he wrote the second lectures on Romans, he would probably have cited this later statement of Ficino's position on the problem in place of, or at least in addition to, the earlier one from the *Theologia Platonica*.

Some confirmation of the view that Colet's reading of the *Epistolae* followed the second Romans commentary may be seen in the fact that the marginalia in the All Souls volume reflect ideas discussed by Colet in both of the early Romans commentaries,[2] whereas neither of the commentaries reflects any knowledge of the *Epistolae* of Ficino.[3]

At about the same time he was reading the *Epistolae* Colet seems to have been reading the *Hierarchies* of the Pseudo-Dionysius and making an abstract of them.

External evidence for the date of Colet's abstract of Dionysius is not very helpful. By comparing Colet's text with the monumental parallel text edition of Dionysius[4] one learns that Colet used the Latin translation of Ambrosius Traversarius (text A in the *Dionysiaca*). The translation of Ambrosius was completed in 1436 and was first published in Bruges in 1480; it was reprinted in Paris in 1498 (see BN catalogue for both editions). The probable *terminus post quem* of Colet's abstract is 1480. The *terminus ante quem* is probably the exposure of the fraudulence of the Pseudo-Dionysius in a lecture at St. Paul's Cathedral by Colet's friend Grocyn. The closest we can come to dating this lecture is the autumn of 1501. In a letter of Sir Thomas More in which he describes the marriage of Catherine of Aragon to Arthur Prince of Wales (14 November 1501) as having taken place 'recently' (*nuper*), he applies the same term (*nuper*) to Grocyn's famous lecture.[5]

Thus the *terminus ante quem* of Colet's abstract must be about 1501. It is true that Lorenzo Valla (1407–57) had exposed the Dionysian writings in 1455,[6]

[1] In a tract entitled 'Quid est foelicitas' (Ficino, *Epistolae*, fols. xxxv–xxxiiiv; the passage concerned begins on fol. xxxir) ; *Opera*, pp. 662–5.
[2] cf. the concept of law and faith in marginalia **25** with *Exposition of Romans*, pp. 107–8, and the concept of form in marginalia **14** with *Lectures on Romans*, pp. 28 and 46. It is true that a similar concept of form appears elsewhere in Ficino (e.g. British Museum MS. Harl. 4695, fol. 30 r-v) but not, so far as I am aware, in the *Epistolae*.
[3] For example, in the *Lectures on Romans* (p. 22). Colet gives an account of the fall of man; this account is probably far less Platonic than it would have been had he read the *Epistolae*; for Colet's fully Platonized version of the fall of man, see marginalia **7**. Lupton rightly compares Colet's account with Ficino's earlier account in the commentary on the *Timaeus* (*Opera*, p. 1471).
[4] See Dom P. Chevalier in *Dionysiaca* (Paris, 1937 and 1950), 2 vols. Cf. Colet, p. 175 with *Dionysiaca*, ii. 831 (an example noticed by Lupton, *Hierarchies*, p. 18), and Colet, p. 169 with *Dionysiaca*, ii. 741.
[5] See *The Correspondence of Sir Thomas More*, ed. E. F. Rogers (Princeton, 1947), p. 4; I am indebted to Professor Josephine Bennett for this reference.
[6] In the *Encomium St. Thomae Aquinatis*. See G. Mancini, *Vita di Lorenzo Valla* (Florence, 1891), p. 312.

but Colet gives no evidence of knowing this. All of Colet's writings known to have been written in Oxford imply unquestioning acceptance of the legitimacy of the Areopagite.[1]

In order to determine the relation between Colet's abstract of the Pseudo-Dionysius and Colet's other works, one has to cope not only with the ubiquity of the ideas of Dionysius in other writers but also with the fact that Colet's abstract of the *Hierarchies* is not all of a piece. He wrote the main part of the abstract, he says, in a few days,[2] covering both the *Celestial* and *Ecclesiastical Hierarchies* in that order.[3] But he later added a supplement to the abstract having to do with matter covered in the *Celestial Hierarchy*.[4] In this supplement Colet quotes a passage from the *Epistolae*[5] of Ficino, showing that he knew the *Epistolae* before he wrote the supplement to the *Hierarchies*. Presumably, however, no supplement would have been necessary had he not already written his abstract of the *Hierarchies* before he read the *Epistolae*;[6] as it is, the supplement not only quotes the *Epistolae* but adds to the discussion of the *Celestial Hierarchy* a concept which, though present in Dionysius, Colet had not thought important until he saw the possible relevance of the passage to his interpretation of St. Paul in the course of reading the *Epistolae*. The nature of this passage I shall explain in due course. For the present we may conclude that after dropping his second commentary on Romans Colet began a study of the Platonists by making an abstract of the *Hierarchies* of Dionysius;[7] he then read the *Epistolae* of Ficino, which prompted him to go back and add a supplement to his abstract of Dionysius. Thus the sequence of Colet's known writings to this point in his career seems to be this:

---

[1] See notes 1 and 2, p. 43.

[2] In the dedication he says that he is writing down from memory what he has read in the last day or two. (*Hierarchies*, p. 1; see next note):

Quapropter, quae heri ac nudiustertius apud Dionysium Areopagitam ... legi et memoria reportavi, ea volo tecum communicare (p. 165).

[3] Edited and translated by Lupton as Colet's *Hierarchies of Dionysius the Areopagite* (London, 1869); the main part of the abstract is on pp. 1–35 (Latin, pp. 165–87).

[4] In Lupton's edition the supplement is printed immediately after the original abstract of the *Celestial Hierarchy*, pp. 36–47 (Latin, pp. 187–96) because that is the order in the St. Paul's School MS., which he is reproducing. The actual relation of the supplement is more clearly shown in the Cambridge University Library MS. Gg. IV. 26, where the supplement appears as a separate tract, on fols. 148b–151. Even in the School manuscript, however, the main part of the abstract, which ends with chapter XV, is followed by the words: Finis Dionysii celestis hierarchiae. *Celestial Hierarchy*, p. 187.

[5] See Appendix D.

[6] This presumption is borne out by the fact that nowhere in the abstract of the *Hierarchies* does Colet make the connexion between the three levels of Dionysius and Paul's triad of faith, hope, and charity. This connexion Colet seems to have seen first in the *Epistolae*, as I have noted below, and it was presumably because of this connexion that he came to write the supplement, in which the connexion is discussed.

[7] cf. *Eccles. Hierarchy*, p. 83, where he discusses the superiority of knowledge to love in the same Ficinian terms which he had applied to Rom. viii (*Lectures on Romans*, pp. 29 ff.).

BIOGRAPHICAL RELATIONS

1. First Commentary on Romans (i–v).
2. Commentary on Genesis.
3. Second commentary on Romans (vi–xi).
4. Abstract of the *Hierarchies* of Dionysius.
5. Reading of *Epistolae* of Ficino.
6. Supplement to abstract of Dionysius.

For what purpose Colet undertook the study of the Platonists which resulted in his reading the *Epistolae* and the *Hierarchies* of Dionysius we do not know; it was probably not for the purpose of resuming his commentary on Romans. At any rate, by the time he had finished reading the *Epistolae*, his mind must have been made up to give his next series of lectures on 1 Corinthians. Not only does he announce that series in the note which we have already discussed,[1] but in another note in the All Souls volume he reminds himself to use in those lectures three particular passages from the *Epistolae* which he cites by folio reference.[2] The lectures on Corinthians as they are preserved in Colet's notes[3] show their derivation not only from the *Epistolae*,[4] but also from the *Hierarchies* of Dionysius.[5] The key concept in Colet's interpretation of 1 Corinthians, his explanation of Paul's triad of faith, hope, and charity, is based upon the parallel triad discussed by Colet in the supplement to his abstract of Dionysius.

After he had finished his lectures on 1 Corinthians Colet returned for a third time to Paul's letter to the Romans, under pressure from 'certain friends':

Though I determined with myself that I would not continue my exposition on this Epistle written by St. Paul to the Romans beyond what was lately delivered by me . . . yet the truth is, being often and pressingly asked by certain friends, themselves also attached hearers of my interpretation of St. Paul (to whom, as in friendship bound, I communicated what I had written on the former part of the Epistle), I was at length induced to promise that I would go on with what I had before begun, and apply to the rest of the Epistle what still remains of my exposition. . . .[6]

---

[1] See marginalia **73**. [2] See marginalia **74**: '99, 51, 51, 98 pro epistola ad corynthios.'
[3] Edited and translated by Lupton as Colet's *Commentary on First Corinthians* (London, 1874).
[4] e.g., *Commentary on Corinthians*, p. 122:
  Nescio an rideam cum Democrito an cum Heraclito defleam hominum vana et perdita studia in hoc mundo . . . (p. 248).
(This is a habitual reference in Ficino's *Epistolae*, see fols. xviv, xviiv, xcvir, xcviv, &c. Cf. marginalia **50**.) See also passages of the *Epistolae* noted by Colet (marginalia **74**) for use in the *Commentary on Corinthians*: e.g. *Epistolae* fol. 51, used in *Commentary on Corinthians*, pp. 26–27.
[5] The *Commentary on Corinthians* also continues to show Colet's knowledge of Pico (see pp. 138–9) and Ficino's *Theologia Platonica* (see p. 140).
[6] *Lectures on Romans*, pp. 57–58:
  At quanquam decreverim mecum non enarraturum me plus in hanc epistolam a divo Paulo ad Romanos scriptam, quam quod modo narratum est a nobis, et productum ad eum usque locum, in

The third and final commentary on Romans,[1] covering chapters xii–xvi, is probably the latest surviving work of Colet's Oxford period. Lupton, too, believed that this commentary followed the Corinthians lectures; but for what I think was an inadequate reason. His reason was that in the third commentary on Romans Colet seems to refer to his lectures on Corinthians:

> ... when I expounded to my hearers the words of St. Paul about the various parts of the Church, I said that these were called Prophets by the Apostle who, drawn towards the one and exalted, surveyed the true causes of things and the right rule of life, in eternity itself; those Teachers, who afterwards delivered that rule to the people in their addresses; and that the Ministers were those between the two, who received from the Prophets what they were to convey to the Teachers.[2]

This passage, as Lupton observed,[3] ought to refer to Colet's comment on 1 Cor. xii. 12–27, where Paul says, in part: 'For as the body is one, and hath many members, and all of the members of that one body, being many, are one body, so also is Christ.' Unfortunately, in the *Commentary on First Corinthians* Colet makes no particular remark on this passage,[4] and says nothing about Prophets. This lack may be explained in part by the fact that our text is only a set of lecture notes, not a verbatim transcript of the lectures, but Colet wrote about the parts of the church several times;[5] I am inclined to think that in the passage noted by Lupton Colet's memory has betrayed[6] him and that he is there merely confusing what he had just said on the subject in the same *Lectures on Romans* (pp. 77–80) with what he had said in his abstract of the *Ecclesiastical Hierarchy* of Dionysius, where he does discuss the Prophets, Teachers, and Ministers.[7]

That Colet wrote the third Romans commentary and the *Commentary on Corinthians* fairly close together is suggested by the fact that Colet uses in those

---

quo Apostolus suam oracionem. . . . hiisce verbis concludit [quotes Rom. ii. 36] . . . tamen certe, multum ac diu rogatus a quibusdam amicis, et eiisdem interpretantibus nobis Paulum fidis auditoribus quibuscum, pro amicicia, quod in superiorem epistolae partem scriptum est a nobis communicavi, adductus fui tandem ut promitterem, quod est ceptum modo me perrecturum [sic], et in reliquam epistolam quod reliquum est enarrationis adhibiturum (p. 175).

[1] *Lectures on Romans*, pp. 57–132 (Latin, pp. 175–227); see note 2, p. 26.
[2] *Lectures on Romans*, p. 90:
 . . . quum auditorio nostro verba Pauli de ecclesiae partibus exposuerimus, nos dixisse prophetas fuisse illos ab apostolo dictos qui in unum et in altum contracti in ipsa eternitate veras rerum raciones ac rectam vivendi normam speculati sunt; doctores vero eos qui eam deinde populo concionibus tradiderunt; ministros medios fuisse illos qui acceperunt a prophetis quod doctoribus referrent (pp. 197–8).
[3] Lupton, *Life*, p. 89, n. 3.
[4] *Commentary on Corinthians*, pp. 123–36.
[5] i.e., the *Ecclesiastical Hierarchy*, the *De compositione*, the *Commentary on Corinthians* (pp. 28–29) and the third commentary on Romans (pp. 66–67).
[6] Colet makes much of his dependence upon memory. He boasts that he always quotes Paul from memory and that he has written his abstract of the *Hierarchies* of Dionysius from memory (see note 2, p. 30). P. S. Allen quotes an anecdote of Wirsung's about Colet's memory; cf. Erasmus, *Epistolae*, iv. 524.
[7] *Ecclesiastical Hierarchy*, pp. 9–19.

two works alone the unfamiliar Greek word, *theanthropon*. In the *Commentary on Corinthians* Colet says: 'A Being, composed of God and man (a Theanthropos, as the Greeks say), lived here on earth.'[1] . . . In the third commentary on Romans, in a passage where he is discussing not Romans at all but the doctrine of faith, hope, and charity from 1 Cor. 13, Colet says: 'This son of God and man, himself God and man, which in Greek, is called *theanthropos*. . . .'[2]

The conclusive reason for believing that the third Romans Commentary followed the *Commentary on Corinthians* is that Colet, completing his exposition of Romans, digresses at length on the subject of faith, hope, and charity, which he had discussed, but apparently not definitively, in the *Commentary on First Corinthians*, where that subject is raised by Paul. It is not merely that Colet is more likely to have gone back to Corinthians than to have anticipated it, but that the discussion itself shows that the third Romans commentary is built on the foundation of all of Colet's previous studies, including his abstract of the *Hierarchies* of Dionysius and his *Commentary on Corinthians*. As I shall try to show in detail in the next chapter the third commentary on Romans goes far beyond either of the first two commentaries on Romans, beyond the *Hierarchies*, and beyond even the *Commentary on Corinthians* in metaphysical complexity.

Thus, using Colet's copy of Ficino's *Epistolae* as a keystone, we may fit together the writings of his Oxford period in the following conjectural order:

1. First commentary on Romans (i–v).
2. Commentary on Genesis.
3. Second commentary on Romans (vi–xi).
4. Abstract of the *Hierarchies* of Dionysius.
5. Reading of *Epistolae*.
6. Supplement to abstract of the *Hierarchies*.
7. Commentary on 1 Corinthians.
8. Third commentary on Romans (xii–xvi).

It will be noted that in addition to the *De compositione*, (see note 6, p. 25), there is one other theological work of Colet missing from this list; it is the *De Sacramentis*, first published by Lupton in 1867. As Lupton's introduction makes

---

[1] *Commentary on Corinthians*, p. 20:
   . . . quod quiddam compositum ex Deo et homine, quod Greci vocant theanthropon, hic vixit in terris . . . (p. 172).
[2] *Lectures on Romans*, p. 63:
   Hic filius Dei et hominis, Deus et homo, qui grece *theonthropon* [sic] dicitur . . . (p. 179).

clear, the *De Sacramentis* shows the influence of the Pseudo-Dionysius, and so presumably followed Colet's abstract of the Dionysian *Hierarchies*, but no satisfactory *terminus ante quem* for the work has suggested itself. Thus, although I believe that the *De Sacramentis* belongs to the period 1498–1501, I have been unable to assign it any particular place in the sequence; a reasonable guess is that it should be added as item **9** and dated 1499.

One other matter which the All Souls volume might be expected to have settled but does not is Lupton's assertion[1] that in Colet's abstract of the *Hierarchies* of Dionysius Colet quotes from Ficino's commentary on Romans. This is clearly a mistake, which Lupton himself elsewhere corrects[2] by tracing the passage not to Ficino's commentary on Romans, but to Ficino's *Epistolae*.[3] But hidden in Lupton's mistake is a different problem which deserves some brief mention. In the note in which he argues for Colet's use of Ficino's commentary on Romans, Lupton refers to a manuscript of the Ficino commentary in the British Museum (MS. Harl. 4695). There is no positive evidence that Colet knew this manuscript, but there are some interesting presumptions involved. If Colet knew of Ficino's commentary on Romans at all, he would have to have seen it in manuscript, since the work was not printed in Colet's lifetime. There are in existence only two fifteenth-century manuscripts of the work,[4] one still in Florence, and the one now in the British Museum (Harleian MS. 4695). The Museum copy is one which Ficino apparently sent to Germain de Ganay, one of his correspondents[5] who was later to become Bishop of Orléans (from 10 August 1514, to 8 March 1521). Professor Kristeller has recently shown that Ficino could not have written this work before December 1496,[6] when Colet was already back in England; if Colet saw it, he must have read it in Ganay's manuscript. We know that Colet stayed in Orléans for a time, but we have no evidence that Ganay was there at the time. Nor is there any way of telling, at present, how Ganay's manuscript came to England. I do not myself believe that Colet knew Ficino's commentary on Romans,[7] certainly not before he gave his own lectures on that Epistle, but Colet's activities at Orléans and his possible relation to Ganay certainly need to be investigated at Orléans before this intriguing relation can be defined more exactly.

[1] *Commentary on Corinthians*, pp. 26–27, in a note on the text at this point.
[2] *Hierarchies*, p. 36.
[3] Ficino, *Epistolae*, fol. liiv; see Appendix D.
[4] See P. O. Kristeller, *Supplementum Ficinianum*, p. lxxxii.
[5] On the relations between Ganay and Ficino see P. O. Kristeller, *Supplementum Ficinianum*, ii. 325.
[6] P. O. Kristeller, *Supplementum Ficinianum*, pp. lxxxii and cxxii–cxxiii.
[7] Another part of Lupton's error about Colet's use of the Ganay MS. was corrected by Albert Hyma, who pointed out (in 'Erasmus and the Oxford Reformers', p. 103) that the manuscript is not a commentary on Romans alone (it covers only chapters i–v of that book), but on the Pauline Epistles in general.

But at least the All Souls volume helps us to define more certainly than we have heretofore been able to do the order in which Colet wrote the major works of his Oxford period. We must now return to our chronological account of Colet's Oxford career; we take up the thread in the autumn of 1499, when Erasmus came to Oxford. That winter Colet seems to have accepted the vicarage of Stepney, near London,[1] but he remained in Oxford, presumably to complete his third year of lectures on the Bible. The next Spring, in March of 1500, he would have completed the requirements for the B.D. degree, and he presumably received it then.[2]

Although the B.D. was required for lecturing on the *Sentences* and the Bible, it was largely a technical degree; the real measure of mastery in divinity, corresponding to the master's degree in arts, was the doctorate, and Colet would have had every reason to wish to go on to that final degree before leaving Oxford. He had only two requirements to fulfil for the doctorate: he would have had to lecture for three more years in order to incept D.D. and then for one additional year in order to fulfil his doctoral regency.

If, as I have argued, Colet received his B.D. in March of 1500, he would have been eligible for inception in the doctorate at the earliest in the spring of 1503, and could have had his doctorate confirmed in March of 1504. This is apparently just what happened. In January, 1504, he resigned the canonry of St. Martin's Le Grand,[3] and in May of 1504, he was appointed Prebendary of Mora at St. Paul's.[4] Within a few months thereafter he was appointed Dean of St. Paul's. By the spring of 1505 he had removed from Oxford to London, where he lived for the rest of his life.

Though we cannot prove that Colet intended from the beginning to go the whole route from Bachelor to Doctor, it is pretty clear that he intended from a relatively early stage to go into theology, and that at a fairly early stage he intended to go on from his M.A. to the Bachelor of Divinity. As for the doctorate itself, he seems to have completed all the statutory requirements for that degree, whether he intended to do so or not, and to have received the

---

[1] The date of Colet's acceptance is uncertain. He is named as incumbent in about 1500 in Reg. Barons Lond. fol. 52ᵛ; cited by Emden. The same Register shows Colet vacating this vicarage in September 1505, possibly because of his acceptance of the Rectory of Lambourne, Berks, the previous June. (See Reg. Audley, Sarum, fol. 21ᵛ; cited by Emden.)

[2] Anthony à Wood says that Colet received his B.D. about 1501 and his D.D. in 1504 (see the *Fasti*, in Wood's *Athenae Oxonienses*, ed. Philip Bliss (London, 1815), II, cols. 7 and 13). Unfortunately Wood had no more access than we do to the missing University Register for the periods. See materials used by Wood noted in *Life and Times of Anthony Wood*, ed. A. Clark, *OHS*, xxx (1895), 87–312.

[3] Vacated 26 January 1503/4, according to Wharton, *Historia de Episcopis*, p. 234. Colet had been made canon of Salisbury and Prebendary of Durnford on 20 September 1502. See Reg. Audley, Sarum, fols. 7, and 79; cited by Emden.

[4] George Hennessy, *Novum Repertorium Ecclesiasticum Parochiale Londinense* (London, 1898), p. 38.

degree in very close to the normal period of study prescribed by the University.[1] These facts suggest that the clearest way to understand Colet's stay at Oxford is to see it in terms of a normal academic career in pursuit of the degree of Doctor of Divinity.

TABLE I

Chronology of the Lives of Colet and Ficino

John Colet		Marsilio Ficino
	1433	Birth
	1462	Undertakes systematic Platonic studies for Cosimo de'Medici.[2]
Birth	1466 (?)	
	1471	*Hermetic Pimander*[3]
	1472	Ordained priest
	1474	*Della religione cristiana*
	1476	*De christiana religione*
	1481	*Contro la pestilenza*
	1482	*Theologia Platonica*
Enters Oxford	1483(?)	
	1484	*Platonis opera*
Receives B.A. degree	1487(?)	
	1489	*De vita*
Receives M.A. degree	1490(?)	
Leaves Oxford; (goes to Orleans?)	1492	*Plotinus*
In Rome March, April, and May	1493	*De sole et lumine*
	1494	Date of latest letter in *Epistolae*
In Paris (November?)	1495	*Epistolae* (March)
[Problem Period; see Table II]	1496/7	*Dionysius* (*Mystic Theol.* and *Div. Names*)
	1497	*Iamblichus*
Ordained priest (March)	1498	*Athenagorae de resurrectione*
Meets Erasmus	1499	Death
Receives B.D. degree	1500(?)	
[Grocyn lectures on Pseudo-Dionysius]	1501	
Receives D.D. degree	1504(?)	
Becomes Dean of St. Paul's	1504	
Founds St. Paul's School	1510	
Convocation sermon	1511–12	
Death	1519	

[1] My computation is based upon the statutes as edited by Gibson (pp. cix–cxii and 48–52); Lyte (pp. 217, 222) and Mallet (i. 198) argue for a shorter period, but as I read the statutes, the times required were as follows:

	years
B.A. study	4
M.A. study	3
B.D. necessary regency	2
B.D. study	7
B.D. necessary lectures on *Sentences*	1
D.D. necessary inception	2
D.D. regency	1
	20

If Colet entered the University in 1483, he would have been eligible for the doctorate in 1503. As we have seen, he seems to have taken one extra year for the process.

[2] See P. O. Kristeller, 'Per la biografia di Marsilio Ficino', *Studies in Renaissance Thought and Letters* (Rome, 1956), pp. 195–8. (First printed in *Civiltà Moderna*, x (1938), 277–98.)

[3] All dates given for works of Ficino are dates of first printed edition.

BIOGRAPHICAL RELATIONS

TABLE II
Tentative Chronology of the Problem Period

1495	November	In Paris
1496	February	Returns to Oxford
1497	July	Ends one year of opponency for B.D. ?
	October	Lady Margaret Professorship begins
		Colet begins to lecture on Bible (?)
	December	Letter to Abbot of Winchcombe
		Ordained Deacon
1498	January	First commentary on Romans (i–v)
	March	Ordained Priest
	April	Reads *Heptaplus* and *Theologia*
		Commentary on Genesis
	October	Second commentary on Romans (vi–xi)
	November	Abstract of *Hierarchies*
	December	Reads *Epistolae*; writes Letter A[1]
1499	January	Supplement to *Hierarchies*
		Lectures on First Corinthians
	April	Letter B received; Letter C written
	September	Letter D received
	October	Third commentary on Romans (xii–xvi)
	November	Meets Erasmus; De Sacramentis [?]

To summarize, there are really three things which we learn about Colet's biography as a result of studying the All Souls volume. First, we learn that Colet had not actually met Ficino, but did correspond with him. Second, we learn something about the chronological order of Colet's major writings before 1500. Third, and most important, we learn that the relation between Colet and Ficino was a small part of Colet's total theological education during a period of twenty-one years when he pursued in fact, if not in intention, the entire Oxford curriculum from undergraduate matriculation to the highest degree given by the University, the Doctor of Divinity.

These biographical conclusions suggest that the important relation between Colet and Ficino was the theological relation, and we must now analyse that relation in some detail.

---

[1] In constructing Table II, I have assumed an elapsed time of about two months for letters travelling between Oxford and Florence. Contemporary accounts of fifteenth-century travel suggest that an average time for personal letters from London to Rome was about fifty days. See especially G. B. Parks, *The English Traveller to Italy*, i. 495–566. Letters which Ficino sent would have gone relatively faster than those he received because he used his own private messenger service. See P. O. Kristeller, *Supplementum Ficinianum*, i. p. lxxxviii.

III: INTELLECTUAL RELATIONS IN GENERAL

(A) Introduction

GENERALLY speaking, modern authorities are divided between two principal interpretations of Colet's place in English thought. One view is that Colet was primarily a humanist,[1] a scholar who completed his education in Italy, who quotes from Ficino and Pico, who introduced Florentine Platonism for the first time into England, who disliked Augustine more than he disliked any other author, who applied humanist methods to Biblical criticism, and finally, who devoted himself enthusiastically to the new humanist education and left as his principal monument St. Paul's School.

The other view of Colet, more popular in recent studies,[2] is that he was primarily a Protestant reformer, an Augustinian hater of this world, who deplored marriage and regarded man as a 'withered fruit, stinking in the nostrils of God', who devoted his time in Italy entirely to the study of the sacred writers, who barred the classics from the curriculum of his school, and who warned his Oxford audience against reading philosophers: 'Those books alone ought to be read, in which there is a salutary flavour of Christ, in which Christ is set forth for us to feed upon. Those books in which Christ is not found are but a table of devils. Do not become readers of philosophers, companions of devils. . . .'[3]

Some of the barbed wire between these two camps of Colet criticism was strung up unnecessarily by Burckhardt, and has since been removed by scholars like Kristeller and Bush, Hyma and Duhamel,[4] with their improved definitions of Christian humanism. But even with the barriers of terminology

---

[1] Principally Lupton, Sidney Dark, Kurt Schroeder, Friedrich Dannenberg, and J. A. R. Marriott.

[2] Principally A. Hyma, 'Erasmus and the Oxford Reformers (1493–1503)', *Nederlandsch Archief voor Kerkgeschiedenis*, N.S. xxv (1932); 'The Continental Origins of English Humanism', *HLQ*, iv (1940–1), 1–25; E. F. Rice, 'John Colet and the Annihilation of the Natural', *Harvard Theological Review*, xlv (1952), 141–63; Karl Bauer, 'John Colet und Erasmus von Rotterdam', *Archiv. für Reformationsgeschichte*, Ergänzungsband V (1929), E. W. Hunt, *Dean Colet and His Theology* (London, 1956) and L. W. Miles, 'Protestant Colet and Catholic More: A Study of Contrast in the Use of Platonism', *Anglican Theological Review*, xxxiii (1951), 30–42. Professor Miles's view has since changed; see p. 47 below.

[3] *Commentary on Corinthians*, p. 110:
Illi libri legendi sunt solum in quibus est salutaris degustacio Christi, in quibus Christus apponitur epulandus. In quibus vero non est Christus, mensa demoniorum est. Nolite fieri vos philosophorum lectores, socii demoniorum (p. 239).

[4] See Douglas Bush, *The Renaissance and English Humanism* (Toronto, 1939); P. O. Kristeller, *The Classics and Renaissance Thought* (Cambridge, Mass., 1955), chap I, and references on p. 94; Hyma references cited in note 2 above; P. A. Duhamel, 'The Oxford Lectures of John Colet', *JHI*, xiv (1953), 493–510.

out of the way, so that we no longer argue about a Christian Colet versus a humanist Colet, the fact remains that the scanty surviving information about Colet does present us with conflicting accounts, one of a man who admired classical philosophy, the other of a man who deplored it. The new evidence from the All Souls volume helps to resolve this conflict by showing that both accounts are correct, but one belongs after the other. Colet apparently had a good deal of enthusiasm for Platonism during the middle twenty years of his life, but very little during the last twenty. Platonism was only a tributary to the main stream of Colet's thought, colouring its waters for a short distance and then disappearing.

(B) Colet and Hellenism

What was the main stream of Colet's thought? To put it in modern parlance, Colet was by heredity an Aristotelian and by environment a Christian. Let me explain each of these, in reverse order. In saying that Colet was a Christian, I mean not only that he was a Roman Catholic, but two other things as well. First, his basic assumption about human life was that life is primarily a search for salvation. Man is born into a fixed theocentric order at a level beneath that of God, and desires above all to rise to God. All human motivation and value, for Colet, rest ultimately on man's awareness of the distance between himself and God and a desire to cross that distance.

Most Tudor Englishmen were Christian in this sense, but Colet was Christian in another sense as well. As I have tried to suggest in my sketch of Colet's Oxford career, from an early period he seems to have thought of the church or at least of Christianity as his vocation. Everyone has a project for himself, some sense of vocation; in the beginning perhaps Colet's project may have been mainly negative, a primitivist reaction against the decadence and aridity of scholastic theology, but this does not mean that Colet was primarily a reformer. Most critics agree that his primary motivation was much more positive than that; his personal project was little less than the vocation of being a new Paul. Relatively early in his career, for what reason we do not know, but perhaps not unrelated to the fact that he was the only survivor among twenty-two children in his family, he seems to have committed himself to a career of teaching and preaching Paul.

Putting both aspects of Colet's Christianity together, I think we may say that the main stream of Colet's thought, running unobstructed from our earliest to our latest record of him, is essentially a desire to understand and teach Pauline soteriology.

But if he was Christian by environment, he was Aristotelian by heredity. I do not mean that he was 'Aristotelian' merely in the sense that he had essentially scholastic training, though that is certainly true. I mean 'Aristotelian' in the sense that Coleridge meant it when he said that every man is either a Platonist or an Aristotelian. Colet was an Aristotelian in the sense that he was a practical man of action, a man of this world. Though his primary concern was the ascent of the soul to God, Colet's intellectual wings were too short for long flights of metaphysical speculation; he had to content himself with the lower levels of the soul's ascent, with the kind of everyday problem which could be reached by writing a grammar, publishing a moral tract, preaching a sermon, investing wealth judiciously, revitalizing a school, or explaining how to read the Bible.[1] What lifted these practical achievements to the level of greatness was Colet's religious zeal. He was interested in action, and he got it by exercising a contagious enthusiasm. Colet had nothing phlegmatic or uncommitted about him; his religious convictions, like those of Augustine and Paul, were intense and commanding. He built his entire career not on superior knowledge or intelligence, or even superior rhetoric, but upon the magnetism of his conviction.

But Colet's zeal for action was not the only dynamic involved in his study of theology. He came to Oxford just at a time when a powerful new external dynamic was beginning to put pressure on traditional Christianity. Just as Christianity in the eighteenth century had to shift gears to adjust to deism, in nineteenth century to evolutionism, and in the twentieth century to existentialism, so in the fifteenth century Christianity in England had to adjust to a revival of Hellenism.[2] The revival of Greek language and literature represented an intrusion into conventional Christian thought which had to be accommodated or surrendered to, and Colet arrived at Oxford just in time to participate in the process of accommodation, a process which may be called the Tudor Hellenization of Christianity.

It is this process which links Colet to the other men with whom he is most often grouped, More, Erasmus, Grocyn, and Linacre. The most important

---

[1] cf. Erasmus in the *Ratio verae theologiae*: 'the principal function of Scripture and sermon is to influence the heart' (*Opera*, V, 81) quoted by E. L. Surtz, 'The Oxford Reformers and Scholasticism', *SP*, xlvii (1950), 556. In saying that Colet 'revitalized' St. Paul's School rather than 'founded' it, I follow the argument of A. F. Leach, in 'St Paul's School before Colet', *Archaeologia*, lxii (1910), 191–238.

[2] The classical treatment of the influence of Hellenism upon earlier Christianity is that of Edwin Hatch, *The Influence of Greek Ideas on Christianity* (London, 1890); recently reprinted with up to date notes and an excellent bibliography of the whole subject, by Frederick C. Grant (New York, 1957).

thing that these men had in common was not their reform instincts or their Latin scholarship but their Greek studies; instead of calling them 'Oxford Reformers' or 'Oxford Humanists', one ought rather to call them the 'Oxford Hellenists'. Their distinctive contribution, as a group, to English culture was their contribution to the Tudor Hellenization of Christianity.[1]

But Colet would not have thought of this Hellenization as a secularizing of Christianity. Like most other fifteenth-century Englishmen Colet had an ontological view of reality. He believed in the separate existence of Truth as a set of absolute and unchanging principles known in its entirety only to God and known to man only to the extent that God has revealed it to us. All knowledge of the Truth is from revelation, and there are only so many authorities whom God has used for that purpose. The wisdom of ancient philosophers, so far as they had any knowledge of the truth, was from the revelation of God.[2] Colet's approach to such authorities was to try to accommodate their truth to the truth already known. His method of accommodating such authorities he borrowed from St. Paul.[3] This approach was to divide all mankind into three groups, the Gentiles, the Jews, and the Christians. By Gentiles Paul meant mainly the Greeks, and this is the meaning of the term accepted by Colet. Colet accommodates the newly discovered wisdom of the Greeks to traditional Christian learning by applying the simple principle of correspondence. 'The Gentiles', he says, had for their guidance 'philosophers, taught by created things; the Jews had prophets, taught by angels, and lastly we Christians have Apostles, fully taught by Jesus, who is God for evermore.'[4] The most important implication in this set of correspondences is that Colet was prepared to accept as a valid account of God's truth any statement of the Gentiles or the Jews which corresponded to, or was implied by Christian authority.

Colet would have been more hospitable than most to the study of the so-called 'Gentile', or Greek versions of God's Truth because his particular idol was Paul, and Paul's writings were thought to be deeply Hellenized.[5] Paul was

---

[1] On Erasmus's study of the Greek New Testament see a forthcoming study by W. J. Brandt. On More's study of the Epicureans see E. L. Surtz, *The Praise of Pleasure* (Cambridge, Mass., 1957). See also N. W. DeWitt, *St. Paul and Epicurus* (Minneapolis, 1954).

[2] *Exposition of Romans*, p. 52:
Quia quod notum est Dei ab illis, et id quod de Deo cognoverunt, quod, quidem suis viribus et sola vestigatione non cognoverunt, sed manifestatione Dei (p. 210).
The italicized passage (underlined by Colet) is a quotation from Rom. i. 19. [3] See I Cor. i. 23.

[4] *Exposition of Romans*, p. 70: Gentiles habuerunt philosophos doctos a creaturis; Judei prophetas doctos ab angelis; Christiani postremo apostolos edoctos a Jesu, Deo eterno (p. 214).

[5] cf. Rom. i. 14: 'I am debtor both to the Greeks, and to the Barbarians.' Albert Schweitzer, in *The Mysticism of St. Paul* (New York, 1955), p. viii, as in his earlier work on Paul, *Paul and His Interpreters* (London, 1912), p. 239, has maintained the thesis that Paul's theology was purely eschatological, and

thought to have been interested in Stoicism because of his correspondence with Seneca and in Platonism because of his personal acquaintance with Dionysius the Areopagite.

Stoicism is the antithesis of the zeal for action which we associate with Colet's own nature, but as a student of Paul he must have read the correspondence between Paul and Seneca,[1] for the legitimacy of that correspondence was not discredited until 1515, four years before Colet's death. Moreover he may have read other works of Seneca or of Epictetus, for in the All Souls volume his marginal comments repeatedly have a Stoic cast, as in the following example: 'Turn necessity into will and be free, free lest you be enslaved. By this one principle you may always be free: simply desire everything to happen as it does happen, and so make the best of everything. This means refining evil with goodness by means of your own goodness. Good will and good love compel everything.' (56) One should not rule out the possibility of non-Pauline and non-Ficinian sources for Colet's Stoicism. For example, since Colet knew no Greek,[2] he was forced to depend upon dictionaries, translations, and reference books for his knowledge of Greek words and terms. One of the reference books which he used most often was Niccolò Perotti's *Cornucopiae*,[3] first published in 1489 and republished nine times before 1500.[4] This work is mainly a dictionary of the Latin and Greek classics, but Perotti also produced a number of Platonic and Stoic works, including a translation of the *Enchiridion* of Epictetus.[5] Any study of Tudor Stoicism in general or of Colet's Stoicism in particular should take Perotti's work into account. On the other hand, it seems most likely that Colet would have been led into a study of Stoicism by the fact that he associated Paul with Seneca.

More impressive to Colet than Paul's association with Seneca would have been Paul's association with Dionysius the Areopagite, for Dionysius had reputedly met Paul in Athens. As we have seen, the legitimacy of this association was not discredited until near the end of Colet's Oxford career, and Colet's

---

that Christianity was not Hellenized until after Paul. Dom Gregory Dix holds a similar view; see *Jew and Greek* (London, 1953). For the reverse view see V. D. Macchioro, *From Orpheus to Paul* (New York, 1930), and Fernand Prat, *The Theology of St. Paul* (London, 1926).

[1] C. W. Barlow in *Epistolae Senecae ad Paulum . . . Papers and Monographs of the American Academy in Rome*, vol. x (1938); see especially pp. 104–5. See also Kurt Deissner, *Paulus und Seneca, Beiträge zur Förderung christlicher Theologie*, vol. xxi (Gütersloh, 1917). [2] See n. 5, p. 48.

[3] e.g. see *Exposition of Romans*, pp. 70, 81, 82, 143, and 144. Colet's reference to the Stoic doctrine of the *logoi spermatikoi* (*Letters to Radulphus*, p. 16) is another example of non-Pauline Stoicism.

[4] For editions see R. P. Oliver, *Niccolò Perotti's Version of the Enchiridion of Epictetus* (Urbana, 1954), pp. 146–7. A copy of the *Cornucopiae* was owned by Colet's friend Grocyn; see M. Burrows, 'Catalogue of Books Belonging to William Grocyn', *Oxford Historical Society Publications*, xvi (1890) (*Collectanea*, II), p. 320. Grocyn also owned a printed edition of the *Opera* of Seneca.

[5] Perotti's *Enchiridion* was not printed in Colet's lifetime; see Oliver, pp. 27, 40–57.

interest in Dionysius as an interpreter of Paul[1] had six centuries of authority behind it.[2] But in Colet's day an interest in Dionysius led directly into an interest in Platonism, for Dionysius, who to Colet was the greatest authority on Paul, to the Florentine Platonists was the greatest authority on Plato.[3] In order to understand Dionysius Colet would have thought it necessary to study also the works of Plato and Plotinus, and especially of Ficino.

Ficino was the ultimate authority on Platonism, not only because he had translated all the ancient Platonists, including Plato, Plotinus, Iamblichus, and Dionysius, and commented in detail upon their relation to the Christian religion, but also because he had written the definitive treatise on the harmony between Christian theology and the Platonic theology, a long work called the *Theologia Platonica* (1482).[4] The publication of this work had provoked a good deal of correspondence in which Ficino had to defend various points against charges of heresy and paganism; Ficino's long letters commenting on the *Theologia Platonica* form a large part of the total correspondence which was published in 1495 under the title *Epistolae*. Anyone who had studied the *Theologia* would have wanted to study the *Epistolae* as well.

This, then, is the chain of associations by which Colet was presumably led to a study of Ficino's *Epistolae*. He began as a theological student interested in preparing lectures on the Bible. Since his particular interest was St. Paul, he naturally became interested in Dionysius the Areopagite. This interest led him to Platonism, and Platonism led him to Ficino's *Theologia Platonica* and thence to the *Epistolae*.

[1] The fullest account of Colet's debt to the mysticism of the Pseudo-Dionysius is that of E. W. Hunt in *Dean Colet and His Theology*, pp. 102–30.
[2] The major translations to Colet's time were as follows: Hilduin (832); Scotus Eriugena (867); Jean le Serrazin (1167); Grosseteste (1235); Ambrogio Traversari (1436); and Marsilio Ficino (1492). For the background of the Dionysian writings see especially Maurice de Gandillac, Introduction to his French translation of the *Les Oeuvres* (Paris, 1943), pp. 7–64 and the works of D. Théry there mentioned (p. 64); Hugo Ball, Introduction to his German translation of *Die Hierarchien* only (Munich, 1955), pp. 19–96; and J. B. Collins, *Christian Mysticism in the Elizabethan Age* (Baltimore, 1940). There is no critical edition of the Greek text of Dionysius; the only modern edition of any of the Latin translations is that in *Dionysiaca*, which is awkward to use for any non-textual purpose. There is only one convenient modern translation of the *Hierarchies*; this is the unreliable translation of J. Parker (London, 1894 and 1897). There is an English translation of the *Celestial Hierarchy* by the Editors of the Shrine of Wisdom (Fintry, 1949) and one of the *Ecclesiastical Hierarchy* in a doctoral dissertation by T. L. Campbell at Catholic University, Washington, D.C.; one section of the dissertation (that dealing with baptism) was published (Washington, D.C., 1955) as a small monograph; its bibliography and notes are extremely useful.
[3] Ficino refers to Dionysius as 'Platonicorum culmen', *Epistolae*, (fol. cxcv^v) and 'primus Platonicorum' (*Opera*, p. 965).
[4] For a detailed analysis of the *Theologia Platonica* see P. O. Kristeller, *Philosophy of Ficino* (New York, 1943). This is not to say, of course, that the union of Platonism and Christianity began with Ficino. For the Alexandrian and Patristic backgrounds of the union see especially Thomas Whittaker, *The Neoplatonists* (Cambridge, 1928), E. R. Dodds, *The Elements of Theology* (Oxford, 1933), and C. Elsee, *Neoplatonism in Relation to Christianity* (Cambridge, 1908).

Colet may have come upon Ficino in a rather more accidental way than this, of course. For example, he may have paid little attention to any of the Platonists until his study of Genesis led him to Pico's *Heptaplus*, and Pico then may have led him to Ficino. But whatever the route, by which Colet was led to the Platonists, his primary interest in the Platonists was probably, as Heinrich Hermelink says, 'die von der Florentiner Akademie entdeckte Verbindung von Plato und Paulus'.[1]

In any case, it is clear that what Colet was looking for in reading Ficino's *Epistolae* was material illuminating the meaning of the Bible,[2] and that his search was based upon the familiar Renaissance assumption that the two major criteria of Truth are authority and correspondence. The foundation of Colet's confidence in the Platonists was the spectacular correspondence between Platonic and Christian doctrine.

The creation of the world by God, for example, was regarded as an autonomous fact, a Truth; we know this truth only on authority, the authority of the Bible; there is in Plato an account of the creation which corresponds in most details with that in Genesis; thus Plato's account must be true also, and Plato in general must have some special authority for the revelation of Truth. One's confidence in the authority of Plato is strengthened by the fact that there is so much correspondence at every point between his account of Truth and the Christian account. According to Christian theology, for example, God is a Trinity; the Platonic theology says the same thing. It is true that the Platonists do not use the names Father, Son, and Holy Spirit (Plotinus, for example, uses the names One, *Nous*, and World Soul; Ficino uses the names Saturn, Jupiter, and Venus). But there can be no doubt that the Platonic account of the Trinity corresponds to the Christian account and so describes the Truth.

The reason why the ancient Platonists used such strange names for divine truth was that God wanted to conceal his secrets from the unworthy pre-Christian mind; thus Ficino gives as his reason for using such mysterious mythological terminology the fact that he wants to protect the divine mysteries from desecration by the uninitiated, unworthy masses (**11**). But the mere difference in terminology did not disguise the essential correspondence between Platonic theology and Christian theology. If Platonists like Ficino seemed to rely rather heavily upon authorities such as Orpheus, Hermes

---

[1] Quoted by Karl Bauer, 'John Colet und Erasmus von Rotterdam', p. 157. See also Lupton, *Hierarchies*, pp. xix–xxxii and *Lectures on Romans*, pp. xxix–xxxv.

[2] For example, in the letter in which Ficino lists the books he has written (*Epistolae*, fol. viir) the only one of the books which Colet notes in the margin is Ficino's commentary on the Gospels (see marginalia **16**).

Trismegistus, and Zoroaster, and to talk rather more about Venus, Minerva, and the Cumaean Sibyl than about Christ and Paul, Colet had only to refine this pagan ore into Christian doctrine by the simple alchemy of 'accommodation', a principle of exegesis advocated by the Pseudo-Dionysius himself.[1]

Once one has established confidence in the authority of the Platonic theology by recognizing various points of correspondence, one can then use the Platonic theology to fill in gaps in the Christian account of the world. For example, the Bible mentions angels in various places, but it does not make clear where in the pattern of the universe all the various kinds of angel belong. One of the great advantages of the Platonic theology is that it supplies this missing information. The works of the Platonic theologian Dionysius, augmented by the commentaries of Ficino, provide a detailed and authoritative account of the nine degrees of angels.

There is a good example of this use of the Platonists in Colet's marginalia. In Romans viii. 1–15 and 1 Corinthians x. 20, Paul refers several times to daemons. The nature and function of daemons are not made clear in the Bible, but they were discussed in detail by Socrates and by the Christian Platonists. Daemons, as Ficino points out, correspond to Christian angels, inhabitants of the spirit world between man and God in the hierarchy of being. In the *Epistolae* Ficino explains in detail in several different letters the nature and functions of daemons, both good and evil. Colet has annotated two of these passages at length: (**61**) and (**64**).

The concept of the daemon is only one detail in which the Platonic theology was regarded as filling in information somehow left out of the Biblical account of Truth. The major omission in Christian theology which the Platonic theology was thought to supply was nothing less than the entire descending, or kataphatic, part of the two way relation between God and man.

The idea that the history of mankind, or of one man, consists of a descent followed by an ascent is extremely common in western culture.[2] Behind most of the pagan mystery religions of ancient Greece there lay the assumption that the soul is a divine spark which has come into an earthly body and seeks to return again by a *Himmelreise*, a soul-journey to heaven. In early Jewish writings, too, the soul-journey is a familiar motif. The soul's journey appears in Origen, in Clement, and in the Gnostics, but in most Christian theology the emphasis is upon the ascent of the soul only.

[1] Dionysius, *Heavenly Hierarchy*, trans. J. Parker, pp. 2–13.
[2] The fullest treatment of the idea in our context is that of Anders Nygren in *Agape and Eros* (London, 1953). My remarks on the ancient Greek and Jewish backgrounds of the idea are based upon M. W. Bloomfield, *The Seven Deadly Sins* ([East Lansing] Michigan 1952), 16–26.

The Christian history of mankind depicts man as first falling from innocence to depravity in Adam and then rising from depravity to salvation in Christ. Unfortunately for us, however, ontogony does not, in this case, recapitulate phylogeny; that is, the life of the individual man today does not recapitulate the fall and rise of the race as a whole. The individual man does not go through the *fall* part of the cycle; he is born fallen and during his own lifetime has nowhere to go but up. The Fall was singular, it occurred once for everyone, but the ascent to salvation is plural and must occur in every individual life. Adam *fell* for everyone, but Christ did not save everyone; he made salvation possible for everyone, but not actual. Thus for most Christians, except Pelagians perhaps, the life of an individual man in this world is an ascent only.

The idea that the soul descends was not lost in Christian theology; it is present in the concept of aversion to God, and turns up in various interesting places. In Donatus, for example. Just as Ovid and Virgil were moralized to make them fit for Christian consumption in the Middle Ages, so Donatus' Latin grammar was moralized for the same purpose. In one version of the moralized Donatus the commentator explains that the various cases in the declension of nouns correspond to the various stages in the declension of the soul from God.[1]

But on the whole the kataphatic, or descending, part of the soul's cycle was scantily treated in Christian theology, and what attracted Renaissance theologians most to the Platonic theology was the fact that it supplied a detailed account of the descending part of the soul's cycle (stressed in the *Timaeus* of Plato and in the *Enneads* of Plotinus) as well as a corroborating account of the ascending part (stressed in the *Symposium* and *Phaedo* of Plato). Renaissance writers did not distinguish between Platonism and Neoplatonism;[2] they regarded Plotinus as merely the most authoritative ancient commentator on Plato. Hence they thought of the Platonic theology in general as providing a well-rounded account of the history of the soul.

We see this interest reflected in the All Souls volume in Colet's detailed marginal paraphrase of the passage in which Ficino himself describes the cycle of the soul's history:

The soul is at first in the presence of God, where it is satisfied and happy. Then, because of its desire for and love of the body, it falls into the body and is united with it. There, like a person drowning in a stormy sea, the soul is overcome by oblivion, the lack of knowledge [of heaven], whence all evils spring . . . but the soul easily passes out of the

---

[1] An example cited by C. E. Mallet, *History of the University of Oxford* (London, 1924), i. 434–5.
[2] See, for example Francesco Vieri, *Compendio della dottrina di Platone* (Florence, 1577).

dense shadows into a remembrance of truer things. At length it recalls its own nature, and, recognizing and despising the meanness of the body, it seeks to return to its natural home [i.e. heaven] and feed once more on nectar and ambrosia, that is, the vision of Truth, and to rejoice in the possession of the Good. It discovers and beats its wings; it comes to life again in its dead body; it is awakened from sleep; it emerges from the river Lethe and, stretching its long-unused [wings of] goodness and wisdom, tries to fly back to heaven. (7)

This appears to be a deliberate secularization of the Christian account of the descent and ascent of the soul, a deliberate translation into Platonic terms, the reverse of the desecularizing process illustrated in the moralized Donatus; but Colet would not have seen it in that way. From his point of view, here, as in the case of the daemons, Ficino provides this Platonic account of the career of the soul as a supplement to available Christian accounts. Colet's motive for entertaining Platonic ideas was certainly not a positive enthusiasm for secularization, or for Platonizing, but only an acceptance of Hellenic truth as additional truth. This is the place of Platonism in Colet's thought; he was interested in the Platonic theology in so far as it explained or illuminated for him matters of Christian theology, and especially of interpretation of the Bible.

(C) *The Extent of Colet's Platonism*

The extent to which Colet was actually indebted to Platonic authorities is difficult to determine. For example, Father Surtz shows that even so Platonic a doctrine as the theory of common property may, in More at least, be traced to the Bible as well as to the *Republic*.[1] Professor Leland Miles, on the other hand, has impressively traced evidences of Platonic influence in all of Colet's writings, and concludes that the key to the whole of Colet's thought is the emanationism of Plotinus.[2] My own study, made independently, has been limited to Colet's debt to Ficino, and my conception of Colet's debt to the Platonic tradition is, perhaps inevitably, somewhat narrower than Professor Miles's.

The evidence most often cited in support of the idea that Colet was profoundly learned in Platonic doctrine is a remark of Erasmus: 'When I hear Colet I seem to be listening to Plato himself.'[3] Unfortunately, Erasmus's com-

---
[1] E. L. Surtz, *The Praise of Pleasure* (Cambridge, Mass., 1957), pp. 161–5; Colet's discussion of this idea is in *Exposition of Romans*, pp. 134–6.

[2] L. W. Miles, *John Colet and the Platonic Tradition* (La Salle, Ill., 1961, London, 1962); see esp. pp. 166–9. I have not been able to take full account of this work, which appeared when the present book was in the press.

[3] Coletum meum cum audio, Platonem ipsum mihi videor audire. Erasmus, *Epistolae*, ed. P. S. Allen (Oxford, 1906–58), i. 273.

parison of Colet to Plato has nothing to do with Colet's Platonism; Erasmus was merely complimenting Colet's eloquence by referring to a humanist tradition, based on Cicero's *Orator* (XIX, 62), that Plato was the most eloquent of all the ancients.

One gets a more accurate notion of the calibre of Colet's Platonic learning by looking at the University curriculum in Colet's day. Of Colet's university training Erasmus says, 'As a youth he studied the scholastic philosophy in his own country, and earned the degree [i.e. the M.A.] which signifies mastery of the seven liberal arts.'[1] Anthony à Wood amplifies this statement to the extent of saying that Colet studied in 'logicals and the philosophicals'; by this he means the seven liberal arts and the three philosophies, still symbolized in the book with seven clasps and the three crowns of the Oxford University seal. The seven liberal arts included the standard trivium and quadrivium; the three philosophies were natural, moral, and divine philosophy. For both the arts and the philosophies specific books were set by the University statutes. The set books required for the B.A. and M.A. degrees[2] included no works which would have been associated with Platonism; and the kinds of disputation questions which we know were assigned[3] show that the University provided only typical scholastic training.

Erasmus, who did not know Colet until 1499, tells us[4] that 'as a student' Colet read Plato and Plotinus, but in fact this reading of Plotinus could not, at the earliest, have occurred until after Colet had received his M.A., for the following reason. Colet knew no Greek until he was fifty years old (i.e. 1516) by his own admission;[5] hence he must have read Plato and Plotinus in Latin. The only Latin translation of Plotinus available, either in manuscript or in print while Colet was at Oxford was that of Ficino; this translation was not published until 1492, when Colet had completed his two years' Master's regency and was about to leave Oxford for the continent. As for Plato, Latin translations of several individual dialogues (notably the *Timaeus*, *Meno*, *Phaedo*, and *Parmenides*) by men other than Ficino were available in manuscript and also partly in print before 1493; about 1455, for example, John Doget, another Oxonian, wrote a commentary on the *Phaedo*, based on a translation by Leonardo Bruni. A Latin translation of the complete works of Plato was published by Ficino in 1484, during Colet's second year at Oxford, so Colet

---

[1] Erasmus, *Epistolae, ed. cit.* iv. 514; the translation is my own.
[2] See Gibson, *Statuta*, pp. xciv–xcvi.
[3] See, for example, the list in A. G. Little and F. Pelster, *Oxford Theology and Theologians*, OHS, xcvi (1934), 287–334.
[4] Erasmus, *Epistolae*, iv. 515.
[5] Erasmus, *Epistolae*, II. 257–9; a letter from Colet to Erasmus dated 20 June 1516.

obviously could have read Plato during his Oxford years; but since Erasmus lumps Plato and Plotinus together, implying that Colet read them at about the same time, since he must have read Plotinus later, and since there is no other evidence at all in his own work that he read them before 1496, I should be inclined to put this part of Colet's Platonic learning off until after his return from the continent in 1496.

As for Colet's studies on the continent, Erasmus tells us that they were entirely theological, and directed towards Colet's preaching career.[1] This again, like most of Erasmus's statements, is doubtless extremely loose, and would not in any case exclude Ficino, except that Erasmus takes the trouble to list a number of the theologians whom Colet did read during that period: Dionysius, Origen, Cyprian, Ambrose, and Jerome. Only the first two are Platonists.

The first concrete evidence we have of Colet's study of Platonists is his use of Pico's commentary on Genesis (the *Heptaplus*) as a model for his own similar commentary on that book.[2] Here the Dionysian principle of accommodation is in full operation, but Colet's commentary is intent upon understanding Genesis, not upon practising or preaching Platonism. The next evidence we have of Colet's study of the Platonists is in his second commentary on Romans. This example is extremely important, not only because it involves his study of the major document in Platonic theology, Ficino's *Theologia Platonica*, but also because his use of that work foreshadows precisely his treatment of Ficino's *Epistolae*. Colet quotes from the *Theologia* at length in his second commentary on Romans.[3] Colet's version of the passage reads, in part, as follows:

But in this life the love of God far surpasses the knowledge of Him, seeing that here no man truly knows God, nor indeed can do. But to love God is in his power.[4] . . . For while the force of knowledge consists rather in separation, that of love consists in union. Hence, of necessity, love is the more impetuous and efficient and swifter in attaining what is good, than knowledge is in detecting what is true. Furthermore it is beyond doubt more pleasing to God himself to be loved by men than to be surveyed, and to be worshipped than to be understood.[5]

---

[1] Erasmus, *Epistolae*, iv. 515. 'iam tum se praeparans ad praeconium sermonis Evangelici.'
[2] See note on *Letters to Radulphus*, chap. II, note 6, p. 27.
[3] *Lectures on Romans*, pp. 29–32 (Latin, pp. 155–7).
[4] *Lectures on Romans*, p. 29:
  Sed Dei amorem in hac vita longe cognicioni prestare, quoniam Deum hic nemo vere cognoscit, nec potest quidem. Amare autem potest . . . (p. 155).
[5] *Lectures on Romans*, p. 30:
  Est enim amoris vis in unione magis, cognicionis in distrectione [sic]. Unde necessario amor magis vehemens et efficax est, et ad assequendum bonum citacior, quam cognicio in vero deprehendendo; plusque eciam necessario possidet bonum quam cognicio verum. Quineciam proculdubio ipsi Deo multo est gracius amari ab hominibus quam prospici, et coli quam intelligi (pp. 155–6).

Colet himself says, as an epilogue to the passage from Ficino, that he has modified Ficino's language as he pleased; on close examination these modifications turn out to be rather far-reaching. Where Ficino cites examples from Plato and Plotinus, Colet systematically changes them to examples from Paul, and Colet so alters the letter and the spirit of Ficino's language that what, in Ficino's original, was an epistemological analysis of the relative functions of love and intellect as speculative faculties by which the soul attains a knowledge of God, becomes, in Colet's version, an argument for preferring the moral goodness of the active life to the metaphysical wisdom of the contemplative life. Both in its general treatment of Ficino, and in the ways in which it differs from Ficino, this passage is a paradigm of what Colet does with the *Epistolae*.

As one reads Colet's comments on the *Epistolae*, the first impression one gets is that Colet is systematically de-secularizing Ficino. Here, for example, is a typical passage from Ficino's *Epistolae*:

When rich and powerful Juno does not hear us, we should not curse our fates before we give that divine power a chance—a power which is omnipresent and amply available to all who seek it. It hears men who have not yet called, as well as those who pray in the normal way. We must seek our help entirely from Minerva, O Salvinus, in order to be able eventually to rise from the earth and escape to the upper air. For no power can lift man to the ethereal head of the universe except one, which has sprung from the very head of Jove. But since Minerva does not respond to anyone who does not pray in the proper way, let us try to seek our aid from her in the right way, my friend. For who rightly worships wisdom unless he worships wisely? But he alone worships wisdom wisely who seeks wisdom from wisdom. Only through wisdom can we seek anything wisely from wisdom or from anything else. This we have learned from Socrates, whom Apollo considered the wisest of men.[1]

We know from another letter in the volume (fol. clxxii[v]) that what Ficino is really talking about here is only the conventional medieval contrast between action and contemplation. The usual pair of figures for these abstractions in a medieval text would have been Mary and Martha; but Ficino, speaking in the mythological jargon of the Platonic Academy, secularizes the abstractions and refers to them as Juno and Minerva.

---

[1] Ficino, *Epistolae*, fol. xcvi[r].
Ubi nos dives potensque Juno non audit, haud prius, nobis culpande sunt Parce quam numen illud experiamur quod, quia viget ubique, affatim adest omnibus qui eidem adesse volunt. Audit hominem nondum vocantem. Exaudit quemlibet rite precantem. Totum igitur auxilium, Salvine, nostrum nobis est a Minerva petendum. Quo possimus quandoque nos tollere humo superasque evadere ad auras. Nempe solum id numen ad ethereum mundi caput hominem potest atollere quod ipso summi Jovis est capite natum. Quoniam vero non exaudit quemquam, nisi rite precantem, conemur, amice, pro viribus, recte hinc auxilium petere. Quis nam sapientiam recte adorat nisi qui sapienter? Sapienter autem hanc solus adorat qui poscit a sapientia sapientiam. Non possumus nisi per illam quicquam vel ab ipsa vel ab alio petere sapienter. Non possumus quicquam ab illa sapienter petere nisi illam. Hoc nos docuit Socrates, vir omnium Apollinis judicio sapientissimus.

In commenting on this passage, Colet ignores Ficino's mythological allegory, substitutes for Ficino's reference to Socrates a reference to Solomon, and interprets the passage as a comment on St. Paul's mention (1 Cor. i. 24) of the two divine attributes of Christ: 'Christ is the power of God and the wisdom of God.' Thus what Ficino had intended as a plea for the contemplative life becomes, in Colet's note, a plea for moral goodness:

'Christ is the power of God and the wisdom of God.' Rich and mighty Juno does not hear us. Let us try the power of God because He is powerful everywhere and because He is present to all who wish to be in His presence; indeed Christ hears even when He is not called; He listens to anyone who prays properly. It is from Christ that we must seek the aid we need to raise ourselves from the earth and escape to heaven. . . . Let us pray to Him properly, that is, wisely . . . [A man prays] wisely who asks for wisdom from Wisdom itself, [and only for such] wisdom as ought wisely and properly to be sought. Hence Solomon asked for wisdom in order that he might distinguish between good and evil, because nothing is good except to the wise and good man. (50)

As in this example, Colet repeatedly translates Ficino's classical references and ideas into Christian terms, showing that his primary interest in the volume is as a source of ideas which may help him to interpret the works of St. Paul. Perhaps the most impressive example is the passage in which Colet substitutes St. Paul for Socrates. Ficino's text reads:

O false judgment of the masses! They thought the philosopher Democritus was stupid when, in his great wisdom, he began to deride human stupidity. Yet he was regarded as the wisest of all by Hippocrates, the most judicious of physicians. Then, too, they condemned the divine Socrates on the grounds of his evil thoughts about the gods, though he was called by their own god [i.e. Apollo] the wisest of all men because his view of God was sounder than theirs. But let the stupid crowd laugh as it pleases: let the philosopher ridicule them in turn as being stupid and impious. Let philosophers join Heraclitus in bemoaning the pitiful laughter of the masses and join Democritus in ridiculing their laughable tears.[1]

Colet's comment on this passage reads as follows:

They are truly ministers of Christ who are possessed of a unique wisdom, and try to bring it about that others become wise [also]. How grievous it is that they are treated so shamefully and irreverently by the masses, that they, who are the salt and wisdom of the earth are thought to be the only mad ones by the masses. The Jews thought Christ was insane, and Agrippa thought the same of Paul. . . . The result is that anyone who is

---

[1] Ficino, *Epistolae*, fol. xcv**v**:
O falsissimum vulgi judicium. Tunc Democritum philosophum putaverunt insipientem, cum maxime sapiens factus coepit mortalium insipientiam deridere; et ab Hippocrate medicorum sapientissimo judicatus est omnium prudentissimus. Tunc Socratem divinum quasi male de diis sentientem condemnaverunt, quando ab ipso eorum Deo, utpote, qui rectius quam caeteri de Deo sentiret, sapientissimus est appellatus. Sed rideat insanum vulgus ut libet; rideat philosophos ut insanos et impios. Interim philosophi et flebilem vulgi risum una cum Heraclito lugeant et ridiculum fletum cum Democrito rideant.

ridiculed by the senseless should actually regard this as something to be proud of, and should himself ridicule them in turn, for it is impossible for him to admire them. Their laughter, which Heraclitus weeps over, is pathetic and pitiable, and their tears, which Democritus laughed at, are ludicrous. (**50**)

Colet's mention of Paul in this passage is typical of his preoccupation with Paul throughout the All Souls marginalia. Three of the passages in Ficino's text which Colet underlines are quotations, acknowledged, or unacknowledged, from St. Paul.[1] In one passage Colet begins his comment with a quotation from 1 Corinthians, and in another with a passage from Romans,[2] and he quotes scraps of Paul's epistles throughout the marginalia.[3] Most important, the issues which Colet selects to discuss in commenting on Ficino's text are again and again issues which are raised by St. Paul, especially in the letter to the Romans and in 1 Corinthians; the issue of the fall and rise of the soul, the mysterious nature of truth, the inter-relation of faith, hope, and charity, the opposition of the flesh and the spirit, the importance of good actions, and the injunction to avoid evil and seek the good.

But it is one thing to read a book with a specific subject in mind, and it is another to be influenced by that book to change one's views about that subject. For example, Colet, like Ficino, tended to interpret Paul as a theocentric rather than as a Christocentric or anthropocentric theologian, but if the first commentary on Romans is any index, Colet had adopted this interpretation of Paul before he ever read the *Epistolae*, and perhaps even before he read the *Theologia Platonica*. One can easily show that Colet read Ficino's *Epistolae* with St. Paul in mind; it is more difficult to show that Colet's reading of the *Epistolae* influenced his interpretations of St. Paul. Positive influence is difficult to show partly because of the multiplicity of possible sources for Colet's ideas; for example, Ficino's favourite image of the sun, and indeed his justification of Plato as a Christian authority, are both anticipated in St. Augustine,[4] and other Platonic ideas of Colet's are traceable to Origen,[5] Clement,[6] the Pseudo-Dionysius, and many other early authorities.[7]

---

[1] See Appendix C, nos. 8, 23, 27.   [2] See **50** and **30**.   [3] See my notes.

[4] cf. L. Miles's review of E. W. Hunt, *Dean Colet and His Theology*, in *RN*, xi (1955), 134, 136; and see marginalia **41** in the light of R. W. Battenhouse, *A Companion to the Study of St. Augustine* (New York, 1955), p. 300. On Augustine's influence on Ficino see especially P. O. Kristeller, 'Augustine and the Early Renaissance', *Review of Religion*, viii (1944), 339–58; reprinted in Kristeller's *Studies in Renaissance Thought and Letters* (Rome, 1956), pp. 355–72. On Augustine's influence on Colet see especially Lupton, *Letters to Radulphus*, pp. xliv–xlvii; E. F. Rice, 'John Colet and the Annihilation of the Natural', p. 161; and A. Hyma, 'Erasmus and the Oxford Reformers', pp. 102, 125.

[5] e.g. *Exposition of Romans*, p. 95 where Pico is the intermediary; for a debt to Philo, see *Letters to Radulphus*, p. 9.   [6] See L. W. Miles, 'Protestant Colet and Catholic More', pp. 31–37.

[7] cf. n. 2, p. 72. A good example is the concept of emanation from sphere to sphere which Colet discusses in the *Letters to Radulphus* (p. 18); one would have said that this was a Neoplatonic idea, from Plotinus or at least the Pseudo-Dionysius, but Colet took it from Cicero's *De Natura Deorum*, ii. 15.

Another difficulty rises out of the fact that there is so little of Colet's writing in which influence of any sort could be revealed. For example, the part of Ficino's *Epistolae* which Colet annotates most fully and at greatest length is Ficino's discussion of the nature of light (**44**); this subject evidently interested Colet very much, yet nowhere in his extant writings is there any indication of his use of this material.

A problem of a different kind is illustrated in Colet's marginalia on the subject of law. The only extended treatment of law in Colet's extant works is in his commentary[1] on Romans ii. 11–29. This commentary appears, on other grounds, to have been written before Colet read Ficino's *Epistolae*. Colet has annotated at least five of the *Epistolae* in which law is discussed (**6, 25, 27, 53, and 66**), but there is little or no relation between Colet's views in the commentary on Romans and those in the All Souls marginalia. In the Romans commentary Colet had made four principal points about law: the superiority of faith to law,[2] the contrast between the Old Law and the New,[3] the identification of law as the will of God,[4] and a classification of law as the law of nature (Adam), the law of obedience (Moses), and the law of grace (Christ).[5] The points made in Ficino's five letters are as follows: all the great law-givers, from Moses through Plato, have regarded law as based on divine authority (**6**); law may be divided into divine, natural, and human (**25**); the allegorical meaning of the parts of the body of a perfect lawyer (**27**); laws are determined not by the stars but by God (**53**); and law is derived from wisdom (**66**). Colet's marginalia on these passages are paraphrases which largely ignore Ficino's preoccupation with defending himself against charges of being more an astrologer than a theologian, and appear to focus on passages which glorify God and depreciate man. Here Colet appears not so much in outright agreement or disagreement with Ficino, as simply out of focus with him; they seem not to be talking about the same things.

Perhaps the best measure of this air of distraction, or preoccupation, about Colet's marginalia is his annotation of Ficino's long essay 'In Praise of Marriage'.[6] This was a subject on which we know that Colet had strong feelings. Though he and Ficino were both bachelors, Ficino defended marriage, whereas Colet vigorously advocated celibacy.[7] Instead of disagreeing with Ficino's

---

[1] *Exposition of Romans*, pp. 107–50.
[2] *Exposition of Romans*, pp. 108–9. On the background of this concept in Paul see V. D. Macchioro, *From Orpheus to Paul*, pp. 195–7.
[3] *Exposition of Romans*, p. 111.   [4] *Exposition of Romans*, p. 129.
[5] *Exposition of Romans*, pp. 141–2, and 150–1.   [6] Ficino, *Epistolae*, fol. xcv^v.
[7] e.g. *Commentary on Corinthians*, pp. 89–97; cf. 1 Cor. vii. 7.

essay on the subject, or ignoring it altogether, Colet merely notes a few of Ficino's arguments:

[Ficino] approves of marriage as acceptable to nature; it creates sons. Socrates [learned moral discipline] from his wife. Marriage does not prevent scholarship. . . . Venus mixes with the Muses. Man is the most sociable [of all animals. It was] for this [reason that nature provided him alone with the faculty of] speech [and the faculty of making] laws. No one lives outside of society unless he is either above man or below man. (**49**)

The neutral atmosphere of these remarks is disarming, and I think the best way to understand them is to think of them as representing a no-man's-land of objectivity between the attitude of enthusiasm with which Colet presumably approached the *Epistolae* and an attitude of antagonism with which I am convinced he left them. I think it very likely that Colet's reading of the *Epistolae* was the means by which he first realized how very far apart he and Ficino were in point of view. It can hardly be accidental that in the very first lectures which he delivered after reading the *Epistolae* Colet delivered his blast against reading philosophers,[1] denied that scripture could be better understood with the help of the heathen philosophers, and asserted that all that was needed was grace, prayer, faith, and the help of Christ.[2]

Colet's direct interest in Ficino appears to have been confined to a period of a few years, perhaps three (1496–9) or at most seven (1492–9), and to have been limited to a plundering of theological tracts as aids in interpreting the Bible.[3] There is no evidence whatever in the All Souls volume that Colet thinks of Ficino as a fellow-reformer, a kindred spirit achieving in Italy the reforms which he himself seeks in England;[4] on the contrary, his attitude toward Ficino in the All Souls marginalia is essentially utilitarian and independent, and on one point, of crucial importance, actually hostile.

As I have suggested, Grocyn's exposure of the Pseudo-Dionysius in 1501 doubtless had a good deal to do with the cooling of Colet's enthusiasm, but the divorce between Colet and Ficino would have come soon in any case, I believe, for their views were fundamentally incompatible. Professor Miles discusses the difference between them in terms of a distinction between two different kinds of Renaissance Platonism: Clementine Platonism, in which Platonism was regarded as merely a hand-maiden of Christian theology, and Florentine

---

[1] See note 3, p. 38.
[2] *Commentary on Corinthians*, p. 110:
. . . quod dum facis, diffidis te per gratiam solam et orationes sacras litteras intelligere posse, atque per adjumentum Christi et fidei . . . (pp. 238–9).
[3] For example, Colet shows no interest at all in Ficino's most elaborate defences of philosophy (*Epistolae*, fols. lxxxiii r, cxxxvi v, and cxliii r).
[4] This is the view of Ficino which one gets in Seebohm, *Oxford Reformers*; see pp. 11, 13.

Platonism, in which Platonism was regarded as a sister-science to Christian theology.[1] Colet, who accepts only certain individual Platonic doctrines, represents what Professor Miles calls Clementine Platonism, whereas Ficino, who insists upon the total equivalence of the Platonic and Christian theologies, represents Florentine Platonism.

Although Professor Miles's distinction is based upon an historical distinction made by Clement of Alexandria himself, I have not seen any evidence in the work of either Colet or Ficino that suggests that they identified themselves with either of these two schools. In any case, there is another difference between the two men, more specific than that suggested by Professor Miles, a difference which perhaps explains *why* they had different views of Platonism and a good many other differences as well. This difference, which is reflected in their work, is that Ficino was an 'intellectualist' theologian in the technical sense of the term common in medieval theology, whereas Colet was a 'voluntarist' theologian.

[1] A similar distinction is made by Robert Ellrodt in *Neoplatonism in the Poetry of Spenser* (Geneva, 1960), pp. 180–2, where he distinguishes between medieval (Augustinian) Platonism and Renaissance (Ficinian) Neo-platonism. This distinction, though useful, is a modern one and does not appear in Renaissance handbooks of philosophy. In any case the difference between Colet and Ficino is best understood, I think, in other terms.

IV: THE INTELLECT-WILL PROBLEM

(A) *The Nature of the Soul*

THE modern reader is tempted to see the cleavage between Colet and Ficino in quantitative terms; it makes some sense for us to say that Ficino was a Christianizing Platonist whereas Colet was only an occasionally Platonizing Christian. But that is not the way in which the men themselves would have said it. Ficino was an ordained priest and regarded himself as a devout Christian throughout his mature life; and Colet, on the other hand, knew more about Platonism than did most other Englishmen of his day. The difference between Colet and Ficino from their point of view was not merely a matter of emphasis, of degrees of religiosity. It was a qualitative difference, a philosophical cleavage too deep to be healed by any redefinition of Christian humanism, and it was the more striking because it asserted itself in a context of extensive common belief.

Both men believed that the human soul is involved in an ascent to God, but they had different concepts of the nature of that soul. They both believed that the soul should arrange its affairs in this world in such a way as to expedite its ascent to God, but they had different views as to what the best arrangement was. They both believed that the soul rises to God through a regular progression, but they differed as to what the stages in that progression were.[1] Finally, they both believed that the soul could attain God, but they differed as to the part which God plays in bringing that attainment about. At all four of these points of common reference the All Souls volume brings the fundamental differences between Ficino and Colet into very sharp focus.

On the nature of the human soul even a cursory glance at the volume is revealing. Colet's marginalia consistently represent the human soul as being in a depraved condition:

Human life is a tragedy, for . . . it exhibits unhappiness whether one lives the life of contemplation, action, or pleasure. (54)
We are prone to lust. (62)
We live in the region of evils; scandals, offences, frustrations and evils are necessary and cannot be eliminated. (64)

---

[1] For the view that Ficino's soteriology is mainly Thomistic see Guiseppe Anichini, *L'Umanesimo e li problema della salvezza in Marsilio Ficino* (Milan, 1937).

This is certainly not the view of man which we associate with Ficino. Ficino has none of Colet's abject humility. Indeed Ficino's view of man in the *Theologia Platonica* is one of the most ecstatically optimistic views in human history. 'Man is the greatest of all miracles of nature', he says; 'man is the miracle of the world'.[1] Ficino sees man alone, of all creatures, as presented with a free choice between God and the world; only of men may it be said that 'the world was all before them, where to choose'. The whole point of Ficino's optimistic and enthusiastic endorsement of the philosophy of love is that the human soul is the centre of the world, the hub and turning point of the universe, where divine love becomes human love, where becoming begins to be being. The soul enjoys this position by virtue of its own weaknesses, its double desire for the flesh and the spirit binding the two spiritual substances above it (God and Angelic mind) to the two physical substances below it (Quality and Body).[2] 'Though at certain periods', says Professor Kristeller, 'Ficino was really convinced of the wickedness of man, his own attitude was far from that of a moral preacher'.[3]

The contrast between Colet's pessimism and Ficino's optimism about man in general is neatly epitomized in Colet's note on Ficino's letter entitled 'There is no escape from sin except to the *summum bonum*'. (54) Ficino's emphasis in the letter is upon the *summum bonum* as the proper end of human effort; Colet's marginal note, however, stresses only the fact that there is no escape from sin.

We begin to see the reasons for this difference in point of view as soon as we turn to a detailed analysis of the conception of the soul in the two men. The Platonic way of explaining the search of the soul for the *summum bonum* is to relate the various parts of the soul to the characteristics of its goal. According to Plato himself that goal involves Truth, Goodness, and Beauty, and the soul correspondingly is equipped with intellectual, moral, and aesthetic faculties. Ficino's account of the organization of the soul seems at first glance considerably more esoteric than Plato's; Ficino lists among the parts of the soul the *mens*, the *ratio*, the *idolum*, and even the body.[4] From the smoke of his terminology, however, emerges the fact that the soul for Ficino really means the individual monad of being, including both body and soul, and that it is motivated in its pursuit of God by three principal faculties which are very much like Plato's: the intellect, the will, and love. But Ficino regards love and will as essentially identical, representing roughly the restlessness of the consciousness, and he sets them off together as differentiated from intellect; thus the

---

[1] P. O. Kristeller, *Philosophy of Ficino*, pp. 118–20.
[2] Kristeller, *Philosophy of Ficino*, p. 106.
[3] Kristeller, *Philosophy of Ficino*, p. 356.   [4] Kristeller, *Philosophy of Ficino*, pp. 368–9, 374–6.

soul's search for God, from Ficino's point of view, involves essentially only these two faculties, intellect and love.[1]

Unfortunately we do not have for Colet, as we have for Ficino, a full and systematic statement by him of his own theology,[2] apart from the doctrines of the church in general formulated in the *Summa theologica* of St. Thomas Aquinas. We may observe from the writings of Colet which we do have, however, two important points of difference between him and Ficino.

First, in spite of the fact that he talks about the World Soul (**61**), there is no suggestion in Colet that he sees the individual human soul as merely a monad in the World-Soul, as Ficino does. The human soul, for Colet, is a discrete entity which does not include the body but is merely imprisoned in it (see **13**). Colet's is the limed soul struggling to be free; its aversion to the flesh is a primary condition of its being, the negative side of its appetite for God. Colet's view of the soul emphasizes the conflict in objectives between God and the flesh, and shares none of Ficino's sublimation of the physical as a means to the ideal. Love, for Colet, is love of God, achieved not by first loving the flesh, but by utterly repudiating flesh.[3]

But the differences between Colet and Ficino as to the nature of the soul are only the beginning of their differences; they also differ on the nature of the soul's ascent to God.

(B) *The Soul's Ascent to God*

Medieval theologians tended to see the problem of salvation in terms of faculty psychology; the soul was said to ascend to God by exercising the faculties of intellect, will, and love, in turn. Medieval theologians had generally agreed that love was the highest of these faculties, but they had not agreed about which of the lower faculties, intellect or will, was the more important. Should one ask, 'What must I do to be saved?' or 'What must I *know* to be saved?' Among scholastic theologians the 'voluntarists' were led by Duns Scotus and the 'intellectualists' by Aquinas. The intellect-will conflict was one of the issues which separated the Benedictines from the Franciscans; and it was a commonplace theme in medieval literature, in debates between characters called Wit and Will, or, as in *Everyman*, Knowledge and Good Deeds. The

---

[1] Ficino, *Opera*, pp. 289–90. The fullest discussion of this particular aspect of Ficino's philosophy is to be found in Walter Dress, *Die Mystik des M. Ficino* (Berlin, 1929); see also Kristeller, *Philosophy of Ficino*, pp. 270–5.

[2] See E. W. Hunt, *Dean Colet and His Theology* (London, 1956), for a synthetic account.

[3] See **7** (fol. iv^r), where Colet specifically rejects Ficino's view of the flesh. See also *Lectures on Romans*, p. 22.

theme continues to appear in Renaissance literature as well, and it occupies a prominent place in the philosophical writings of Ficino.

Ficino first stated his position in an early commentary on Plato's *Philebus*.[1] In that commentary, which was never published in Colet's lifetime, Ficino, still the philologist, physician, and philosopher, rather than the cleric-theologian, expressed the view that intellect was higher than will. Later, in the process of working out a Platonic Christian theology, he reversed his position, at least in writing, and so in the *Theologia Platonica* he asserts that will is higher than intellect.[2] But the way in which he manages this is to identify will with the third faculty, love; the will involved is the Augustinian doctrine of will, but the love involved is not the Christian *caritas*. Ficino's Latin term, *amor*, cleverly keeps the Christian flavour of *caritas*, but it is for him essentially an epistemological term meaning desire for truth; thus love, even when one identifies the Platonic Good with God, remains for Ficino essentially an intellectual rather than an emotional process. It is only by keeping everything on a purely intellectual level that Ficino succeeds in harmonizing so many different religious and philosophical points of view; the triumph of holding in the mind all at once the views of Plato, Christ, Plotinus, the Cabala, Zoroaster, the astrologers, Hermes Trismegistus, Moses, the Pseudo-Dionysius, St. Augustine, St. Thomas, St. Paul, and many others, is primarily an intellectual achievement.

It is true that in the *Epistolae* volume Ficino several times asserts[3] that will is superior to intellect, and because of the early and inconclusive character of the early *Philebus* commentary, Professor Kristeller has suggested that we must regard the superiority of will-love as representing Ficino's mature view on the subject.[4] There is in the same *Epistolae* volume, however, another kind of evidence which would have given Colet the reverse idea of Ficino's point of view.

Ficino was in the habit of identifying the three functions of the soul: intellect, will, and love, by the kind of life to which they led: contemplative, active, and voluptuous; these modes of life he commonly represented by the mythological figures Minerva (Contemplative), Juno (Active), and Venus (Voluptuous)[5]. When he uses these figures in the *Epistolae* volume, he consistently advocates the contemplative rather than the active life,[6] suggesting

---

[1] Ficino, *Opera*, pp. 1251–2. See Kristeller, *Supplementum Ficinianum*, I, p. 79.
[2] See Ficino, *Opera*, p. 324, and Kristeller, *Philosophy of Ficino*, pp. 270–6.
[3] e.g. Ficino, *Epistolae*, fols. xxxv–xxxiii r, especially fol. xxxiv. See also a passage entitled 'Voluntas deo fruitur magis quam intellectus', fol. liv.
[4] Kristeller, *Philosophy of Ficino*, p. 276.   [5] e.g. Ficino, *Epistolae*, fol. clxxii v.
[6] This fact is also represented mythologically by the superiority of Saturn to Jove. See Chastel, *Ficin et l'Art*, pp. 167–8. Cf. *Epistolae*, fols. xcvi r and cxxxii v.

that he regarded the principal objective of the soul as an intellectual objective. Ficino does not see the life of the soul as a war against evil; nor does he see it as a three-stage mystical ascent through purgation, illumination, and identification; he sees it rather as a continuous process of intellectual growth, building first on physical experience and then on successive levels of intellectual abstraction until at last the point of the pyramid is reached and the soul understands God.

It is true that in his *Symposium* commentary[1] Ficino describes this ascent of the soul to God as a pursuit of divine Beauty; and identifies personal human love with the cosmic force of divine love, but Ficino is not there or anywhere else really interested in erecting a moral or aesthetic rule of life. Although he talks about love as the unifying force in the universe, he preserves the primacy of the intellectual life by the way in which he defines that love. Love and intellect are for him actually parallel forces; love motivates what intellect does; their being parallel is the key to his identification of Platonism and Christianity. They are for him simply two different aspects of the soul's pursuit of God. But the fact is that he believes that in practice the soul must concentrate on the intellectual faculty; it is only when he is pressed to admit the ultimate superiority of God to man that he is willing to say that love actually takes precedence over intellect. His whole life testifies to the fact that the supreme value is for him intellectual.

When we turn from Ficino to Colet, we see that Colet, too, had a special interest in the intellect-will problem, but not because he was a Platonist; Colet wanted to solve the problem because at the time he read the *Epistolae* he was about to interpret publicly the famous passage in 1 Corinthians in which Paul talks about faith, hope, and charity. For a Renaissance audience, this would have meant discussing the three virtues in terms of their corresponding faculties of intellect, will and love.[2] Accordingly Colet treats Ficino's discussions of intellect and will as a commentary on faith and hope, and the intellect-will problem turns out to be the most important single issue in the whole volume, involving the correspondence as well as the marginalia. I shall try to trace the growth of Colet's treatment of the problem through all of his works.

The Pauline text involved is 1 Cor. xiii. 13: 'And now abideth faith, hope, and charity, these three, but the greatest of these is charity.' The literal interpretation of the passage would mean that intellect (the faculty of faith) was the lowest faculty, will (the faculty of hope) the next higher, and love (the faculty of the virtue of charity) the highest. But this is too simple for Colet.

[1] Ficino, *Commentary on Plato's Symposium*, trans. Jayne, pp. 208–15.
[2] See *Dictionnaire de Théologie Catholique*, 'Esperance' and 'Foi'.

The theme of faith, hope, and charity first appears in Colet's writings in the first commentary on Romans.[1] There Colet placed faith immediately below charity (hope being omitted),[2] using the image of a candle, in which the whiteness of faith is set aflame by charity. Colet's whole discussion of faith in this passage is quite unplatonic, but implicit in it is the standard patristic view of faith as the virtue of the intellect and love as the virtue of the will.

When Colet came to write his second commentary on Romans, he had read the *Theologia Platonica*, and in that commentary he tries to relate the intellect-will problem to Ficino's concept of *spiritus*: 'Now the intellect of the spirit is faith in God, and its will is charity and the love of God.'[3] But Colet still sees the problem essentially as a dualism of faith and love,[4] though he has adopted the Platonic image of the ray of the sun in place of the candle image of the earlier commentary:

This faith is a kind of light infused into the soul of man from the divine sun, by which the heavenly verities are revealed without uncertainty or doubt, and it so far excels the light of reason as certainty does uncertainty. . . .[5]

Now this infused light is Faith, by which the mystery of incarnation is discerned, and believed unto salvation; whilst Love, which takes possession of the soul along with Faith, and rarifies it, so to speak, and expands it, is that whereby, so far as can be done by man, God and his Christ are received and worshipped. These two, as it seems to me thus differ, not in reality, but in a kind of interchangeableness, namely in faith being a less united and, as it were a more diffused love; love, on the other hand is a more condensed and united faith.[6]

The obscurity of Colet's distinction here arises from the fact that though he regards the virtues of faith and love as infused virtues, in standard Thomistic fashion, he wants to treat them as faculties of the soul as well. This confusion is

---

[1] *Exposition of Romans*, p. 118. See E. W. Hunt, *Dean Colet and His Theology*, pp. 104, 116.

[2] Hope is discussed separately in Rom. viii. 24–25 and by Colet briefly in *Exposition of Romans*, pp. 62 and 147.

[3] *Lectures on Romans*, p. 46: Intellectus autem spiritus est fides Deo; voluntas veros eiusdem est charitas et amor Dei (p. 167).

[4] It is significant that Colet seems never to have been attracted by Ficino's doctrine of Platonic love. Colet nowhere seems willing to admit the force of pleasure in beauty as a manifestation of the *appetitus* for God. Though he is aware of the Platonic definition of love as a desire for beauty and distinguishes between physical and spiritual beauty, he shows no sympathy with Ficino's concept of love. Cf. Ficino, *Epistolae*, fols. xxviiv–xxviiir and xxxr–xxxiiir and marginalia 30 and 34.

[5] *Lectures on Romans*, p. 44:
. . . quod lumen est quoddam a divino sole infusum in humanam animam, quo certo et indubitanter divinae veritates revelari cognoscuntur; quod tam prestat lumini racionis, quantum certum incerto . . . (p. 165).

[6] *Lectures on Romans*, p. 46:
Lux autem haec infusa fides est, qua misterio verbi incarnati cernitur et creditur ad salutem. Amor vero una cum fide simul animam occupans, et eam (ut ita dicam) rarefaciens ac amplificans, est id quo, quantum ab homine fieri potest, Deus et eius Christus capitur et colitur. Haec duo, ut mihi videtur, ita inter se differunt, non re quidem sed quandam racione reciproca: ut fides minus unitus et quasi sparcior amor, contra amor coactior et unitior sit fides (p. 154).

also shown in a later passage in the same commentary, where he relates them to hope for the first time: '. . . all his [i.e. man's] hope of salvation is placed in faith, that men should trust in God alone; and in hope, that they should look for God Himself, and in love, that they should most ardently return the love of God.'[1]

In the *Hierarchies* of the Pseudo-Dionysius, which Colet seems to have studied next, he found two new aspects of the soul's relation to God. At the very beginning of the *Celestial Hierarchy* Dionysius quotes James i. 17 as Biblical authority for treating the soul as a ray of light;[2] Dionysius equates the light of the ray to the intellect and its heat to the will. In addition, Dionysius divides the distance to be covered by the soul in its rise to God into three territories, to each of which Dionysius assigns a specific group of celestial beings.[3]

This Dionysian account of the three virtues of Paul is discussed by Ficino in the *Epistolae*,[4] and Colet has annotated the relevant passage in detail, reproducing in tabular form the correspondences between the Pauline virtues and the three levels of the *Celestial Hierarchy*. The order of the three virtues in this Dionysian account is the conventional medieval ascending order:

Charity   Love, that you may enter on the way.
Hope   Hope, that [God's grace] may be given you.
Faith   Believe, that you may understand. (**41**)

Elsewhere in the marginalia, however, Colet is seen working toward an important new sequence, in which hope is put at the foot of the triad:

	true love	charity
God is	true light	faith
	true good	hope (**54**)

This is the order of the virtues which Colet finally settles on in his later work. His reasons for choosing this order are probably to be found in the very *Epistolae* volume in which the order first appears. But before we examine these reasons, we should first follow out the remainder of the history of the triad in Colet's thought. The next step in that history is the introduction of the idea of unity as an attribute of God and a goal for the soul. Colet had talked about the union of form and matter in his exposition of Genesis,[5] and he had seen

---

[1] *Lectures on Romans*, pp. 32–33: . . . sed spem salutis omnem esse positam in fide, ut homines soli Deo confidant, et in spe ut ipsum Deum expectent, et in amore ut amantem Deum ardentissime redament. . . . (p. 158).
[2] See Dionysius, *Heavenly Hierarchy*, trans. Parker, p. 1.
[3] See Dionysius, *Heavenly Hierarchy*, trans. Parker, pp. 13–42.
[4] Ficino, *Epistolae*, fol. liv. This is one of the three passages which Colet specifies for use in the commentary on 1 Corinthians; see marginalia **73**.   [5] See *Letters to Radulphus*, p. xx.

THE INTELLECT-WILL PROBLEM

unity discussed as a value in both of the *Hierarchies* of Dionysius.[1] In reading the *Epistolae* of Ficino he adds an independent comment on unity and simplicity to a part of Ficino's text,[2] and he paraphrases two other passages where Ficino echoes the Dionysian concept of unity.[3] But Colet does not apply the concept of unity to the Pauline triad of faith, hope, and charity until he writes the supplement to his abstract of the *Hierarchies*. In that supplement, which we know, on other grounds, followed Colet's reading of the *Epistolae*, 'unity' is introduced as follows:

good	1st Hierarchy of Angels
wise	2nd Hierarchy of Angels
one	3rd Hierarchy of Angels
good	1st member of each Hierarchy
true	2nd member of each Hierarchy
one	3rd member of each Hierarchy.[4]

When, at last, Colet comes to comment on 1 Cor. xii. 13, itself, where Paul's triad of faith, hope, and charity is stated, he puts the three virtues in the order hope, faith, charity and, using the new principle of unity, sets up equivalents as follows:

charity	faith	hope
will	intellect	
heat	light	unity[5]

The order hope, faith, and love represents a deliberate and final rejection of Ficino's view of the matter; hope for Colet, corresponds to the first level because one is sustained through the trials of purgation of fleshly sin only by the hope of knowing God; one proceeds to a knowledge of God only by Grace, which comes from faith; and one's final knowledge of God is not really knowledge at all, but only love, or charity.

But Colet is still not quite through with Paul's triad. Faith is, as it should be, the intellectual virtue, but he still has no third faculty of the soul in spite of

---

[1] See Dionysius, *Heavenly Hierarchy*, trans. J. Parker, pp. 29–31; and Colet, *Ecclesiastical Hierarchy*, p. 72 (Latin, p. 213).   [2] See Ficino's *Epistolae*, fol. xlvii^r and marginalia **40**.
[3] See marginalia **10** and **30**.
[4] *Celestial Hierarchy*, pp. 41–42:

Bonus	Prima	hierarchia	
Sapiens	Secunda	hierarchia	
Unus	Tercia	hierarchia	
Bonum	Primi	cuiusque	hierarchiae
Verum	Secundi	cuiusque	hierarchiae
Unum	Tercii	cuiusque	hierarchiae

(pp. 191–2)   [5] *Commentary on Corinthians*, p. 119; see also pp. 57–58.

the help given by the three-fold analogy with light. If he had followed Ficino's lead, he would have made the third faculty spirit, but he was evidently unwilling to do so because this metaphysical refinement had no precedent in Paul, for whom spirit was obviously the antithesis of the flesh, and not Ficino's *spiritus*. In spite of all of his experiments, Colet was still thinking in terms of the basic dualism between intellect and will which he had first seen in Romans. This relation Colet again emphasizes in the commentary on Corinthians, using the terms which Paul had used in Romans iii:

Paul speaks of three kinds of man: the Jews, the Gentiles, and Christians.... The Jews were ignorant because of depravity of will, and the Gentiles were depraved of will because of their ignorance.... The Gentiles lacked the light of faith and were foolish, whereas the Jews lacked [the heat of] love and were weak.[1]

Colet now applies these terms to the meaning of Paul's statement 'Christ is the power of God and the wisdom of God' (1 Cor. i. 24). This, says Colet, is Paul's way of saying that Christ's version of divine truth incorporates and surpasses both the moral emphasis of the Jews (the 'power' and heat of moral action) and the intellectual emphasis of the Greeks (the 'wisdom' and light of reasoned speculation).[2] In spite of the fact that in the commentary on Corinthians Colet works out more fully the mystical and celestial triads from Dionysius, specifying all the classes of angels as well as heat, light, and unity and the three stages of unification, illumination, and purgation,[3] the two faculties of the soul, intellect and will, still stand apart, without a third faculty to complete the correspondence.

Colet does not really supply the missing piece in his table of equivalents for the Pauline triad until he comes to the final commentary on Romans. We may see his first concern with the missing part in the *Epistolae* where he noticed (as we know from his marginal note) Ficino's discussion of the three qualities of God as truth, goodness, and being (see **36**). The importance of this concept trickled down only slowly into his thought, possibly because of his prior interest in *doing*. But we see him mentioning being as an attribute of God in the supplement to his abstract of Dionysius[4] and again as the third member of his

---

[1] *Commentary on Corinthians*, pp. 12–13: Tria apud Paulum sunt hominum genera; Judei, gentes, et ex hiis vocati Christiani. In Judeis fuit cecitas ex depravatione voluntatis; in gentibus pravitas et [i.e. ex] ignorantia.... Qua luce destituti gentiles ad bonum Christi nuncium stulti fuerunt.... Judei autem, potenti amore carentes, infirmi.... (pp. 166–7). [The text is evidently corrupt here; I have altered Lupton's translation to reflect the balance which Colet presumably intended] (pp. 166–7).
[2] *Commentary on Corinthians*, p. 16. This passage is an excellent example of the really superior powers of analysis which made Colet's lectures on the Bible so illuminating.
[3] *Commentary on Corinthians*, pp. 118–36.
[4] *Celestial Hierarchy*, pp. 39–40.

THE INTELLECT-WILL PROBLEM

triad of human faculties (with action and knowledge) in the *Commentary on First Corinthians*.[1] Thus being becomes for him the third function of the soul, and in the process of completing his commentary on Rom. xii–xvi, he brings up once again the Corinthian triad of faith, hope and charity, and applies to it the concept of being. This final version of the triad we may represent in tabular form thus:

charity	faith	hope
heat	light	unity
will	intellect	being
goodness	truth	power[2]

The full complexity of the concept is better represented in Colet's own statements. The soul, he explains, is a ray of the divine sun, involving three powers: light, heat, and unity, which are equivalent to the Pauline trinity of faith, hope, and charity:

For from unity, comes compactness and power, from light truth and uprightness, from heat, honesty and good action. From its union with God, by the uniting ray of grace, the soul is born again and has a new existence, for nothing can have existence save unity. From its [the soul's] illumination, it trusts and believes in God, and in its faith has the clearest vision, in its vision the clearest faith. Lastly, from its heat, it loves and longs for God, and for all divine things for the sake of God.[3] ... In laying down three things by which the soul exists in its new and divine life, namely Hope, Faith, and Charity, I placed Hope under the head of union and being, Faith under that of illumination and wisdom, Charity under that of heat and love.[4] ... No doubt these three things, faith, hope, and charity, are infused into the soul at the same moment by the one good and beautiful Spirit of God. But still if there is nothing to forbid precedence being imagined in things instantaneous, and our arranging a first, second and third; then certainly reason demands that faith should precede charity, and hope faith. For hope consists in union, faith in light, charity in heat. And if the order of things requires that everything should be in a state of unity before it is in that of light, and should have light before heat, then of course it would be necessary for Hope to hold the first place, being as it is a kind of unity and steadfastness of mind; Faith the second, being an illumination of the mind and recognition of God; Charity the third and last, as it is a

[1] *Commentary on Corinthians*, p. 119.
[2] *Lectures on Romans*, pp. 62–63 and 67–69.
[3] *Lectures on Romans*, p. 62:
   Ab unitate enim solliditas et potencia; a luce veritas et rectitudo, a calore bonitas et proba actio. Ex unione in Deum, ab uniente gracia et radio, regignitur anima et est denuo. Esse enim nihil est aliud quam unitas. Ex illuminacione confidit Deo creditque, ac credens cernit clarissime, et cernens credit. Ex calore denique amat et desiderat Deum, divinaque omnia propter Deum (p. 178).
[4] *Lectures on Romans*, p. 67:
   Quoniam, quum tradidimus tria quibus anima nova vita et divina constat, spes, fides, et charitas, spem in unione posuimus et esse, fidem in illuminacione et sapere, charitatem in ardore et amore. (p. 182)

love of God when known, and a longing for him.[1] . . . Such a one and beautiful goodness, and good and beautiful oneness, and one and good beautifulness is the very life of the soul, rendering it strong, beautiful and active for good. Its unity is sure hope; its beauty shining faith; its goodness burning charity.[2]

With this statement in the third commentary on Romans, we reach the end of the history of the Pauline triad in Colet's writings; we are now ready to return to the question of what persuaded Colet in the first place that the order of the virtues should be: hope, faith, and charity.

For those who see Colet as a reformer, it is tempting to see this issue as an example of the way in which Platonism contributed to the English Reformation, for one of the points of doctrine on which reformers differed from Roman Catholics was precisely this issue of the relation between faith and hope.

The standard Roman Catholic position is that faith is an intellectual virtue and hope is a moral one, that the soul proceeds from faith in God to hope of God, and that hope is a necessary stage in the progress of the soul toward God because, in depending upon works as well as faith to achieve salvation, one hopes that one's works will find favour in the sight of God. The Protestant position, however, is that faith alone is enough; neither works nor prayer are really efficacious, and to admit hope as an adjunct to faith is merely to question the validity of faith in the first place. From the Protestant point of view faith is both intellectual and moral: an intellectual assent to truth beyond the grasp of intellect, motivated by the will, which is moved by the love of God. Thus, from the Protestant point of view, hope, if it is admitted at all, can only be admitted first, as a stage of initial wishing preceding the intellectual stage of faith; from faith one moves directly to the experience of the love of God.

So far as Colet is concerned, however, there is no evidence that he preferred putting hope first from motives of reformation. The first place where we see this order in Colet is in the All Souls volume, and his initial choice of this order is probably attributable to the influence of Ficino. We may reconstruct the matter as follows:

---

[1] *Lectures on Romans*, pp. 68–69:
Sunt quidem haec tria, fides, spes, et charitas, a Dei spiritu uno bono et pulchro simul eodem momento in animam infusae. Verumtamen, si nihil prohibeat quin in momentaniis ordo excogitari possit, et primum, secundum, et tercium statuere, profecto ratio exposuit ut fides charitati, spes fidei antecedat. Quandoquidem spes unitione, fides lumine, charitas ardore consistit. Quod si rerum ordo exigit ut prius quodque sit unione quam luceat, prius luceat quam ardeat, profecto tum necesse sit, ut primum locum teneat spes, quae est quaedam unitio et stabilitas animi; ecundum fides, quae illustratio mentis et Dei cognitio; tercium et ultimum charitas, qui amor es cgniti Dei et desiderium (pp. 182–3).

[2] *Lectures on Romans*, pp. 69–70:
Haec una et pulchra bonitas, et bona et pulchra unitas, et una ac bona pulchritudo, ipsa vita est animae, reddens eam fortem, formosam, et beneficam, quae unitas est firma spes, pulchritudo splendida fides, bonitas ardens charitas. (p. 183).

Colet had set out to interpret St. Paul. Paul had set the order of the virtues as faith, hope, and charity. According to medieval doctrine, this meant the order intellect, will, and love. Given Colet's voluntarism, this would have been a perfectly satisfactory order for him. Unfortunately he turned to Ficino for assistance in interpreting Paul and found in the *Theologia Platonica* that Ficino identified will with love. For the purposes of Paul's triad this meant that will correspond with charity, and intellect with faith, but there was no faculty left to correspond with the middle virtue, hope.[1]

It is this difficulty of finding a place in the triad for hope which explains Colet's various experiments with the triad in the All Souls marginalia (e.g. **40, 53, 54**). In the end, as we have seen, Colet finally settled on the faculty of *being* as the faculty corresponding to hope, and since *being* was inferior to both intellect and will, he put hope at the bottom of the triad.

The *Epistolae* themselves probably did not give Colet much help in solving his problem because Ficino continually speaks there in terms of two faculties only, intellect and will. At any rate, Colet seems to have been sufficiently disturbed about the problem to write to Ficino and ask him where in the hierarchy will should stand. Colet's letter of inquiry (possibly the lost remainder of Letter C) seems not to have survived; but we do seem to have Ficino's reply to that inquiry, in Letter D of the All Souls' correspondence. In that reply Ficino takes an unequivocally intellectualist position; he says specifically that intellect is higher than will. He also says that intellect is higher than love, but he evidently identifies love with will, as he does in the *Theologia Platonica*; thus intellect is primary and love-will is secondary. (The entire letter is relevant; see pp. 82–3).

Translated into the terms of Paul's triad, Ficino's letter puts hope-charity on the bottom and faith on the top; thus it may have been Ficino who suggested to Colet putting hope below faith, as he does in his commentary on 1 Corinthians. On the other hand, it is doubtful that Colet had received Ficino's letter D before writing that commentary; he seems to have given his lectures on Corinthians relatively soon after reading the *Epistolae* volume, and he probably did not have time to write and receive Ficino's reply before he actually gave the lectures.

In his final lectures on Romans, Colet makes a particular point of defending his order of hope, faith, and charity, as though his lectures on Corinthians might have drawn some criticism, but he nowhere cites Ficino's authority in support of his position; instead he protects himself by saying that all three

---

[1] See P. O. Kristeller, *Philosophy of Ficino*, pp. 256–88.

virtues are actually infused simultaneously, of course, but since they must be discussed in order, he puts hope first, as being '. . . the beginning of man's journey towards God, a collecting of the soul and a uniting and a drawing of it to God, that it may be illumined and inflamed.'[1]

Though Ficino's Letter D or Ficino's other *Epistolae* may have prompted Colet to put hope first, since it is in the All Souls marginalia that we first see Colet adopting the order hope, faith, and charity, the same Letter D and the rest of the *Epistolae* would also, paradoxically, have revealed to Colet the fundamental philosophical chasm between him and Ficino. As his letters show, Ficino was essentially an intellectualist, whereas Colet is consistently a voluntarist. This fundamental difference reflects the crucial difference between them; it is the reason why Colet would never have been a disciple of Ficino, and why his interest in Ficino never went beyond the point of seeking possible help in interpretation of the Bible. Once one recognizes this difference one understands why they differ on most other theological issues. I shall discuss only three of those issues.

(C) Action versus Contemplation

The first is the issue of the active versus the contemplative life. Whereas Ficino emphasizes the contemplative life, Colet emphasizes the active life. We have already seen (p. 51 above) how, in quoting from the *Theologia Platonica* Colet twisted Ficino's argument for contemplation to an argument for right action. Similarly, one of the dominant themes in the All Souls marginalia is the necessity for moral action:

Human reason imitates God . . . when it wills from right reason, and with a habitual and customary rightness, so that it behaves justly toward God, toward itself, and toward others. . . . (**25**)

From a great act of learning comes a good intellect and a stable will. From this come good actions, and from these come good habit and custom. (**31**)

No one makes good use of anything except by goodness, and unless he himself knows the good. It is by good usage that goods are good, and the same argument applies to evil things; by bad usage evils become worse and goods evil. The quality of the action is determined by the quality of the doer. (**50**)

In one passage (**69**) Colet specifically criticizes Ficino for dwelling too much on intellectual problems and neglecting moral problems; in another (**50**) he simply ignores Ficino's argument for contemplation. In still another passage

---

[1] *Lectures on Romans*, p. 68:
Quae spes inicium est humanae profectionis in Deum, quae est collectio animae et counitio ac contractio in Deum ut illuminetur et incendatur (p. 182).

(**64**) Colet emphasizes Ficino's admission that even religious and philosophical contemplatives do not entirely escape trouble in this world; if they escape physical torments of the flesh, they are subject to spiritual torments.

The proper life of the soul, for Colet, is a succession of 'good' actions; by 'good' Colet usually means 'aversive to the flesh'; good and evil he ordinarily distinguishes by reference to the flesh: 'From the soul's desire for the body came about the ruin of the soul . . . to scorn the body and hold it in contempt is to set out on the road back to life and to the incorporeal world from which souls originally come'. (**7**) Colet appears to be much interested in Ficino's exposition of the theory of demons as the cause of evil in the world, but even here he emphasizes the fact that the demons themselves are evil because of their seduction by the flesh: 'It is the same with demons as with men: men who are masters over their bodies are good, but those who are slaves of their bodily appetites are necessarily evil and wicked. So also is the case of demons. . . .'. (**61**) And he concludes: 'The saintly man, whose soul is dedicated to God and is divine, pure, and holy, clasping to itself a body impenetrable [by demons] (that is, a body that is chaste and pure), cannot even be harassed by demons'. (**61**)

Rejection of the flesh is of course only the aversive value corresponding to the appetitive value of desire for God. Thus Colet also holds that 'Irreligion and neglect of God[1] is the source of all evils.' By contrast, Ficino asserts that 'The cause of evil is the stupidity and ignorance of man.'[2] Colet believes that where evil exists it can be overcome only by good[3] actions and that good actions derive from good character, that is, the road to righteousness is a moral rather than an intellectual road, involving right moral choices rather than increased intellectual power. The Platonic doctrine of 'knowledge is virtue' has a special meaning for Colet. For Socrates it meant, 'no one knowingly does what is not best for him'; for Colet it means 'the good man thinks everything is good (because he never questions the will of God)'.

One of the ways of assuring right choices is to cut down on the number of choices; for Colet, as for the Pseudo-Dionysius,[4] evil is associated with multiplicity; he stresses this issue in a long comment which begins with a quotation from St. Paul (Rom. xii. 9).

'Do not remember evil things if you wish to retain the good.' . . . Avoid multiplicity, confusion, and tumult; seek simplicity, tranquility and peace. Have few thoughts, and share them with few people; that is, better thoughts with better people. Avoid the

---
[1] *Exposition of Romans*, p. 55: Irreligiositas negligentiaque Dei omnium malorum fons est. (p. 203)
[2] Ficino, *Epistolae*, fols. xviv–xviiv (*Opera*, pp. 636, 640).
[3] *Lectures on Romans*, pp. 86–87 (Latin, pp. 194–5).
[4] cf. *Ecclesiastical Hierarchy*, p. 72.

crowded way. Follow the bypaths; seek not the broad way but the straight way, the way which few know and few go. Then you will find what few find and enjoy what few enjoy. (30)

In seeking simplicity, as in avoiding the flesh, it is a moral issue which is at stake; the key to salvation is moral. Of the three stages of the soul's search, purgative, illuminative, and unitive, the first or moral stage is the one to which Colet urges man's primary attention. Yet the ultimate object of that search Colet calls *sapientia*, or wisdom, just as Ficino does. What does Colet mean by the term *sapientia?*

(D) Sapientia

In a recent informative study entitled *The Renaissance Idea of Wisdom*,[1] Professor Eugene F. Rice argues that the concept of wisdom during the Renaissance was gradually secularized from an intellectual to a moral virtue. Using a series of humanistic treatises from Italy, and then a parallel series from France, Professor Rice traces in both countries a shift in values, under the secularizing influence of humanism, from an emphasis upon contemplation to an emphasis upon action.

Paralleling this humanist activity, says Professor Rice, was a different kind of movement, what he calls an Augustinian-Pauline revival, a reversion to 'medievalism', which had representatives in various countries, including Luther in Germany, Savonarola in Italy, Jacques LeFèvre d'Étaples in France, and in England John Colet. In keeping with the idea that the objectives of these thinkers were essentially reactionary by contrast with the progressive secularism of the humanists, Professor Rice goes on to argue (p. 176) that Colet's concept of wisdom is essentially contemplative, and is to be contrasted with the thoroughly worldly emphasis on action in men like Petrarch and Erasmus.

Professor Rice is certainly right about Colet's affinities with Augustine and Paul, but the All Souls volume, about which Professor Rice could not have known, certainly disputes his view of Colet's conception of wisdom. Just as Augustine was a voluntarist, preferring action to contemplation, so his disciple Colet was also. Colet appears to have been a voluntarist from the start; he was misled into the study of Platonism by his supposition that it could assist him in the interpretation of Paul, but when he discovered, in reading Ficino, that Platonism was really a form of contemplative intellectualism, he rejected it, just as he had rejected the arid intellectualism of Aquinas. It is true that Colet's

[1] (Cambridge, Mass., 1958); see especially chaps. 3 and 5.

motives for preferring action to contemplation were not at all those of the humanists whose treatises Professor Rice shows to be leading in the same direction; certainly Colet's conception of wisdom can hardly be said to be a secularized conception, but it is nevertheless a voluntarist conception from beginning to end, as I shall try to show.

The problem of the nature of wisdom is a major preoccupation of Ficino in the *Epistolae*, and Colet's marginalia show that the problem interests him also; but his marginal comments do not often agree with Ficino. He seems to agree with Ficino that wisdom is the 'knowledge of things divine', and that divine truth is fundamentally arcane, but here their agreement ends. If Ficino, like Colet, emphasizes the mysterious character of that wisdom, its unattainability by the average man, he does so for reasons very different from Colet's. Ficino emphasizes that mystery in order to magnify the dignity and power of the human soul, especially, of course, those gifted human souls at Careggi, whom he presumed to have penetrated the mystery, whereas Colet stresses the mysterious character of God's truth in order to illustrate and emphasize the weakness and unworthiness of man.

Ficino consistently couches his ideas in mythological allegory, using figures such as Minerva, Saturn, Jove, Venus, and Prometheus.[1] This habit, which contributed so much to the popularity of his works with Renaissance poets and painters,[2] rose not merely out of his desire to affect learning or his desire to cultivate a specific language for the Careggian Academy, but out of a philosophical principle at the heart of his system, that the myth, incorporating as it does meaning within meaning, is the natural semantic tool for dealing with divine truth; to speak in allegory is to speak as God speaks. Conversely, one arrives at divine truth by unpeeling layer after layer of the meaning of the myth in the mind. Mysterious and unknowable by ordinary epistemological processes, God can be known through internal analysis of remembered knowledge, for innate knowledge of God is present unconsciously in the soul.[3] Thus for Ficino the doctrine 'know thyself'[4] means 'study man in order to know

---

[1] See *Commentary on Symposium*, trans. Jayne, pp. 185, 187, &c.; *Epistolae*, fols. cxxxiv–cxxxiiiv; and Chastel, *Ficin et l'Art*, pp. 136–40.

[2] See especially E. Panofsky, *Studies in Iconology* (London and New York, 1939), chaps. V and VI; Chastel, *Ficin et l'Art*, and Edgar Wind, *Pagan Mysteries in the Renaissance* (London and New Haven, 1958).

[3] See Appendix C, No. 8: 'And so St. Paul and St. Dionysius the Areopagite, the wisest of all Christian theologians, say that for everything which has been created there is an invisible counterpart in the mind of God. In relation to this everything in the visible world may be regarded as in this sense divine. Plato says that human knowledge may be taken as a paradigm of all wisdom.' See also Ficino, *Epistolae*, fol. xxixv, 'Knowledge of and reverence for oneself'; notice Colet's superficial marginalia (33).

[4] On this doctrine in St. Augustine see R. W. Battenhouse, ed., *A Companion to the Study of St. Augustine*, pp. 404–7. See also 1 Cor. xi. 28; especially W. K. Ferguson, 'Renaissance Tendencies in Erasmus', *JHI*, xv (1954), 499–508; and E. G. Wilkins, *'Know Thyself' in Greek Literature* (Chicago, 1917).

God', that is, by intellectual introspection penetrate the word within the word until the word becomes God; contemplate the idea of the Good, and find inside it God. Repeatedly in the *Epistolae* Ficino urges his correspondents to the study of philosophy as the road to wisdom. Colet replies sourly 'the road to wisdom is justice and good actions'. The soul's first business is to 'be purged of vice' (**30**). 'Do not remember evil things if you wish to retain the good.' (**30**) For Colet one loves God and may be shown the idea of the Good as a reward.

Colet shows little enthusiasm for Ficino's exhortations to philosophy and learning (e.g. **11, 12, 30, 32, 50**). It is true that in the *Commentary on Corinthians* (p. 61) Colet defines *sapientia* in the usual Renaissance way as 'the knowledge of things divine' (as opposed to *scientia*), but he shows that he believes that that knowledge is achieved not by intellectual analysis of ideas, but by passive reception of insight granted by God to the morally good soul.[1] Colet reasons that since truth is obscure, one ought not seek it at all; seek moral virtue, and God will give you truth. Men who trust in themselves rather than in God 'trust in falsehood rather than in truth' (**54**); the only sure path to wisdom is to perfect one's moral nature and have faith that God will grant 'attainment' of Himself to those 'whom he most loves' (**41**); and that he loves best those who are morally pure and good.

The best illustration of this point of view is perhaps Colet's comment on Ficino's discussion of the nature of light.[2] At a passage in which Ficino is speculating as to the sense in which one may speak of each of the planets as twins —twin Venuses, twin Mars, &c.—Colet says: 'Things which have very little [visible] light are investigated [by getting] closer to them . . . The brightest things, however . . . are open for us to see of their own nature; only let the eye prepare itself to receive the light; that is, let them [the eyes] purify themselves and turn themselves [towards the light]'. (**69**)

As this passage shows, Colet, too, argues for self-knowledge, but for him the doctrine 'Know thyself' means 'understand your moral obligations by con-

---

[1] His attitude is well exemplified in his defence of the Pseudo-Dionysius as having taken "the greatest pains to appear to have no wisdom of the world, thinking it unworthy to mix human reason with divine revelation", *Commentary on Corinthians*, p. 19 (Latin, p. 171). Cf. also his silent translation of Ficino's meaning for wisdom into his own in marginalia **50**.

[2] cf. *Epistolae*, fols. lxii r, xlviii r, and clxxxvii v; see also his *De sole et lumine* (*Opera*, pp. 965–86). For some of the patristic background of this figure (e.g. in Clement, Cyril, Basil, and Gregory) see H. Koch, 'Pseudo-Dionysius Areopagita in seinen Beziehungen zum Neuplatonismus und Mysterienwesen', *Forschungen zur christlichen Literatur und Dogmengeschichte*, i (1900), 236–42. Ficino himself presumably was strongly influenced by the Dionysian account in the *De divinis nominibus*, which he translated and commented upon; see *Opera*, p. 1057. For discussions of the scientific view of light in the Renaissance see Kester Svendsen, *Milton and Science* (Cambridge, Mass., 1956), pp. 261–2. See also 1 Cor. xv. 41; Rom. xiii. 12, and James i. 17.

sulting your conscience'. Thus wisdom itself becomes a moral rather than an intellectual objective: 'Hence Solomon asked for wisdom in order that he might distinguish between good and evil, because nothing is good except to the wise and good man'. (**50**)

The fact that Colet refers to Solomon as his authority is significant; Ficino himself refers to Socrates at that point. Although one usually associates with Platonism the view that knowledge is virtue, the thinking behind Colet's conception of wisdom is unplatonic, for it is utterly divorced from epistemology.

So the difference between Colet and Ficino on the subject of wisdom is ultimately the difference between emphasizing the moral faculty of the soul and emphasizing the intellectual faculty of the soul. On the question of wisdom, however, the nature of the soul is not the only element at issue; the question of how much the soul may learn of God involves also certain assumptions about the degree to which God intervenes in human affairs.

(E) Justification and Grace

It has sometimes been asserted[1] that Colet, like Augustine, denied human free will altogether, putting the whole responsibility (including, presumably, that for the soul's ascent to God) upon God. The All Souls volume does not support this view; though Colet obviously imputes much less power to man than Ficino does, he clearly holds the human will in some way responsible.

That the freedom of the soul is seriously inhibited for Colet is undeniable; there is no doubt that the demands of the flesh, the fundamental weakness of the human mind, and the omnipresence of evil constitute much more formidable barriers for Colet than they do for Ficino. Ficino actually glorifies man's freedom to deal with the passions as being man's distinctive privilege, and since there are no necessary physical limitations upon the activity of pure intelligence (from Ficino's point of view), as there are upon moral actions, the human soul is very much more free in Ficino's conception than it is in Colet's.

Yet everywhere in the All Souls volume we see Colet urging man to right action. To urge a man to the choice of right action is to assume that the human will is free to choose between right and wrong.

Colet's marginalia thus involve a paradox: on the one hand he asserts that unassisted man is basically weak and incapable of effective progress, and on the other he repeatedly enjoins man to accept his moral responsibility and do good instead of evil. The solution to this paradox, I believe, is that Colet did

[1] E. F. Rice, Jr., 'John Colet and the Annihilation of the Natural', *Harvard Theological Review*, xlv (1952), 141-63.

not believe that free moral choice was impossible; he only believed that knowledge of God by human effort alone was impossible. Insofar as *wisdom* meant a developed moral consciousness, Colet believed it could be acquired by man. Insofar as *wisdom* meant knowledge of God, Colet believed it could be acquired only by the grace of God.

In the end, of course, Ficino has to admit, in order to preserve the superiority of God to man, that knowledge of God, the ultimate mystery, can be given only by God, and thus he seems to come to the same conclusion as Colet. So in Ficino's imaginary 'Dialogue between Paul and the Soul' Paul is represented as explaining that he did not get to heaven by his own effort, but was carried there by God: 'It is impious insolence to wish to rise to heaven [by our own efforts]; for we are not meant to glory in revelations of that kind. Our glory rests entirely with that one King of Glory to whom no one ascends, but is raised.'[1]

One should observe, however, that this is only what Ficino has represented Paul as saying in the dialogue, and is not necessarily what he himself might have said. Even in the short letter entitled 'No one ascends to heaven to whom God himself has not *in some way* descended'[2] (italics mine), the short phrase 'in some way' conceals a world of substantive difference between the two men. Colet believed that because in the end one achieves God only by the grace of God, one should proceed on that principle from the beginning, winning God's grace by moral action. Ficino, on the other hand, believed that God in the end helps the soul over the last impossible Zenonian fraction of the remaining gap of ignorance only if the soul itself has reduced that gap to a minimum; therefore the proper course for the soul is to seek as full comprehension of God as possible.

I do not mean to imply that Ficino was being hypocritical in acknowledging the ultimate necessity of divine grace to the soul's attainment of God, nor do I mean to ignore the fact that he obviously did say, and probably believed, that the mind alone could not go the whole way. What I am saying is that the effect of Ficino's writing is to urge upon man that the major burden for achievement of God rests upon the exercise of the human intellect. Translated into theological terms, this means that in advocating works along with faith as the condition necessary to win God's grace, the works Ficino has in mind are primarily intellectual achievements.

Colet's view of justification is somewhat more ambiguous. In his first commentary on Romans he says, '... righteousness comes from faith, not from

---

[1] Ficino, *Epistolae*, fol. li^r; I quote Colet's paraphrase (41).
[2] Ficino, *Epistolae*, fol. lxx^r, paraphrasing John vi. 44.

the reason of the Gentiles, nor from the law of the Jews.'[1] But when he comes to the critical passage in Romans (iii. 28), where Paul says, 'Therefore we conclude that a man is justified by faith, without the deeds of the law', Colet explains that by 'deeds of the law' Paul means only the rites and ceremonies of the Jews, and Colet concludes: 'Leaving out of account all of these works of the law, let any one but *work* Christ, and he will be justified, whether Jew or Gentile' (italics mine).[2]

On the basis of this and other passages in Colet's works apart from the All Souls volume, modern scholars have concluded that Colet's view of justification was based on the scholastic principle of *fides formata cum charitate*, in which faith implies works.[3]

The All Souls volume bears out this interpretation of Colet's position. The marginalia repeatedly emphasize the importance of God's rather than man's part in justification: 'Souls must be justified and made just through the grace of God.' (**7**) 'It [i.e. attaining heaven] is entirely a matter of God's raising us, not of our own effort. God lifts up and takes to heaven those whom He most loves.' (**41**) But Colet everywhere shows that 'those whom God most loves' are those who have taken the step of purging their sins (an act of will) before demonstrating their faith (an act of intellect); thus 'works' are clearly necessary for Colet, as for Ficino, but Colet's 'works' are moral rather than intellectual.

The fact that the intellect-will conflict is the central issue between Ficino and Colet is significant for several reasons. For one thing it shows that the conflict between intellect and will, or contemplation and action, is one of the major problems of Renaissance theology, as it is in the fields of metaphysics and politics discussed by Professors Rice and Baron. The example of Colet suggests, however, that though a shift from contemplative to active did take place in England, as it did on the continent, in England it was not so much a shift from other-worldliness to this-worldliness, that is a tendency toward secularization, but rather a reaction from Hellenic intellectualism back to Augustinian voluntarism. The example of Colet suggests that Renaissance thinkers were backed into voluntarism in the process of trying to accommodate intellectualist Hellenism to Christianity. Colet's voluntarism may be seen as a return to Augustinian theology, as a defensive reaction against the excessive intellectualism required, by a man like Ficino, to accommodate the new Hellenism to the Christian order.

[1] *Exposition of Romans*, p. 53:
    . . . justicia autem fidei, non rationis gentium, nec legis Judeorum (p. 202).
[2] *Exposition of Romans*, p. 108:
    His operibus legis omissis, si quispiam operetur Christum, justificabitur, sive Judeus sive gentilis sit. . . . (p. 242)   [3] E. W. Hunt, *Dean Colet and His Theology*, pp. 64-65.

Interest in the intellect-will problem remains a dominant theme in English literature to the end of the Renaissance. Spenser's concern with intellect and will, in Book I of *The Faerie Queene,* is pointed out by Milton in his remark that Spenser is a better teacher than either Scotus (the voluntarist) or Aquinas (the intellectualist).[1] John Davies discusses wit and will repeatedly throughout the second part of *Nosce Te Ipsum,*[2] and Cudworth devotes a whole sermon to the problem.[3]

On the surface most later Renaissance statements of the intellect-will problem in England seem to follow the direction pointed out by Colet, toward emphasis upon the will, but the ultimate outcome of the conflict is in identification of the two faculties as reflected in *Paradise Lost* in Milton's observation that 'Reason also is choice',[4] and in Bacon's *Advancement of Learning,* where Bacon hopes 'that contemplation and action may be more nearly and straightly conjoined and united together than they have been'.[5]

[1] *Areopagitica*, M. Hughes, ed., *Complete Poems* (New York, 1957), 728–9.
[2] See especially A. B. Grosart, ed. (London, 1876), I, 78–81.
[3] Reprinted in part in H. J. C. Grierson, *Cross-Currents of the Seventeenth Century* (London, 1951), 227–8.
[4] *Paradise Lost*, iii. 108.   [5] Ed. R. F. Jones (New York, 1937), p. 214.

V : CONCLUSION

In attempting to reconstruct the point of view from which Colet annotated his copy of Ficino's *Epistolae* I have not meant to imply that I think of the marginalia as fragments of a Greek vase, which needs only to be put back together again to recover its integrity. The All Souls marginalia do not constitute a coherent treatise; nevertheless they do reveal something about the mind that put them there, and, together with the correspondence, add significantly to our understanding of Colet's life and thought.

To summarize briefly, on the biographical side the All Souls volume shows that though Ficino and Colet did not meet, they did correspond with each other. The volume further adds to our knowledge of Colet's life by providing evidence which suggests that Colet's major activities at Oxford during the period 1496-9 took place in the following order:

1. First commentary on Romans
2. Commentary on Genesis
3. Second commentary on Romans
4. Abstract of *Hierarchies*
5. Reading of *Epistolae*
6. Supplement to abstract of *Hierarchies*
7. *Commentary on First Corinthians*
8. Third commentary on Romans

As for Colet's thought in general, the All Souls volume tends to clarify and emphasize the fact that his work should be understood primarily in the framework of Christian soteriology. One concludes that Colet was interested in Platonism mainly in the Oxford years of his career, and almost exclusively as a source of material for his required theological lectures on the Bible. The marginalia emphasize his moral fervour, his Augustinian view of human frailty, and his acceptance of St. Paul as the pole star of his life.

On the particular question of Colet's debt to Ficino, the All Souls volume speaks with unique authority, for here alone may one see the views of the two men stated side by side. The volume tends to emphasize the differences between the two men rather than their similarities, contrasting Colet's moral zeal with Ficino's intellectual enthusiasm, Colet's search for order and pattern with Ficino's search for mystery and sophistication, Colet's Augustinian ethics with Ficino's Platonic metaphysics.

Even this, however, is probably not in itself the whole difference, but rather a part of the larger difference between a practical mind, concerned with Doing and the Actual, and a theoretical mind, concerned with Truth and the Ideal. The speculative life was all very well for a man like Ficino, protected by a benevolent patronage and subsidized for the purpose; it is little wonder that for him Jewish morality and Greek knowledge should fuse in the positive glow of Platonic love high above the grimy, bloody streets of Florence. For Colet, the resolution of Hellenism and Christianity was more negative; for him Jewish moral weakness and Greek stupidity added up to total human depravity, demonstrated every day in the frustration, disgust, and fear experienced by any idealist who has to live and work in society. It is hardly surprising that Ficino and Greek thought generally should have ceased to interest Colet after he left the relative seclusion of Oxford for the turmoil of London.

Colet had been led to study Ficino by the practical need for help in interpreting the letters of Paul, but Colet's mind, even in his idealistic youth, was not essentially a theoretical mind, and it was perhaps inevitable that, as we have seen, he should retreat from Ficino's pure reason to his own practical reason. For in Coleridge's sense at least, though Ficino was certainly a Platonist, Colet was an Aristotelian.

In pointing out the moral focus of Colet's work, I have not intended, of course, to deny all intellectual elements. What I have meant to show is that by comparison with Ficino, Colet had relatively little confidence in man's ability to reach God by intellectual means. But one may well ask, if Colet's point of view had been so anti-intellectual as I have suggested, why would Colet have read Ficino at all? If efforts of intellect had meant so little to him, why would he have read anyone or preached to anyone? Colet would obviously not have revived a school if he had not believed that moral training involves intellectual discipline. There is a genuine paradox in Colet's career which the All Souls volume does not solve. Perhaps it is the same kind of insoluble paradox which one sees in Augustine, in Schopenhauer, in Nietzsche, and in anyone who takes the trouble to communicate to others a relatively pessimistic view of the human condition.

TEXT AND TRANSLATION

I. Correspondence

II. Marginalia

LIST OF ABBREVIATIONS

AHR	*American Historical Review*
DNB	*Dictionary of National Biography*
EHR	*English Historical Review*
HLQ	*Huntington Library Quarterly*
JHI	*Journal of the History of Ideas*
MLQ	*Modern Language Quarterly*
MP	*Modern Philology*
OHS	*Proceedings and Papers of the Oxford Historical Society*
RS	*Rolls Series*
SP	*Studies in Philology*
STC	A. W. Pollard and G. R. Redgrave, *A Short Title Catalogue of Books Printed in England, Scotland, and Ireland . . . 1475–1640* (London, 1926).

I: CORRESPONDENCE

Letter A: Colet to Ficino (December 1498?)

[missing]

Letter B: Ficino to Colet (February 1499?)

Marsilius Ficinus Florentinus Johanni Colet colenti pariter et colendo.

Solent amantes amati vulti [sic] vultum vera facie pulchriorem in se ipsis effingere. Vis enim amoris est non solum amantem transformare mirabiliter in amatum, sed etiam amati formam apud se in melius reformare. Siquidem naturalis amor est generationis et augmenti principium. Tu igitur, amantissime mi Joannes, quum primum spiritus nostri lucem in scriptis ferme sicut lunam in aquis lucentem intuitus es, quasi tuo spiritui congruam ardentius amavisti et amore captus subito solem accipisti [sic] pro luna. Itaque me solem sepe vocas. Solem quidem tibi pariterque amantibus, ceteris vero luna; felix mihi plane tua hec opinio, mi Colette, pulchriorem videlicet Marsilium tibi reddens quam aspexerit. Felicissima certe fores [i.e. foret] si ceteris reddiderit eque pulchrum. Utina[m] ardens et eligans tua epistola ita placeret aliis atque mihi, ut ego ita placeam aliis atque tibi.

Vale, amantissime pariter et amatissime, mi Colete.

Marsilio Ficino, of Florence, to John Colet, an admirer to be admired:

It is customary for lovers to imagine that the face of someone they love is more beautiful than it actually is. It is the power of love not only to change the lover in a marvellous way into the shape of the beloved, but also to change for the better the shape of the beloved in the lover's eye. The reason is that natural love is the beginning of generation and increase. So, my dear John, as soon as you saw the light of my spirit reflected in my writings as the moon is reflected in the water, you fell ardently in love with it because you thought it akin to your own spirit. And so, overpowered by this sudden love, you saw me, not as the moon, but as the sun. So you keep referring to me as the sun.[1]

I may seem a sun to you and to others who love me as much as you do, but to everyone else I am a moon; it is fortunate for me that you have this opinion of me, dear Colet, since it is obviously reflecting to you a much more beautiful Marsilio than the one whose image it is receiving. It would be even more fortunate for me if your conception of me could make me equally beautiful to everyone else. I wish that your devoted and elegant letter could impress others as much as it has impressed me, so that I might impress others as much as I have impressed you.

Farewell, my loving and beloved Colet.

[1] Colet may have borrowed this image from Ficino's own *Epistolae*, fol. lxii^r; see item **44** below.

Letter C: Colet to Ficino (April 1499?)

[Draft 1]

Tuis [sic] libros / legens ut videor, vivo, quant*um*[1] *viverem* [quan]to magis te vivens viderem te ipsum vidende et colende Marsile. Tua epistola non solum vivo sed etiam bene vivo.

[Draft 2]

Tuos libros legens, ut videor *viso* vivo, quanto magis te videns viverem vidende et colende Marsile. Tua *epla* epistola non solum vivo, ut videor, sed bene vivo. Te ipsum si iam videre et cernere potero, beatus erro [i.e. ero]. Spe vivo videndi tui et spem [sic] morior, expectans (ut videor) nimium contemplationem me sustine vita tui. At interea *interea me* sustine in ea vita tui [?] partiali. Hunc annum tua epistola me temuisti [i.e. tenuisti] in vita. Ei alteram adde et alter*um* ann*um* am vivam. Tu *si ab hinc tertium vixeris* Tu si deinde tertio vixerero vixero anno[2]

While I am reading your books I seem to live, just as I should be more alive if I could see you in person, Marsilio, whom I long to see and pay homage to. Because of your letter I seem not only to live, but to be living the good life. If I can only look upon you and see you in person, I shall be truly blessed. I live in expectation [of seeing you],[3] and I [also] die from expectation, having waited too long, as it seems, for a glimpse of you. Meanwhile sustain me in this half-life. For this year you have kept me alive with your letter. Add another to it, and I shall live another year. Then, [if you are still alive three years hence][4] if I am still alive in the third year. . . .

Letter D: Ficino to Colet (July, 1499?)

Hoc inter intelligentiam et amorem interesse puto: quod Intelligentia prior est, amor posterior. Intelligentia parit amorem: amor funditur in Intelligentia. Intelligentia magis intus stat. Amor magis foris extat. Intelligentia denique simplicior, serenior, et verior est. Amor quodammodo compositior, crassior et concretior est. Unde fit ut quamquam amor ex Intelligentia pendeat, tamen quia posterior est, et foras magis eminet quam intelligentia: quicquid obiiciatur anime quovis modo quumque: id prius ametur quam intelligatur. Nam in externis objectis oportet quod posterius est quodque propius objecto prius apprehendat quam quod prius est intus et remotius. Hinc est quidem quod ignis prius

The difference between intellect and love, I think, is this: intellect is primary and love is secondary. Intellect produces love, love is brought forth in intellect. Intellect faces inward; love faces outward. Intellect, finally, is purer, clearer, and truer; love is more mixed, denser, and thicker.

Thus, although love depends upon intellect, nevertheless, because love is secondary and projects outwardly more than intellect does, whatever is brought to the attention of the soul, by whatever means, is loved before it is understood. For [in perceiving] external objects, the soul necessarily apprehends [first] the part of the object which is secondary, [external], and near at hand, before it

---

[1] Words printed in italics are crossed out in the original.

[2] In this sentence Colet has neglected to delete the word *Tu* before *si ab hinc* . . . and the word *vixerero*, which is his first effort to write the future perfect of *vivo*.

[3] cf. Rom. viii. 24–25.

[4] Passage in brackets is Colet's first version, crossed out in favour of the more tactful final version.

calefacit quam illuminat, et apposita califaciendo [sic] rarifacit [sic] ut ea penitus et intime illustret. Hinc est etiam quod omnis appetitio ferventior est sensu ipso cuius est appetitio: et voluntas magis ceca et temeraria quam inttellectus [sic]. Nam ex intellectu prodiens et in crassius degenerans minus considerata et ad omnia magis cita evadit. Volo, mi Joannes, hoc mysterius [i.e. mysterium] intelligas voluntatem scilicet crassum esse intellectum. Intellectum autem serenam et liquidam voluntatem. Itaque voluntas cognoscit et intellectus vult. Immo in hiis quicquid est intellectus est. Sed intelligentia ipsa intellectus est sibi sufficiens aut saltem minus egens quam voluntas. Voluntas autem intellectus est quidam egens, atque ob id avida et desiderans. Hec rebus ipsis proprior [i.e. propior] quam intellectus et prius cupide nimis sensiens [i.e. sentiens]: id admittit et probat bonum: quod ad liquidum intellectum si perveniret non probaretur. Quod ipsum quoque tandem apprehensum ab intellectu: si id intellectus respuat: tamem [sic] tamen[1] id repudiari non sinit voluntas; que vicinior rei, rei cognite magis et tenatius heret.

apprehends the part that is primary, internal, and further away. Hence it is that fire heats things before it illuminates them; by heating objects placed near it, fire rarefies them in such a way that it lights them up internally and inwardly.

By the same token, every appetite is more ardent than the sense of which it is the appetite, and will is blinder and more impetuous than intellect. Proceeding from intellect, and degenerating into something cruder, [will] turns out to be less careful and more rash about everything [than intellect is].

I wish you, my dear John, to understand this mystery, namely that will is crude intellect; and intellect, on the other hand, is pure and refined will. Thus the will apprehends and the intellect wills. Rather what ever it is [which is] in both [intellect and will] it is [some kind of] awareness. But intellect is awareness which is self-sufficient, or at least less needy than will. Will is a type of awareness [which is] in need of something and for this reason is hungry and acquisitive. Since will is closer to physical objects than intellect is, and becomes aware of them sooner and very hungrily, will may accept and approve something which would not be approved if it penetrated to the more refined intellect. As it is, even when such a thing ultimately reaches the intellect and is there disapproved, the will does not permit it to be rejected altogether; the will, being closer to a thing which it apprehends [than intellect is], clings more to the thing and holds more tenaciously to it [than the intellect does].[2]

---

[1] This is one of Colet's numerous mistakes in copying; one *tamen* is accordingly omitted in the translation.

[2] This theory of knowledge is essentially St. Augustine's; see *De Trinitate*, IX. 12.18, and R. W. Battenhouse, *Companion to the Study of St. Augustine* (New York, 1955), pp. 300–4. Cf. also Ficino's own discussion in the *Epistolae*, fol. xxxii[r].

II: MARGINALIA

TABLE OF MARGINALIA

Item	Folio		Title
1	title^r		[Title page]
2*	i^r		Prologus
3*	i^r–v^v	BOOK I	Quae sit ad foelicitatem via
4*	i^v		Imitatio utilior est quam lectio
5*	i^v–ii^v		Dialogus inter Deum et animam theologicus
6	iii^r		Lex et Justitia
7	iii^v–v^r		De divino furore
8	v^r		Excusatio prolixitatis
9	v^v		De divinatione et divinitate anime
10	v^v		Solitariae vitae utilitas
11	vi^r		De laude platonicorum interpretum
12	vi^r		Exhortatio ad scientiam
13	vi^v		Consolatio in alicuius obitu
14	vii^r		De virtutibus civilibus purgatoriis …
15	vii^r		De sapiente et foelice viro
16	vii^r		Bona scribere praestat quam multa
17	viii^v–ix^r		Laudes Laurentii Medicis mire
18	xiii^r		Causa peccandi. Spes. Remedium
19	xiv^v		De toleranda iniuria
20	xiv^v–xv^r		De constantia adversus fortunam
21	xvi^v		Stultitia et miseria hominum (1)
22	xvii^v		Stultitia et miseria hominum (3)
23	xvii^v		Quod amicus est in amico
24	xviii^r		Divinatio de amico
25	xxv^v–xxvi^r		De lege et iusticia
26	xxvi^r		De anima
27	xxvi^v		Legitimi iurisconsulti partes
28	xxvii^r		Fontes potius quam rivulos sectari debemus
29	xxvii^r–v		Virtutum definitio officium finis [fol. xxviii^r]
30	xxvii^v–xxviii^r		Praecepta ad memoriam
31	xxviii^r–v		Virtutum definitio officium finis
32	xxviii^v		Tres vitae duces
33	xxix^v		Cognitio et reverentia sui ipsius
34	xxx^v–xxxii^v		Quid est foelicitas
35	xxxiii^v		Oratio ad deum theologica
36	xxxix^r–xlii^r	BOOK II	Questiones quinque de mentis motu
37	xliii^r–xliv^r		Mens dei radio reflexo intelligit creata
38	xlv^r–xlvi^r		Elementa moventur mobiliter

* Not in Colet's hand.

MARGINALIA

Item	Folio		Title
39	xlvi^v–xlvii^r		Forma corporea dividitur et movetur ab alio
40	xlvii^r–l^v		Compendium Platonice theologiae
41	li^r–lvi^r		De raptu Pauli ad tertium caelum
42	lvi^{r-v}		Argumentum in Platonicam theologiam
43	lxi^v–lxii^r		Qualis est amor talis amicitia
44	lxii^r–lxiii^v		Quid sit lumen in corpore mundi ...
45	lxx^r	BOOK III	Omnes omnium laudes referantur in Deum
46	lxx^v		Nemo ascendit ad Deum nisi ... Deus ipse descenderit
47	lxx^v		Nugis vulgus pascitur
48	lxx^v		Amicitia vera est quam religio vera concilliavit
49	xcv^v	BOOK IV	Matrimonii laus
50	xcvi^{r-v}		Philosophia sapientiam gignit
51	xcvi^v		Disputatio contra iudicium astrologorum
52	xcvii^v		Montes non seperant animos montibus altiores
53	xcviii^r	BOOK V	Leges divinae fides scientia confirmatur [sic]
54	xcviii^v–xcix^r		Nullum in malis refugium est
55	xcix^v		Nullus incontinens potest sapiens esse
56	cix^r		Patientia sine religione haberi non potest
57	cx^r		Non ex humanis divina: sed ex divinis humana
58	cxi^r		De salute philosophorum ante Christi adventum
59	cxxi^v–cxxii^r	BOOK VI	Orphica comparatio solis ad Deum
60	cxxxv^v–cxxxvi^v	BOOK VII	Divina lex fieri a coelo non potest
61	cxlviii^r–cl^r	BOOK VIII	Platonici Deo et anime mundi ... sacrificant
		BOOK IX	
62	clxxiv^r	BOOK X	Heroicorum virorum laboriosa ... vita ...
63	clxxxii^v–iii^v	BOOK XI	Excerpta ex Proculo [sic] in Rem publicam Platonis
64	clxxxvii^{r-v}	BOOK XII	Nullus mala poenitus et curas extirpare potest
65	clxxxvii^v–viii^r		Solem non esse adorandum
66	clxxxviii^{r-v}		Copula philosophiae cum legibus
67	clxxxix^r		Similitudo Mercurii cum Saturno
68	clxxxix^r		Apologia in librum suum de Sole
69	clxxxix^v		Sepe in coelestibus gemini sunt
70	cxc^r		In librum de sole
71*	cxcv^r		De Jove amicabili et Apolline
72	cxcvi^r		Cur providentia permittat adversa

* Not in Colet's hand.

86 JOHN COLET AND MARSILIO FICINO

Item	Folio	Title
73	flyleaf^v	[none]
74	flyleaf^v	[none]
75*	flyleaf^v	Dr. Kinge
76*	flyleaf^v	Lib[ri] Log[ici]

* Not in Colet's hand.

TEXT AND TRANSLATION

Note: Number references in left margin are to folio and line in the printed text of Ficino's *Epistolae* (Venice, 1495).

[title page^r]   1 [**Title page**][1]

Sanctitas	severa	vis pietatis in deo [sic] totum	Saturnus
Sapientia	benigna	vis pietatis ad homines	Juppiter
Fortitudo	austera	necessitas belli	Mars
Sol		pax finis bellis	Sol pacis
Mercur[ius]	nuncis [sic]	legati nu[n]cii	Angeli
	libedo [sic]	voluptas gaudium	Venus
	generatio	le[2] generatio crescere et multiplicare	

1 [**Title page**]

holiness	strict	piety entirely towards God	Saturn
wisdom	kind	piety towards men	Jupiter
courage	austere	a requirement of war	Mars
sun		peace, the end of war	sun of peace
Mercury	messenger	agents, messengers	angels
	desire	pleasure, joy	Venus
	procreation	procreation, growth, multiplication	

[i^r]   2 **Prologus**

6	nota[3]
10	scilicet praedictum[4]
12	nota[5]

2 **Prologue**

note
that is, [Plato's] precept
note

---

[1] cf. marginalia **67**. *Mercur* is crossed through in the original. I have rearranged Colet's rough notes a little to clarify their columnar order.

[2] This syllable is crossed through.

[3] Calls attention to passage underlined in text: *nihil ad aegregias res agendas accommodatius esse quam prudentium doctorumque virorum benevolentiam.*

[4] Passage underlined in text: *Aureum hoc Platonis praeceptum.*

[5] Calls attention to passage underlined in text: *Longe ditior hominum, prudentiae justitiaeque ditissimus.*

MARGINALIA

[i^r] **3 Quae sit ad foelicitatem via**[1]   **3 The way to happiness**

29–42   Charegium est gratiarum ager. Duodecim sunt hominum bona: devitie [sic], sanitas, forma, robur, nobilitas generis, honores, potentia, prudentia, justitia, fortitudo, temperantia, et sapientia que quidem vim omnem felicitatis complectitur.
Careggi is the land of the Graces. There are twelve goods for men: wealth, health, beauty, strength, nobility of birth, honors, power, prudence, justice, fortitude, temperance, and finally, wisdom, which indeed comprises the whole meaning of happiness.

[i^v]

1–2   summum sapientie bonum
The highest good of wisdom [i.e. which wisdom seeks].

5–6   Bona non prosunt nisi utuntur [sic].
Goods [such as strength, wealth, &c.] are meaningless unless they are used.

10   periti officium
The task of the craftsman.[3]

12   Bona sunt utenda ratione.
Our use of goods [such as strength, wealth, &c.] must be controlled by reason.

16   male agens est miser.
He who does evil is unhappy.

18–19   Bona non nuncupantur bona per se.[2]
These so-called goods are not intrinsically good.

25   scientie officium
The task of knowledge.

26–27   studio quis fit sapientissimus
One becomes wisest by desiring [piety].

28   Deus est sapientia
God is wisdom.

[i^v]   **4 Imitatio utilior est quam lectio**   **4 Imitation is more instructive than reading**

28   Nam viva vox plus efficit quam mutus magister.
For the spoken voice has more effect than the silent teacher.

30–31   Plato grecos composuit dialogos.
Plato composed dialogues in Greek.

32–33   Habeo gratiam, et agere gratias.
I am thankful, and to give thanks.[4]

[i^v]   **5 Dialogus inter deum et animam theologicus**   **5 Theological dialogue between God and the soul**

41   Dialogus theologicus
Theological dialogue.

43–44   Moralia usu, naturalia ratione querenda.
Moral [truths are to be acquired by use], natural [truths] are to be investigated by reason, [and divine truths to be sought by prayer].

---

[1] In lines 1–5 of this letter several words are glossed interlinearly: *primum* (l. 1) glossed *quamprimum*, *quam* (l. 1) glossed *valde*, *accipe* (l. 2) glossed *intellige*, *paucis* (l. 3) glossed *verbis*, *calcem* (l. 4) glossed *finem* and *censui* (l. 5) glossed *indicavi*.

[2] Perhaps a contraction of 'Quae bona nuncupantur non nuncupantur bona per se'.

[3] Ficino is saying that the good man makes right use of goods as the craftsman makes right use of his tools.

[4] The annotator seems here merely to be reminding himself of the idioms involving *gratia*, and especially of the fact that *habeo* takes the singular *gratiam*.

[ii^r]
1	Platonis praeceptum¹	a precept of Plato's.³
5–6	Deus et anima sunt inteloqutores [sic].	God and the soul are the speakers [in this dialogue].
7	murne no more²	mourn no more.⁴
8–9	Deus est medicina salusque.	God is our remedy and our salvation.⁵
10–11	I wold be as mery as a cryket.	I would be as merry as a cricket.⁶
[ii^v]	[Here the notes in Colet's hand begin].	
12–13	sapiens vestigatio dei	The wise way to learn the nature of God.
foot (cf. ll. 10–21)	Deus constans lux uniformis invisibilis, simplex omniformitas, omniformis simplicitas.	God is a never-flickering light, uniform and invisible, simple universality, and universal simplicity.

[iii^r] **6 Lex et Iustitia**   **6 Law and Justice**

16	anima	lex	the soul	law
18	spiritus	medicina	the spirit	medicine
19	corpus	mercatura	the body	business
21	Moysem		Moses	
23	Osiris		Osiris	
24	Zautrastes		Zautrastes⁷	
26	Xamolsis		Xamolsis⁸	
27	Minos		Minos	
28	Solon		Solon	
29	Prometheus		Prometheus	
30	Lycurgus		Lycurgus⁹	
32	Numa		Numa¹⁰	
33	Maumethes		Maumethes¹¹	
35	Plato		Plato	

foot (cf. ll. 29–31)	Juppiter summus	juvans providentia	Deus	
	Mercurius	Jovis nu[n]cius	Angelus	

Jupiter, the Supreme   protecting providence   God
Mercury   the messenger of Jove   Angel

---

¹ Passage underlined in text reads: divina ob vitae puritatem revelari potiusquam doctrina verbisque doceri. (Cf. p. 141 below.)

² The word *aspiret* at the end of this line is glossed immediately above: *favet*.

³ That divine truths, because of the purity of their nature, are revealed rather than taught by doctrine and words.

⁴ This translates an underlined phrase in the text: Pone iam finem, o filia, lachrymis. (Cf. p. 141 below.)

⁵ The following is underlined in the text: En assum tibi pater tuus. Assum medicina salusque tua. (Cf. p. 141 below.)

⁶ This translates an underlined phrase in the text: laetitia insanirem. (Cf. p. 141 below.)

⁷ Zoroaster.

⁸ Zalmoxis; the Getan mentioned by Apuleius (*Apol.* 26), Plato (*Charmides* 156D) and Herodotus (IV, 94–96).

⁹ Spartan law-giver (fl. 800 B.C.?)

¹⁰ King of Rome (715–673 B.C.).

¹¹ Mahomet, who is said to have been visited by Gabriel; see also Appendix C, no. 7.

[iii^v]	**7 De divino furore**	**7 On the divine madness**
head (cf. ll. 23–30)	Ex appetitione animi ad corpus evenit animi interitus. Amor et coitus cum corpore genuit anime oblivionem, ignorantiam, mortem, miseriam; corpus odio habere contemnere est ad vitam proficisci et incorp[o]rea unde veniunt. Justificentur oportet et justi fieri ex dei gratia.	From the soul's desire for the body came about the ruin of the soul. Physical love and intercourse with the body begat in the soul forgetfulness, ignorance, death, and misery. But to scorn the body and hold it in contempt is to set out on the road back to life and to the incorporeal world from which souls originally come. Souls must be justified and made just through the grace of God.
16–17	Deus { fons / lumen	God [is both] { the source [and] the light
21	idee	Ideas [in the mind of God]
22	divine essentie	Divine essences
23	prime nature	prime natures
25	ambrosia—dei cognitio	Ambrosia—knowledge of God
26	nectar—perfectum gaudium	Nectar—perfect joy
27	Letheus—oblivio divinorum	Lethe—forgetting of things divine.
30	justicia—morum[?]	[Socrates calls the virtue of] action justice
31	sapientia—spiritus[?]	[and the virtue of] the spirit wisdom.
32–33	Ale { justicie actio / sapientia contemplatio	[The][1] wings [of the soul] { justice action / wisdom contemplation
36	furor divinus furor ≡	the divine madness madness ≡[2]
[iii^v] foot (cf. ll. 23–35)	[Ani]mus primum apud deum expletus et exultans, appetitu amoreque corporis decidit in corpus, coitque cum corpore unde quasi [obr]uto alicui aquis turbulentis nata est anime oblivio, ignaratia [sic] unde omnia mala nascuntur. Habet hic mundus corporeus divini mundi illius umbras quibus visibilibus monemus [i.e. monemur] ut invisibilia conjectemus. Animus facile excitur quod illic [su]apte natura tendit. Illa quoque effecta umbratilis ut in	The soul is at first in the presence of God, where it is satisfied and happy. Then, because of its desire for and love of the body, it falls into the body and is united with it. There, like a person drowning in a stormy sea, the soul is overcome by oblivion, the lack of knowledge [of heaven], whence all evils spring.[3] This physical world embodies reflections of that divine world; by these visible signs we are advised to conjecture [the nature of] things invisible.[4] The soul is easily aroused [to a desier for heaven] because it tends in that direction by reason of its very nature. The

[1] The figure is from Plato's *Phaedrus*, 246B–248E.
[2] This is Colet's shorthand sign to indicate that a thing has a given number of parts or classes. Here he refers to Ficino's observation that Plato says there are four kinds of madness, but Ficino does not name them, and hence Colet does not either, here; but see p. 92.
[3] Colet apparently thinks of Ficino's passage as a paraphrase of Rom. I. 21.
[4] cf. Rom. I. 20.

corpore crassa evadens facile a crassis umbris [... ?] cita venit in memoria[m] rerum magis verarum ac tandem sui ipsius reminiscitur et naturales suas sedes ut corporis vilitatem agnoscens ac fastidiens appetit redire ac rursus ambrosia et nectare i.e. veritatis [v]isione pasci boni possessionis gaudeo [sic] exultari [sic]. Alas reperit et quatit, reviviscit in mortuo corpore, expergiscitur somno, emergit e fluvio Letheo, [excitat] bonitatem et sapientiam segnes, conatur in altum volare redireque.

soul is plunged into shadow, as is to be expected when it is in a dense body, but the soul easily passes out of the dense shadows into a remembrance of truer things. At length it recalls its own nature, and, recognizing and despising the meanness of the body, it seeks to return to its natural home [i.e. heaven] and feed once more on nectar and ambrosia, that is the vision of Truth, and to rejoice in the possession of the Good. It discovers and beats its wings; it comes to life again in its dead body; it is awakened from sleep; it emerges from the river Lethe and, stretching its long-unused [wings of] goodness and wisdom, tries to fly back to heaven.

[iv^r] head (cf. fol. iii^v, l. 42–fol. iv^r, l. 26)   Ut ignis calor a solis calore degenerat. Ita corporee pulchritudinis amor ab amore divini pulchritudinis; hic enim castus et reverens est ac perpetuus. Ille lascivus, petulans, ac fastidiens; hic corporis ardor urit, infestat, cruciat. Ille consolatur [?] fovet, mulcet, recreat uti solis calor.

As the heat of fire is a degenerate form of the heat of the sun, so in the same way the love of physical beauty is a degenerate form of the love of divine beauty. For the love of divine beauty is chaste, reverent, and everlasting; whereas the love of physical beauty is lewd, insolent, and scornful. Love of the body consumes, destroys and tortures; [but the love of God] consoles, cherishes, soothes and re-creates, like the heat of the sun.

[iv^r]
1–2 divine sapientie umbre — reflections of the divine wisdom
5 pulchritudinis spiritualis — [the physical representation of] spiritual beauty
9 reminiscentia animi — the soul's memory [of divine beauty][2]
16 divinus amor — divine love
21–22 Philosophus amator sit corporee pulchritudinis. — The philosopher should be a lover of corporeal beauty.
25 amoris diffinitio — definition of love
30–31 Aspice co[r]pora ut admonearis, non ut ames. — Look on the body not in order to love it, but in order to be reminded [of divine beauty].
31 mens[1]
37–38 alienatio furor } divinus — divine { distraction [and] madness }
41–43 musica { eterne mentis globorum — music { of the eternal mind of the spheres

[1] Merely corrects a typographical error in the text (*meas*).

[2] Leland W. Miles, in 'Protestant Colet and Catholic More', *Anglican Theological Review*, xxxiii (1951), 30–42, discusses the influence of the Platonic doctrine of memory upon Colet's view of the sacraments. Cf. also Ficino, *Epistolae*, fol. xxvii^v, a letter on the function of the memory; Colet's marginal note on the letter is item **30** below.

MARGINALIA

foot (cf. fol. iii^v, l. 42–fol. iv^r, l. 26)	Deus sapie[n]s concinnus pulcher. Sapientia illius sensibus nostris parum indicatur et occulte. Nam in corporibus parum vel umbratilis sapientia apparet. Ad sapientiam enim corpora ineptissima sunt. Ad concentum harmoniam pulchritudinem representa[n]dam quanquam crassiora tamen magis apta. Ab ordine, concinnitate &[1] pulchritudine animus maxime excitur; ipse quoque se ponens in ordine concinnitate et pulchritudine, id est justus et bonus accedit tantum ut sapientiae umbrarum capax sit. Homini autem nulla umbra sapientie magis in promptu est quam sua ignorans natura. Hinc cognosce te ipsum. Ad hoc via est justicia et bona actio.	God is wise, harmonious, and beautiful. His wisdom is revealed to our senses very rarely and secretly, for wisdom rarely or only obscurely appears in bodies, because bodies are ill-suited for wisdom. Bodies, although they are more solid, are more suitable for representing God's harmony and beauty [than His wisdom]. The soul is roused, above all, by order, harmony, and beauty; it also makes itself orderly, harmonious, and beautiful (that is, it becomes just and good) to the extent that it is capable at all of reflecting [the divine] wisdom. There is no clearer image of divine wisdom available to man than his own unknowing nature. Therefore 'Know thyself'. The road to this goal is justice and right action.
[iv^v] 2	cuntiis [sic]	[The soul uses] all [its faculties, in listening for the music of the spheres.]
9	musica sonorum	the music of sounds
13–14	poete divino furore afflati	Poets [are] inspired by a divine madness.
15–17	Poesis imitatrix divine armonie	Poetry [is] an imitator of the divine harmony.
25	furor poeticus	the poetic madness
26	Muse	the Muses
27	Muse: celestes cantus	The Muses [are] heavenly songs.
32	siren	the Siren
35	Juppiter: anima mundi	Jupiter [is] the world soul.
37	Muse sperarum anime	The Muses [are] the souls of the spheres.
40	Virgilius[2]	Virgil
foot (cf. fol. iv^r, l. 33–fol. iv^v, ll. 8, 29–35)	Pulchra fingamus ut divine pulchritudinis memores esse possimus. Concentus effingamus ut divine harmonie memoria nos teneat. Nonem [i.e. novem] illa numina presedentia orbibus novem muse sunt.	Let us make beautiful objects that we may remember the divine beauty. Let us make harmonies that we may remember the divine harmony. The nine goddesses who preside over the [nine] spheres are the nine Muses.

[1] This word looks like *per*, but it may be an ampersand, formed, not in Colet's usual way, but, as Mr. J. B. Trapp has ingeniously suggested, by converting the *p* of *pulchritudine*, which Colet started to write first by mistake. Alternatively the correct reading may be *perpulchritudine*.

[2] Explains Ficino's phrase: *Platonicus ille clarissimus*.

[v^r]				
1–2	Orphicus de Jove		Orpheus on the subject of Jove[2]	
7	misteria		mysteries	
8	vaticinium futurorum		prophecy of future things	
10	mysteriorum dictio		the revelation of mysteries	
12	supersticionem vide		note superstition	
14	divinatio		divination	
15	furens divinatio		inspired divination	
17	conjectio		prophecy	
			[kinds of madness]:	
19	vaticinium—	Appoli[ni] [sic]	prophecy	Apollo
20	mysteria —	Dyonisio [sic]	mysteries	Dionysus
21	poesis —	Musis	poetry	the Muses
22	amor —	Venus	love	Venus

[v^r] **8 Excusatio prolixitatis** — **8 An apology for prolixity**

29–30 In brevi et compresso multa complectuntur quae si explicaveris explicatior et produxtior [sic] eris.

In a short and condensed [statement] many things are included which would be clearer but also more tedious if explained.

[v^v] **9 De divinatione et divinitate anime** — **9 On divination and the divinity of the soul**

5   sacerdotes deum — [See that the] priests [pray] to God [for me][3]
17   divinatio anime — divination of the soul
21   heroum: anime bonorum virorum — [The souls of] heroes [are] the souls of good men.

[v^v] **10 Solitarie vitae utilitas** — **10 The value of a life of solitude**

30   motu et multitudine — [Go] from motion and multiplicity to stability and unity [in order to attain God].
31   [...?] statum et unitatem

[vi^r] **11 De laude platonicorum interpretum** — **11 In praise of the interpreters of Plato**

8–24 Plato, cuius aurea et splendida erat[1] sapientia quum dignas verborum vestes reperire non poterat, putavit honorifice[n]tius se agere non posse

Plato, whose wisdom was so golden and glorious that suitable words could not be found in which to clothe it, thought that the best thing to do with this gold was to conceal it. He believed that since its true value could

---

[1] Colet seems to have begun to write *fuit* and changed to *erat*, as Mr. J. B. Trapp has suggested.

[2] The reference here is to the theogony in the Orphic hymns. See W. K. C. Guthrie, *Orpheus and Greek Religion* (London, 1952), V. D. Macchioro, *From Orpheus to Paul* (New York, 1930), and especially D. P. Walker, 'Orpheus the Theologian and Renaissance Platonists', *Journal of the Warburg Institute*, xvi (1953), 100–20. See also D. P. Walker, *Spiritual and Demonic Magic* (London, 1958) and Edgar Wind, *Pagan Mysteries in the Renaissance* (New Haven, 1958).

[3] Ficino is telling how Alexandra asked her daughter to see that the priests prayed for her.

MARGINALIA

quam aurum celari, et eg[it?] ut dignitas rei quum digne ostendi non poterat, digne sal[tem] occultaretur. Itaque obs[curo] et squallido hab[itu] induit ut lateret, ut a stultis pretermitteretur. Sapientibus forsan agnoscatur ac perspiciant qui secum lumen deferunt. Alioqui ceci reperiant obscurius.

not be properly displayed, it should be fittingly hidden. And so he clothed his ideas in obscure and repellent dress in order to hide them and make the stupid reader miss them. By the wise, perhaps, [Plato] may be understood, and those who bring their light with them may penetrate his mysteries. Otherwise, being blind, people find Plato obscure.

[vi{r}]

12 Exhortatio ad scientiam

12 Exhortation to learning

30–33

Homo magnificus ceteros amat vivitque ad alios; ingeniosus sibi vivere debet.

A high-minded man loves others and lives for others, but a man of superior intellect ought to live for himself.[2]

foot (cf. ll. 40–41)

Hodie esse vivere valere discere sapere debemus, esse[1] non cras quidem. Procrastinatio propulsio vite est; tempus nostrum est quod instat atque adest. Quod preteritum quodque futurum est, nostrum non est. Quod autem nostrum est, non perdamus. Curemus ut in eo simus, vivamus, et agamus. Quum hec disserimus interia [sic] non sumus. Non autem debeamus non esse ut sci[a]mus, sed potius esse quum possimus ne quum velimus non possimus. Instans tempus frugaliter expendatur et eius parcus esto.

We must live, be strong, learn, and know today, not tomorrow. Procrastination puts off life itself. It is the time which is present and immediate which is ours. The past and the future do not belong to us. What is ours, let us not lose. Let us take care that in that time we exist, live, and act. Even as we are discussing these things we are not being. We ought not to give up living for the sake of learning; we ought rather to live while we can lest we wake up one day to find that we want to live but cannot. Let the present be expended frugally; be thrifty with it.

[vi{v}]

13 Consolatio in alicuius obitu

13 Consolation on the death of someone

head (cf. fol. vi{r}, l. 44–fol. vi{v}, l. 8)

Homo id est quod maxime est. Is animus est antiquus, constans, effectrixque hominis. Is quam diu hic est defertur a sua felicitate. Causa eius esse et verior anima est eius idea in mente divina, in quam qui rediit vere et constanter est quidem.

Man is that which most truly exists [i.e. the soul rather than the body]. That [part of man] is the soul which is ancient [i.e. older than the body] and unchanging, and which makes man human. As long as the soul is on this earth, it is lowered beneath its proper happiness. The 'cause' of [the soul's] being (and thus [in itself] a truer soul) is the idea of the soul in the mind of God. He who has returned to that idea [i.e. one who has died] does indeed exist truly and unchangingly.

---

[1] Colet seems to have written this second *esse* twice, by mistake; I have accordingly ignored it in the translation.

[2] Ficino is commenting on the fact that his correspondent has praised Lorenzo de' Medici for his conflicting virtues, his high-mindedness and his brilliance.

[vii^r]	**14 De virtutibus civilibus . . .** [see last two lines of fol. vi^v]	**14 On the public virtues**
head (cf. ll. 1–8)	civilitas expiatio purgatio informatio	political virtue[1] expiation purgation reattainment of pure form

[vii^r]	**15 De sapiente et foelice viro**	**15 On the wise and happy man**
9–18	Qui nihil timet eorum quae timentur, nihil ex[s]pectat, nihil movetur, nihil allicitur, nihil incenditur; sed ab hiis abductis et contemptis in maiori [sic] stabilitate quieta.	[The happy man is he] who fears none of the things which are normally feared, has no vain hopes, and is not swayed, enticed, or enflamed by passion, but [lives] withdrawn and aloof from all these in peaceful equanimity.

[vii^r]	**16. Bona scribere praestat quam multa**	**16 In writing, quality is more important than quantity**
27 29	libri in evangelia	books [written by Ficino; a bibliography][2] on the gospels [i.e. commentaries on the gospels written by Ficino]

[viii^v]	**17 Laudes Laurentii Medicis mire**	**17 The wondrous praises of Lorenzo de' Medici**
36–foot (cf. ll. 36–43)	Difficile est non invidere, sed bonus non invidet. Immo gaudet et gratulatur alicui sive is eliganter loquitur, sive aucute [sic] probat, sive dulciter mulcet, sive concitat vehementius. Nam turpe est ociosum veteranum in philosophia ab occupato tyrone cito et facile superari. Ut invidemus alienis, ita gaudemus propriis et fruimur.	It is difficult not to envy, but the good man does not envy. Rather he rejoices in and congratulates [the accomplishments of] anyone who speaks eloquently, makes an acute proof, calms the passions sweetly, or rouses them by impassioned [oratory]. For it is disgraceful for a veteran [like Ficino], who pursues philosophy at leisure, to be quickly and easily surpassed by a novice [like Lorenzo], who is busy with his affairs. Just as we envy others [what they have], so we rejoice in and enjoy what we have.

[ix^r]
head (cf. ll. 8–12)

{ Splendor mentis | Sapientia }   Florida mens
{ Leticia voluntatis | Gaudium }
{ Viriditas corporis fortunaeque   Floridum corpus }

---

[1] This is a summary of Ficino's exposition of the stages by which one advances from ordinary worldly virtue to 'divine' (i.e. ideal) virtue. Cf. Plotinus, *Enneads* I, 2 and Macrobius, *In Somnium Scipionis*, I, 8.

[2] This important letter is reprinted by P. O. Kristeller, in *Supplementum Ficinianum*, I, p. 1; see also discussion, pp. clxvii–clxxxi.

MARGINALIA

Radiance of mind	} Wisdom }	Vigorous mind }
Happiness of will	} Joy }	
Thriving body and fortune		Vigorous body }

Hiis gratiis homo redditur maxime gratiosus et Deo et hominibus. Qui-[bus] hec [sic] gratie aspirant hii beati sunt. Aspirant autem hiis quibus Deus vult ac tam diu quam gratis [sic] illas[1] a Deo solo gratias illas [sic] se accipisse [sic]. Obscuritas et tenebrae mentis; dolor et tedium voluntatis; ac deinde corporis ariditas, squallor et feditas, hoc est stultitia malicia et turpitudo difformitas hominem horrendum abominandumque efficiunt.

These graces make man especially valuable both to God and mankind. Those men are blessed to whom these graces are sent. They are sent to those men whom God chooses and for as long as [they recognize] that they have received those graces as an act of grace from God alone. Obscurity and darkness of the mind; grief and apathy of will; and then the withering, foulness and decay of the flesh—that is, folly and envy [on the one hand] and ugliness and deformity [on the other]—make a man loathsome and abominable.

[xiii^r] **18 Causa peccandi. Spes. Remedium**

40 nota[2]

18 The cause of sin. Hope. The remedy

Note[4]

[xiv^v] **19 De toleranda iniuria**

15 plebs polippus [i.e. animal multipes sine capite]

19 On the necessity of tolerating insult

The populace [is like] a polyp. [i.e. because it is an animal with many feet, but no head.]

[xiv^v] **20 De constantia adversus fortunam comparandam**[3]

36–37 Creator anime Deus, corporis mundus.

foot (cf. ll. 36–37) quia corpus a corporeo mundo regitur si quidem pars a toto

20 On steadfastness in the face of fortune

The creator of the soul is God, [but] the creator of the body is the world, for the body is ruled by the physical world, just as a part is ruled by the whole.

[xv^r] head cf. ll. 7–8) prudentia { sanctitas deo / justicia hominibus

1 fuga

prudence { holiness towards God / justice towards man

[Ficino says that] flight [from evils is the only way to avoid them, since they cannot be eliminated].

---

[1] This *illas* appears to be a mistake of anticipation of the phrase to come; I have accordingly omitted this *illas* in the translation.

[2] Calls attention to an extended passage, ll. 39–44, by means of a bracket.

[3] There is a cross-mark in the margin opposite the first line of this letter; in this line Ficino mentions the *Theatetus*.

[4] This note calls attention to the first six lines of this letter, in which Ficino asks a question ('Since souls are divine, why do they live so impiously'), and gives as his answer, 'Because they live in such an impious place [i.e. the earth]'.

6	sanctitas actio deo	holiness [is] action which is proper to God
7	justicia actio hominibus	justice [is] action which is proper to man
8	prudentia visio	prudence [is] foresight

[xvi^v] **21 Stultitia et miseria hominum (1)**

21 The stupidity and wretchedness of man (1)

(cf. ll. 20–21) foot

Misiri [?] sunt qui semper habent mentem intentam in futurum, quod nihil est; relinquentes quod habent, quo carent copiunt [sic], ac in nihil sunt quum in aliq[u]o esse possunt, et moriuntur quum possunt vivere.

Wretched are those whose minds are always fixed on the future, which is nothing. Forsaking what they have, they long for what they lack; when they could be in something, they are actually in nothing, and when they could be alive, they are dying.

[xvii^v] **22 Stultitia miseriaque hominum (3)**

22 The stupidity and wretchedness of man (3)

head (cf. ll. 6–14)

Omnes affectiones nostri [sic] sunt vero contrarii; vitam morte[m] et mortem vitam existimamus. Ita nos oblectat mors ut finem moriendi exhorreamus. Homines sumus sed supra homines surgendum est commendandique sumus deo.

All the desires of men are contradictory. We think death life and life death. The process of dying[1] [i.e. life] pleases us so much that we are horrified to think about its coming to an end [i.e. in death]. Although we are mortal, we are supposed to rise above our mortality and commend ourselves to the care of God.

[xvii^v] **23 Quod amicus est in amico**

23 That a friend is in his friend[2]

foot (cf. ll. 34–36)

Tanta vis est amicicie ut qui mutuo se amant mutuo quodammodo se absentes vident simul et agunt; quum alter alterum suo ipsius animo speculatur et presentem habet et cernit.

So great is the power of friendship that men who love each other mutually may somehow, even when they are apart, mutually see each other and act at the same time; for each holds the image of the other in his own mind, and so has him with him and sees him face to face.

[xviii^r] **24 Divinatio de amico**

24 Divination about a friend

17 matutina somnia

morning dreams[3]

---

[1] Ficino (and Colet) may be thinking here of the Socratic doctrine of the philosophical life as a search for death, but they are more probably thinking of the doctrine of mortification from the Pseudo-Dionysius. See Colet's abstract of the *Ecclesiastical Hierarchy*, trans. Lupton, pp. 100-1. Cf. also Heraclitus:
  Immortal mortals, mortal immortals, living their death, dying their life.
Quoted by V. D. Macchioro, *From Orpheus to Paul*, p. 172.

[2] For the background of this concept see Laurens J. Mills, *One Soul in Bodies Twain* (Bloomington, Indiana, 1937).

[3] This phrase refers to Ficino's statement that dreams dreamed just before waking have greater prophetic value than those dreamed earlier in the night, as Ficino says he has explained in his *De immortalitate animae* [i.e. *Theologia Platonica*], XIII (Basle ed., p. 293, bottom of page).

MARGINALIA

[xxv^v] 25 De lege et iusticia

25 On law and justice

head (cf. ll. 6–10)

Quia amat legem, quotiens debet totiens vult ut legittima sint voluntaria. Quia amorem colit, quotiens [amat] totiens debeat [sic] existimare se debere ut voluntarium in amore sit legittimum. Voluntas ex amore, debitum ex lege. Amanda lex, et lege perficiendus[?] amor.

Because he loves the law, the more he has to submit his will to law, the more willing he is that his wishes be lawful. Because he values love, the more he loves, the more he ought to think himself obligated [to see] that his wishes in love should be lawful. Willingness rises from love, obligation rises from law.[2] The law must be loved, and love must be perfected by law.

13 divina lex — divine law
15 scripta lex — written law
20 justicia — Justice

19–21 [l]ex { divina / naturalis / humana }   Law { divine / natural / human }

22–23 Religio justicia in deum.

foot (cf. ll. 11–30)

| divina lex | legittima voluntas | lex scripta |
| divinitas | natura | civilitas |

Religion is justice towards God.

| divine law | right will | written law |
| divinity | nature | society |

justus { deo pius / in se pulcher / in alios benignus }   The righteous man is { reverent to God / beautiful in himself / kind to others[3] }

Divina voluntas decernit creatque; creata institutum servant. Homines instituta imitantes instituunt.

The divine will decrees and creates; His creatures comply with His plan. Men create their own institutions in imitation of His.

[xxvi^r] head (cf. fol. xxv^v, ll. 16–24)

[top line cropped]. Illa summa ratio diffiniens volensque divina lex est. Ad eius exemplar opera Dei se exercentur; id agunt naturali lege. Humana ratio Deum imitans diffinit et vult quae volens recta ex ratione et in rectitudine habituata ex consuetudine, ut ad Deum, in se, ad alios recte agat. . . .[1]

The highest ruling and willing reason is divine law. By its pattern God's works operate; they do this by natural law. Human reason imitates God in both ruling and willing when it wills from right reason, and with a habitual and customary rightness so that it behaves justly toward God, toward itself, and towards others . . .

[xxvi^r] 26 De anima

26 On the soul

21 nam scientia est ex cogn[itione] — For knowledge is derived from inquiry.
25 ratio — reason

---

[1] Illegible.   [2] cf. Rom. xiii. 10.   [3] cf. Marginalia 74.

foot
(cf. ll. 18–39)

anima substantia incorporea rationalis immortalis rectrix corporis

agnoscit substantiam
agnoscit incorporea
quia ratiocinatur

cognitio ex cognatione [sic]

The Soul is:	substance	non-physical	rational	immortal	the ruler of the body
	knows substance	knows the non-physical	because it reasons		

knowing by the affinity [of the knowing for the known]

[xxvi^v] **27 Legitimi iurisconsulti partes**   **27 The parts of the perfect lawyer**[1]

foot
(cf. ll. 28–32)

lex {
anima dei cultus
spiritus legis cura
cerebrum perspicax iudicium
oculi ⎱
li[n]gua ⎰ doctrina
pectus memoria tenax
cor recta voluntas
pedes perseverantia
totum equitas
}

The Law [for each part of the lawyer] {
the soul — the worship of God
the spirit — regard for the law
the brain — clear judgement
the eyes ⎱
the tongue ⎰ learning
the breast — a retentive memory
the heart — right will
the feet — perseverance
the whole — equity
}

[xxvii^r] **28 Fontes potius quam rivulos sectari debemus**   **28 The source is more important than the stream**

5   philopompi   showmen
8   Cantabrigienses   members of Cambridge University[2]

[xxvii^v] **29 Virtutum definitio officium finis** [see fol. xxviii^r]   **29 The definition, function and goal of the virtues**

foot
(cf. fol. xxvii^v, l. 34)

Cognitio nostri speculari ex quibus es.   To know oneself is to consider whence one comes.
Amor nostri diligere pulchritudinem.   To love oneself is to love beauty.
Usus nostri exercere ordine suum quodque officium.   To use oneself rightly is to do one's duty properly.

---

[1] Colet's interest in this passage seems to be explained by a passage in the first Commentary on Romans (*Exposition of Romans*, p. 163) where he criticizes the excessive legalism of the clergy, and refers to various clerics as 'unworthy lawyers'.

[2] This term appears opposite a sentence which translated reads: 'When they [i.e. the pseudo-philosophers] talk in the classroom among boys they always seem to know a great deal, but if you wisely ask them something at home, you will see that they know little about physics, less about mathematics, and least about metaphysics.'

MARGINALIA

	Cognoscere nobis cognatos homines prudentia.	To know	one's fellow man is prudence.
	Diligere nobis cognatos homines charita[s].	To love	one's fellow man is charity.
	Uti eiusdem ad . . . [bottom line cropped].	To use	one's fellow man is [illegible].

[xxvii^v]
head
(cf. fol.
xxviii^r,
ll. 30–
34)

cognitio	dei	intellectus	sapientia ⎫
cultus	dei	voluntas	amor ⎬ religio
consecutio	dei	fruitio	felicitas ⎭
cognitio	nature	admiramur	
appetitus	nature	imitamur	
usus	nature	representamus	

Knowledge of	God	intellect	wisdom ⎫
Worship of	God	will	love ⎬ religion
Attainment of	God	enjoyment	joy ⎭
Knowledge of	Nature	we wonder	
Love of	Nature	we imitate	
Use of	Nature	we represent	

[xxvii^v] **30 Praecepta ad memoriam**
19–foot
(cf. ll.
19–37)

30 Precepts for memory

Noli recordari mala si vis tenere bona; purga abjice vilia ut preciosa teneas. Multiplicitatem turbationem tumultum fuge; simplicitatem, tranquillitatem quietem secta. [P]auca cum paucis, id est meliora cum melioribus; relinque via[m] popularem. Diverticulam [sic] [te]nere; non latam sed rectam viam ingre[d]ere, quam pauci noverunt, qua pauci eunt; tum invenies quod pauci invenient et frueris quo pauci [f]ruuntur. Qui sagax est et eligit et diverticulas [sic] novit, abdita invenit; et qui fortuite et temere, circumvagantur. Ex imo in altum, ex amplo in angustum te contrahe, ubi bonum latet: quamque rem ad rationem refer. Bona pulchra, utile iucundum, nutrie[n]s oblectans.[1] Tenere

'Do not remember evil things if you wish to retain the good.'[2] Clear out and throw away what is worthless in order that you may keep what is valuable. Avoid multiplicity, confusion and tumult; seek simplicity, tranquillity and peace.[3] Have few thoughts and share them with few people, that is, better thoughts with better people. Avoid the crowded way. Follow the bypaths; seek not the broad way but the straight way, the way which few know and few go.[4] Then you will find what few find and enjoy what few enjoy. The man who is wise, who knows and chooses the bypaths, finds what is hidden; but those who go by chance and accident wander about aimlessly. Withdraw yourself from the depths to the heights and from the broad to the narrow, where the good lies hidden. Measure every issue by the standard of reason. The good is the beautiful, the useful is the

---

[1] Following this series of pairs Colet seems to have started off on another tack, writing *oblectans nutri* and then crossing out the *nutri* only and beginning a new sentence with *Tenere*.

[2] Rom. xii. 9.

[3] Colet expands on the Neo-Platonic distinction between simplicity and multiplicity in his *Commentary on First Corinthians*, trans. Lupton, pp. 58–59 (Latin, pp. 82–84). See also *Eccles. Hierarchy*, trans. Lupton, p. 72.

[4] cf. Rom. xiii. 12, and *Lectures on Romans*, p. 102.

26	ratio	Reason
30	Aristoteles	Aristotle
31	Simonides	Simonides[2]
42	aloe	aloe[3]
43	cinnami	cinnamon[4]
44	maiorana	maiorana[5]
	pur[gandum est cerebrum][1]	the brain should be purged [by aloe].

diutius, ordine dispone[re], et degere continuata serie. Que apprehendimus, mandimus, terimus, decoquimus. Sic que discimus meditanda, decantanda, decoquenda ut dura mol[l]escant, cruda maturescant, ut sapida et salutaria esse possint.

enjoyable, the nourishing is the pleasant. Retain things [in the mind] for a long time, arrange them in order, and organize them in connected sequence. Things which we take [into our mouths] we chew, masticate and digest. In the same way things that we take into our minds must be meditated upon, repeated, and digested in order that the hard may be softened and the unripe ripened, and [the things] may become savoury and beneficial.

[xxviii r] head (cf. l. 1) Purgandus animus a malis ut impleatur bonis. Ut tersa specula imagines facile capit [sic], ita purgatus animus notas facile inurit.

The soul must be purged of vice in order to be filled with virtue. As polished mirrors readily catch reflections, so the purged soul readily receives the imprint [of truth].

[xxviii r] **31 Virtutum definitio officium finis**

31 The definition, function and goal of the virtues

9	virtus		virtue
11	speculative		speculative virtues
12	morales		moral virtues
15–19	sapientia scientia prudentia ars	} speculative	wisdom knowledge prudence art } the speculative virtues
21	justicia		justice
22	fortitudo	timor	courage cowardice
23	temperantia	libedo	temperance lust
32	cognitio dei		knowledge of God
34	cultus dei		worship of God
35	consecutio dei		attainment of God

[1] This note, in the gutter of the book, appears to be incomplete; Ficino points out in the text that aloe is a purgative, but that the other herbs mentioned above are sedatives.

[2] Greek poet (*c.* 556–468 B.C.), here as the inventor of a mnemonic technique. Cf. Cicero, *De oratore*, II, 86–88, and Quintilian, *Inst. Orat.*, XI, 2. 357.

[3] A bitter herb used as a purgative. See *Herbal of Rufinus*, ed. L. Thorndike (Chicago, 1946), p. 15.

[4] The common spice, also used as a remedy for indigestion. See *Herbal of Rufinus*, p. 93.

[5] Usually called *sansucus*, an herb used as a sedative. See *Herbal of Rufinus*, p. 176.

MARGINALIA

foot	Clarus	intellectus et lucidus	Status	Speculatio repetita	claritas
	Ardens	appetitus et illuminatus	Stabilis	Bona actio repetita	stabilitas

Intellect [is] clear and radiant	certain	repeated speculation	[results in]	clarity
Will [is] strong and enlightened	stable	repeated good action	[results in]	stability

(cf. ll. 19–34) Ex magna cognitione bonus [intellectus][1] stabilisque appetitus; ex hoc bone actiones; ex his bona consuetudo et mos. Ex speculatione sapientia. Scientia prima cognitio dei. Primus appetitus dei. Prima actio cultus [dei], ex quo consuetudo colendi et [mos] religiosus. Hec pietas et justicia deo omnia alia colere propter deum [last line cropped].

From considerable learning comes a good intellect and stable will. From this come good actions, and from these come good habit and custom. From speculation comes wisdom. The highest knowledge is the knowledge of God. The highest desire is the desire for God. The highest action is worship [of God], from which develop the custom of worship and the habit of piety. This is piety and justice towards God [namely] to worship all other things for the sake of God.

[xxviii^v] head (cf. fol. xxviii^r, ll. 17–18) quare potest, quum possunt prudentie [sic] et caritas continere se ab infimis, non terreri ab horre[n]dis.

Therefore, since prudence and charity cannot be harmed by even the basest things, the soul cannot be alarmed by anything frightening.

[xxviii^v] **32 Tres vitae duces . . .**

32 The three guides of life

foot (cf. ll. 34–41) Ratiocinare diligenter. Experiri diu. Collige autoritates et presentia et preterita cerne. Reperies optimum secundem [sic] mentem vivere utique mente ac, quoad natura humana patitur, assidue et vigilanter meditare. Sperne corpus quod validius etiam non quaerentes [habent] quam sapiens habet. In quiete quale [sic] vita est perpulchra.

Reason diligently. Gain wide experience. Gather authorities and take into account both past and present. You will find it best to live the life of the mind, use your mind and, as far as human nature will allow, meditate long and rigorously. Despise the body, for even those who do not seek [wisdom] have stronger bodies than the wise man has. In peace such as this lies the most beautiful life.

[xxix^v] **33 Cognitio et reverentia sui ipsius**

33 Knowledge of and reverence for oneself

5–6	cognosce te animam auream
13	reverere te ipsum
20	homo stella nube
34	numeri
35	magnitudo

know [that] you [are] a golden soul
have proper respect for yourself
a man [is like] a star [wrapped in] a cloud
numbers
size[2]

---

[1] The entire note is hurried, as is shown by the omissions in the following lines. The word which I have here emended to read *intellectus* actually reads *stabilis*; Colet was evidently thinking ahead to the next phrase.

[2] Ficino is here expressing the opinion that numbers, being abstract, are finitely small but infinitely large, whereas size, being material, is infinitely small but finitely large.

[xxx^v]	**34 Quid est foelicitas**		**34 What happiness is . . .**
40	pecunia	Mida	money Midas
41	Augustus		Augustus
42	honor		honor
43	benevolentia		benevolence
44	dominatio	in Cesar [sic]	power in [the case of Julius] Caesar[1]
[xxxi^r]			
1	robor sanitas		strength health
3	Milo		Milo[2]
4	Herillus	pulchritudo	Herillus[3] beauty
7	Aristippus		Aristippus[4]
10	sensus:	voluptas	sense: pleasure
24	virtus		virtue
25	Stoici		Stoics
26	Cynici		Cynics
33	contemplatio ⊫		contemplation ⊫[5]
34	Democritus		Democritus[6]
35	Anaxagoras		Anaxagoras
37	Aristoteles		Aristotle
41	Plato		Plato
44	Avicenna		Avicenna
[xxxi^v]			
12	ambrosia visio		ambrosia the sight [of God]
13	nectar gaudium		nectar the enjoyment [of God]
41–42	voluptas summum bonum		pleasure [as the] highest good
[xxxii^r]			
4	intellectus intus		Intellect faces inward
5	voluntas extra		Will faces outward.
13–14	Amor transformat, non scientia.		Love, not knowledge, transforms [the soul]
21	voluntas extra		Will faces outward.
36	amor		love
37	visio		vision
43–44	Plus potes amare quam videre.		You can love more than [merely] what you can see.
[xxxii^v]			
17–18	de fruitione dei		on the enjoyment of God
24–26	Varia fruitio sed cuique sufficientia.		The enjoyment of God occurs in different ways, but for each man there is a sufficiency.

[1] A reference to the story, alluded to by Ficino, that Caesar is supposed to have said that he would rather be first man in a village than second man in Rome (cf. Plutarch, *Julius Caesar*, XI).

[2] Greek athlete who defeated Sybarites in 511 B.C.

[3] Stoic philosopher (fl. 250? B.C.); disciple of Zeno.

[4] Greek philosopher (435?–356? B.C.); founder of Cyrenaic school.

[5] Colet's usual sign indicating the number of classes or parts in a thing. In this case it refers to the three classes of contemplation distinguished by Ficino, that of sub-lunary things, of celestial things, and of supra-celestial things.

[6] Greek philosopher (460?–370? B.C.); commonly associated with Heraclitus as representative of comic and tragic views of life. (Cf. Ficino, *Epistolae*, fol. xcvi^v.)

MARGINALIA

[xxxiii^v] **35 Oratio ad deum theologica**

foot (cf. fol. xxxiii^r, l. 12– fol. xxxiii^v, l. 37)
  O chosyn virgin, unto that grete and wonderos meracle to be the moder of Christ bothe god and man!
  O mervelous moder and berer and brynger forthe of hym that browthe forth all others,
  And made the also of nowt that thou shoulde conceve hym of sumwhat.
  O dere dowter of good the wyche warte made the moders of Jesu Christ be the holy gost. O clere growde of lyve. Of Christ howse of goodehe.
  O comfrotable rooth of helth, of the sprange the gret phisicion, restorer and heler of man kynd.

35 A theological prayer to God

O virgin chosen unto the great and wondrous miracle to be the Mother of Christ, both God and Man![2]

O marvellous mother and bearer and bringer forth of Him that brought forth all others,

And made thee also from nought that thou shouldest conceive him from somewhat.

O dear daughter of Goode [God], which wert made the mother of Jesus Christ by the Holy Ghost!

O clear ground of life! O house of Christ's godhead!

O comfortable root of health, from thee sprang the great physician, restorer and healer of mankind.

[xxxix^r][1] **36 Questiones quinque de mentis motu** (cf. fol. xxxviii^v)

34–35	ens: in maxime comunitate [sic]
41	bonum
42	ens
[xxxix^v][1]	
33	ens
[xli^v]	
2	Prometheus
[xlii^r]	
25	resurrextio [sic]

36 Five questions about the motion of the mind

Being: the most universal concept [for the Aristotelians][3]
The Good [is broader than] Being [for the Platonists]

being[4]

Prometheus[5]

the resurrection[6]

[xliii^r] **37 Mens dei radio reflexo intelligit creata . . .**

9–11   sol   Deus

37 The mind of God perceives God's creatures by reflection from them

the sun   God

---

[1] This folio is misnumbered xlix.

[2] With this prayer to the Virgin cf. the prayers of Erasmus, *Opera* (Leyden, 1703–9), cols. 1227D–1234C. See also the *Fifteen Oes*, discussed by Helen C. White, *The Tudor Books of Private Devotion*, (Madison, 1951), pp. 216–29.

[3] Ficino says that according to the Aristotelians *being* includes both the true and the good, that is the objects of the intellect as well as the will; he asserts that there is nothing which is not or cannot be included in the term *being*; whereas according to the Platonists the concept of the good is broader than the concept of being.

[4] Here Ficino goes on to say that the true object of the soul (both intellect and will; that is, the real 'true and good') is God, but he begins the paragraph by talking again of the 'evil' of the soul and Colet says *Being* in the margin, perhaps thinking of the previous discussion.

[5] For Ficino's allegorization of Prometheus as human providence (as opposed to divine providence) see Appendix C, No. 7. Here Ficino calls the soul, imprisoned in its earthly body, 'that unhappy Prometheus'.

[6] This note appears opposite a passage in which Ficino explains that the soul is immortal even though it inhabits a mortal body.

	stelle angeli	the stars angels
	luna anima	the moon the soul
26–28	solaris Deus	God [is] solar
	stellaris angelus	the angels [are] stellar
	lunaris anima	the soul [is] lunar

	deus	God
35–42	an ⟨⟩ geli	an ⟨⟩ gels
	anima	the soul

[xliii^v] 8–18	comparatio solis ad deum	comparison of the sun to God
[xliv^r] 22	sol videt	The sun sees[1]

[xlv^r]	**38 Elementa moventur mobiliter . . .**	**38 The elements are in motion and are always ready for motion**
33–34	Animi motus circularis	The motion of the soul is circular.
[xlv^v]		
4	empireum	the Empyrean
5	terra	the earth
21–22	celestia moveri a substantia spiritali	The heavens are moved by spiritual substance.
[xlvi^r] 1–4	Deus	God[2]
	mens	the [angelic] Mind
	anima	the [World] Soul
	natura	Nature
	corpus	the [World] Body

[xlvi^v]	**39 Forma corporea dividitur et movetur ab alio**	**39 Bodily form is separable and is moved only by something else**
13–14, 16	Deus in se generat; extra creat.	God generates [form] within Himself; He creates [matter] outside Himself.
[xlvii^r]		
1	finis mundi	the end of the world
3	reditus in fontes	the return to the source
5	catholica illustratio	universal illumination

[1] This refers to Ficino's explanation that the Platonists attribute life to the sun and follow Orpheus in calling it the 'eye of the world'.

[2] Here Ficino lists the Neoplatonic hypostases.

MARGINALIA

[xlvii^r]	40 Compendium Platonice theologiae			40 A compendium of Platonic theology		
14–15	unitas simplicitas } potentia		p[ater]	unity simplicity } potency		the Father
16–17	puritas claritas } veritas		fil[ius]	purity clarity } the truth		the Son
23	vita			life [i.e. soul]¹		
33	angeli			angels		
41	mentes			minds		

[xlvii^v]
14   Deus causa   God is [mind as final] cause.
16   mens formaliter   Angels are [mind as formal cause].
            mens   mind²
             /   /
18–20   ratio   reason
             /   /
            vita   life

[xlviii^r]
42   intellectus   mens
foot   sol veritatis intellectui   intelliguntur magis veridica
(cf. fol. sol luminis   visui   videntur   magis illuminata
xlviii^r,
l. 42–fol.
xlviii^v,
l. 5)

The mind [part of the soul] is the intellect.

The sun of truth [makes things visible to] the intellect (for it is the things which are truest that we understand), [just as]

the sun of light [makes things visible to] the sight (for it is the things which are best illuminated that we see).

[xlviii^v]
head   Deus { bonus   voluntas   God { [as] good [is the object of the] will.
(cf. ll.   { verus   intellectus   { [as] true [is the object of the] intellect.
8–10)
                                                    [as it is] warm [is the object of] desire
           sol { calidus   appetitus   The sun
               { lucens   sensus oculi   [as it is] bright [is the object of] sight

---

¹ This and the two following notes label three of the four grades of incorporeal substance distinguished by Ficino; the fourth is God.

² This diagram summarizes the idea in the preceding paragraphs of Ficino that the soul involves not two functions only (passion and reason), but three: passion ('life'), reason, and mind (intellect). This doctrine of the *mens* is expounded more fully in Ficino's *Theologia Platonica*; see P. O. Kristeller, *Philosophy of Marsilio Ficino*, pp. 375–88.

9	Angeli oculi				Angels are like eyes.[1]		
24	deus				God [is the object of both intellect and will].		
[xlviii^v]							
foot (cf. ll. 12–27)	bonum verum	bene esse vere esse	bonitas veritas	voluntati intelligentie	bonus deus verus [deus]	suavis implens clarus illuminans	
						[facit] felicem facit sapientem	

the good the true	to be good to be true	goodness truth	for will for intellect	God as good, [God] as true,	sweet, and fulfilling clear, and illuminating makes [man] happy. makes [man] wise

[xlix^r]
39   lumen videt   The light sees [all things; i.e. the sun is the eye of the world].

[l^r]
7–14 impleta   filled
      sistentia   stand still
      rapta   taken up
      tracta   drawn up   [The order of effects of God upon
      mota   moved   His creatures (to be read from
                                           bottom to top).]

      vivificata   given life
      fota   then fostered
      facta   Things made

[l^v]
head   Voluntas dei facit bonum.   The will of God makes the Good.
(cf. fol. Voluntas hominis capit bonum.   The will of man admits[2] the Good.
l^r, l. 43–fol. l^v, l.4)

1–11   providentia Dei   The providence of God [is the diffusion and consecration of the Good].
18   finis   final
19   agens   efficient
20   forma   formal
21   materia   material [the four kinds of cause]
20   claviculus [sic]   That tendril of a vine [which is called] 'the
21   capreolus   weight-bearing tendril' [exists solely for the purpose of gaining control over the nearest tree. In this case the act of conquering is the cause of the vine's having risen.][3]

[li^r] 41 **De raptu Pauli ad tertium caelum**   41 **On the taking up of Paul to the third heaven**

[1] Ficino has been saying that if you could change your whole soul to intellect alone, you would then be like an angel, and that that would be like changing your whole body to an eye.

[2] Ficino's text says *vult, desires* the Good.

[3] As my translation of Ficino's context suggests, Ficino is using the vine as an illustration of the difference between the four kinds of cause.

MARGINALIA

27–30   In illud cuius radiis inflammati nos una tam diu vitam celestem in terra agimus.

To that [heaven] by whose rays we are illuminated and for so long live a heavenly life together on earth.

33– foot (cf. ll. 33–43)   Est superba impietas velle ascendere in celum: in eiusmodi revelationibus non enim nobis gloriandum. Nostra gloria omnis in solo illo rege glorie est, ad quem nemo ascendit sed rapitur. Gravitas terrene nature non patitur ut ascendatur [sic]; pati potest ut trahatur. Ut enim gravia non petunt alta nisi ab altis trahantur, ita quoque homines terrene huius orbis terrarum incole in celum gradus non ascendunt quidem, nisi eos celestis potestas attraxerit. Est res tota in tractu dei non in conatu nostro. Trahit autem ille et rapit quos amat ardentius.

It is impious insolence to wish to rise to heaven [by our own efforts], for we are not meant to glory in revelations of that kind. Our glory rests entirely with that one King of Glory, to whom no one ascends, but is raised. The heaviness of earthly nature does not permit [the soul] to rise of its own accord; it is capable only of allowing itself to be raised. As heavy things do not seek the heights unless they are drawn up by things above them, so also men, the earthly inhabitants of this earth, do not climb the steps to heaven unless some heavenly power draws them up. It is entirely a matter of God's raising us, not of our own effort. God lifts up and takes to heaven those whom He most loves.

[liv]

1   sol luna   As the sun [is related to] the moon [so is God to the soul].

4   imago speculum   as the image is to the mirror

20–21   sol quarto celo Venus amorem   In the fourth heaven the Sun is Venus, [giving earthly] love.

25   fides   faith
27   spes   hope
29   charitas   charity
34   Helias   Elijah

34–36   caritate   pulses
         spe   petas
         fide   queras

Knock in charity, seek in hope, and ask in faith

38–40   morte   vita   death [produces]   life [produces]   [to be read from bottom to top.]

         tenebris   lumen   darkness [produces]   light [produces]

         frigus   calor   cold   heat

foot (cf. ll. 18–31)   Sanctus Dei spiritus charitas et amor Dei
     seraphin amati   caritas   ames ut ingrediare
     principatus in tercia spera   spes   speres ut detur
     angelus veritatis   fides   credas ut intelligas

God's holy spirit, charity, and the love of God
     beloved seraphim   charity   Love, that you may enter on the way.
     principalities in the third sphere   hope   Hope, that [God's grace] may be given you.
     the angel of truth   faith   Believe, that you may understand.

[lii^r]

11–17	spere septem	the seven spheres
	spera octava	the eighth sphere
	chrystallinum	the crystalline sphere
	aque supra celos	waters above the heavens
	empyreum	the Empyrean

foot (cf. fol. lii^r, ll. 22–44), fol. lii^v ll. 20–25)

    seraphin ⎫
    cherubin ⎬
    throni ⎭

Ut anima se habet ad corpus, ita spiritus ad animam, ita denique deus ad spiritum. Anima a subcelestibus ad celestia ac deinde ad supracelestia transferre se debeat.

    D[omi]nationes ⎫
    Potestates ⎬
    Virtutes ⎭

    Principatus ⎫
    Archangeli ⎬ [bottom cropped.]
    [Angeli] ⎭

    Seraphim
    Cherubim
    Thrones

As the soul stands in relation to the body, so does the spirit stand to the soul, and so, finally does God stand to the spirit. The Soul ought to rise from the sub-celestial to the celestial and then to the supra-celestial.

    Dominations
    Powers
    Virtues

    Principalities
    Archangels   [bottom cropped]
    [Angels]

[lii^v]

27–28	malignorum spirituum turbe 9	The nine orders of evil spirits
33	Seraphin amor	Seraphim [seek God by] love[1]
34	Cherubinorum scientia	Cherubim [seek God by] knowledge

foot (cf. ll. 20–25)

Seraphini	Seraphim
Cherubini	Cherubim
Throni	Thrones
Dominationes	Dominations
Virtutes	Virtues
Potestates	Powers

[1] In this passage St. Paul, as a speaker in the dialogue, says that before he went to heaven he often wondered whether it was better to seek God by love or knowledge, and when he arrived in heaven he found out that love was better, for the Seraphim, who seek God by love, are closer to God (in the chain of being) than the Cherubim, who seek God by knowledge.

MARGINALIA

		Principatus Archangeli [Angeli] [bottom cropped]	Principalities Archangels Angels
[liii^r]	9–10	exemplar bonorum	[There must exist one supreme] exemplar of the Good.
	15–17	pater filius S[piritus] S[anctus]	Father Son }[1] [Deity] Holy Spirit
	32	septem munera	the seven gifts [of the Holy Ghost; given to counteract the seven deadly sins]

foot (cf. ll. 23–29)

sol { forma, figura, lux }   propagans / propago } amor } Deus

the sun { form[2], shape, light }   parent / offspring } love } God

[liii^v]	27	materia	[The forms of objects are understood by abstracting them from the] matter [of the objects].
	34–35	idee in deo	The ideas are in God.
	43	pater	The Father [is the divine light.]
	44	gratia	Grace [is the name given to the rays of God's influence.]
[liv^r]	22	ethernitas	Eternity [is the truth and truth is eternity.]
	31–32	anima etherna	The soul is immortal.
[liv^v]	21	nox	'The night [is my illumination in the time of my pleasure.']³
	22	D[e] D[eo]	On God⁴
foot (cf. ll. 15–23)		Expletio animi non comprehendere.	The fulfilment of the soul is not to comprehend, [but to comprehend that God is incomprehensible.]
[lv^r]	2	charitas	Charity [penetrates where knowledge cannot altogether go.]⁵
	8–9	contenta voluntas	The will is contented [i.e. it enjoys the Good infinitely, without want or satiety, whereas the intellect is finite in its satisfaction.]

---

¹ Colet's usual sign for parts of a whole.
² Ficino, in the person of St. Paul, is describing the unity of God, and he here points out that in the third heaven all aspects of the sun are one and the same.
³ Ficino here appears to be running together Ps. cxxxix. 11–12 and Isa. xxi. 4.

⁴ The initials D.D. may stand for *David* referring to the quotation preceding, but they may also stand for De Deo, the subject of the next letter.
⁵ The title of this section is: *Voluntas deo fruitur magis quam intellectus*, 'Will enjoys God more than intellect does'.

34	Nota similitudinem.			Note the similitude [i.e. Ficino's comparison between the light of the sun and the light of God as being visible only when they strike objects.]	
[lv^v] head (cf. ll. 15–23)	Deus	Is[1]		God	Himself
	anima	imago		soul	image of God
	corpora	umbre		bodies	shadows of God
28	veritas Dei in se			The truth of God is in Himself.	
30	veritas anime in se			The truth of the soul is in itself.	
32–33	imago Dei in anime speculo			[One sees] the image of God in the mirror of the soul, [as one sees] the image of the soul in the mirror of the body.	
34–35	imago anime in corporis speculo				

foot (cf. ll. 33–36) Deus, vultus Dei aspiciet nos. Aspici est aspicere, et aspicie[n]s inspicit se et respi[cit]; et inspectum respicit a se ipso. Imago Dei exemplar universi exactu[m].

speculum mentis {
 extra umbram: facie ad faciem clare. Respice te imaginem Dei, radium reflexum in solem summum supracelestem, imaginem veritatis.
 in umbra: in enigmate et obscuritate.
}

mos, pietas { cultus Dei / justicia } compone refor[ma]

umbra corporis

God, the face of God, will look on us. To be looked at is to look, and that which looks beholds itself and looks back at itself. That which is looked on looks away from itself. The image of God is a complete exemplar of the universe.

the mirror[2] of the mind {
 beyond the shadow [of the body one sees God] face to face clearly. Look upon yourself as an image of God, a ray reflected to the highest sun above the heavens, an image of the Truth.
 Within the shadow [of the body one sees God] in mystery and obscurity.
}

custom, piety { [by] the worship of God [and] [by] justice, } compose and reform yourself

The shadow of the body.

---

[1] These notes actually apply to the paragraph headed: '*Corpora sunt umbrae dei; animae vero dei imagines immortales*' (ll. 15–29).

[2] For a useful discussion of this point and its relation to 1 Cor. xiii. 12, see Gordon W. O'Brien, *Renaissance Poetics and the Problem of Power* (Chicago, 1956), pp. 1–20.

MARGINALIA

[lvi^r] head (cf. ll. 2–6)

per Deum et eo ipso Deo gaudemus, et beate gaudemus quod ipsum est gaudium. Deus ipsum gaudium; per ipsum duntaxat gaudium beate gaudemus.	We rejoice through God and for that reason in God Himself; and we rejoice in bliss because God is joy itself. God is joy itself; it is only through joy itself that we rejoice in bliss.

2–4 actio { ut consequare gaudium / vitandus dolor }   Action { to achieve joy / to avoid sorrow }

[lvi^r] **42 Argumentum in Platonicam theologiam**

32–33 foot (cf. fol. lvi^r, l. 31-fol. lvi^v, l. 23)

Celum		sine materia
supernaturales	forme	sine materia et qua[n]titate
celestia[les]	forme	cum quantitate sine materia subjectum [sic] motui
naturales	forme	cum quantitate et materia

42 A preface to the Platonic theology

Heaven: without matter
supernatural forms: without matter or quantity
celestial forms: with quantity, but without matter and subject to motion
natural forms: with quantity and matter

[lvi^v]

1–4

sine materia et quantitate	anima	without matter and quantity	soul
sine quantitate	spiritus	without quantity	spirit
cum materia et quantitate	corpus	with matter and quantity	body

38–39 orbis [i.e. orbes] magis lucere quam stellas   [The Aristotelians say that] the planets shine brighter than the stars.

[lxi^v] **43 Qualis est amor talis amicitia**   **43 The quality of love determines the the quality of friendship**

head (cf. ll. 9–18)

anima { appetit levitas / discernit lux / repellit animositas }   the soul[1] { desires lightness / perceives light / rejects wrath }

7–9
ratio   reason
ira   wrath
concupiscentia   concupiscence

10 Una anima plures vires.   A single soul [has] several powers, as fire [not only] glows, [but also] rises and is warm.
11 Ignis lucet, ascendit, calet.
14 appetitus levis volat in Deum   Soaring desire flies up toward God.
15 ratio lux { verum / bonum }   Reason, light { the true / the good }

---

[1] All the notes on this page reflect Ficino's discussion of the Platonic division of the soul into three parts as shown in the first note: the reason, the appetitive passions, and the aversive passions.

16	Animositas repellit contraria.		Animosity repels contraries.	
17–18	anima { volat / decernit / repellit }		the soul { flies up / judges / rejects }	
32	ratio revocans		Restraining reason[1]	
33–34	concupiscentia ad blanda sensibilia		the passion for smooth sensibilia	
37–38	ratio { irascitur / concupiscit }		Reason { can be angered / can desire }	
foot (cf. ll. 23–26)	anima { revocans ab humilibus / appetens humilia }		the soul { recalling from baser things / desiring baser things }	

[lxii^r]

1–3	ratio	purissima	fa[vet]	reason	purest	assists
	ira	purior	fer[vescit]	wrath	more pure	seethes
	concupiscentia	vilis	al[licit]	desire	base	[?attracts]

[lxii^r] **44 Quid sit lumen in corpore mundi**

44 The nature of light in the physical world

8–20 Christiani solis radiis humana et fidelis mens gravida quasi seminibus eniti debet solem parere [sic] et referre Christum, sed indegam [sic] luminis lunam parit: que dicanda est Christo ut illius radiis illustretur qui suo ingenti splendore potest obscura reddere clariora. Odiose tenebre sane tenebrosaque omnia. Amabile lumen luculentaque omnia.

The human mind, when touched by faith, being pregnant by the Christian sun's rays, as it were with seeds,[2] ought to strive to produce a sun and resemble Christ. But instead it only produces a light-needing moon, which must be dedicated to Christ, to be illumined by His great light, Who can make dark things lighter. Truly, hateful are darkness and all things dark. Lovely are light and all things light.

[lxii^r]

	[lumen] / tenebre }		light / darkness }
		aureum [i.e. aereum]	are aerial
21–24	sonus / silentium }		sounds / silence }
	vapores	odorantur	odours are smelled
	liquores	gustantur	liquors are tasted
	co[r]pulenta	tanguntur	bodily things are touched

26–foot (cf. ll. 26–39) Lumen est splendor spiritalis a spiritalubus [sic] captus et indicatas [sic] quod emanat subito et latissime a corporibus. Nam omne corpus suapte

Light is a spiritual radiance received and taken [?] from spiritual things. It emanates suddenly and extensively from bodies. For every body, of its own nature, pours fourth

---

[1] In the margin at this point Colet has drawn a rough semicircle with a dot in the centre, intended to illustrate Ficino's observation that just as the centre of a circle can stand still while the circumference revolves, so the reason part of the soul can remain stable while the passions are active.

[2] cf. *De Sacramentis*, trans. Lupton, p. 60, where the sexual image appears in its proper context of the marriage of man and God in the Church.

MARGINALIA

natura aliquid fundit sue nature sine detrimento. Que eman[a]tio in diaphanis et transpicuis nitor est. Et quod emanat a dyaphanis, transpicuis, nitor videtur et nitiditas. Nam transpicua nitent. Ab iis, que non sunt dyaphana et transpicua, et transpicua[1] que opaca sunt, funditur color. Lux omnicolor, si[ve][2] lumen opacum in solidiore obscuriorique [sic] materia. Tolle terra[m] quae facit colo[ra]tionem i.e. facit lumen evadere in crassum lumen i.e. colorem. Tum restabit quaedam qualitas, immo claritas quaedam, non opaci actus, actus sed perspicuus, et quidam floridus vigor unicolor et virtute omnicolor. Opaca lux, color: clarus color, lux, et quasi flos colorum et puritas suprema, [?] intemerata, et vigor colorum, unicolor et omnis [?sic] color, actu et virtute, quia lux evadit multiplex in opacitatibus et virtute est omne [? sc. genus], hoc est, possit[3] potest talis evadere. Una lux et simplex, multiplex et [?] varia evadit.

something without loss to its own nature. This emanation, in diaphanous and transparent things, is sheen, and that which emanates from diaphanous and transparent things is seen to be sheen and a shining light.[5] Transparent things glisten. From those things which are not diaphanous and transparent, which are opaque, colour is poured out. Light is of all colours, or it is opaque light in matter which is more solid and obscure. Take away the earth which produces colouring, i.e. makes light become thick light, i.e. colour. Then there will remain a certain quality, or rather, a certain clarity, which is not the actuality of the opaque, but a clear actuality, a certain beautiful vigour, which is uniform in colour and *potentially* multiform in colour. Opaque light is colour, clear colour is light, and, as it were, the flower of colours, a supreme inviolate purity, the vigour of all colours. It is uniform and multiform in colour, actually [uniform] and potentially [multiform], because light becomes multiform in opaque bodies and is potentially of all kinds, i.e. it can become such. Light is one and uniform, it becomes multiform and differentiated.

[lxii^v] head (cf. fol. lxii^r, l. 41–fol. lxii^v, l. 6)

Adumbratio luminis est hic vigorosus [sic] in se et expressus [sic] in colores et opaca lumina.[4] Non pichtura longe [?] minus veritas. Solem oculis inest deum [sic] lumen quo nihil luminosius, quo item nihil obscurius. Omnia deum obstrepetant [sic], ut qui [non] audit nihil eo surdius sit; quamquam omnia deum circumsonant. Tamen nihil tenebrosius est quam sibi putare deum esse clarissimum; s[t]ulticie putare te deum scire omnino et insanie omnino nescire.

The beclouding of light shows itself here on earth more strongly and manifestly in colours and opaque lights; not a picture, still less is it the truth. To our eyes God is represented by the sun. [God is] a light than which no light is brighter yet harder to see. The whole world resounds so loudly of God that nothing is more deaf then the man who does not hear this, although all things are resonant with God. Nothing is darker than the darkness of thinking that God is perfectly understood. It is stupid to think that you know God completely, [but it is] insane to think that you do not know Him at all.

---

[1] This second *et transpicua* is apparently a mistake, and I have therefore omitted it in the translation.

[2] This reading is supplied from Ficino's text.

[3] This subjunctive appears to be an error corrected in the following *potest*; I have therefore omitted *possit* in the translation.

[4] This sentence is clearly very corrupt.

[5] Up to this point Colet's note is a fairly close paraphrase of Ficino's text. From this point on, Colet seems not to understand what Ficino is saying.

[lxiii^v]
25–28 | In mundano hoc templo lumen refert deum, res veneranda aspectu ampla, larga, subita, latissima. | In this worldly temple the light stands for God; it is a thing awesome to behold, great, abundant, sudden, and ubiquitous.

[lxx^r] **45 Omnes omnium laudes referantur in deum . . .** | **45 All praise of all things should be referred to God**

29–39 | palinodia, recantatio dici potest a palyn, quod est iterum, et odos, cantus. Est quidem quum male de quopiam scribentes, deinde rescribentes de eodem bene scribamus mutato canto [sic]. | *palinode*[1], that is, a recantation, from *palyn*, which means *again*, and *odos*, which means *singing*. [The word] is used when we write wrongly on a subject, and then, by rewriting, change our tune and treat the same subject rightly.

[lxx^v] **46 Nemo ascendit ad Deum nisi . . . Deus ipse descenderit** | **46 No one rises to God unless . . . God has descended to him**

10–13 | Non ascendes ad Deum nisi ad te Deus quodammodo descenderit. | You cannot rise to God unless God somehow first descends to you.

[lxx^v] **47 Nugis vulgus pascitur** | **47 The common man feeds on trifles**

19–20 | celum sine materia
elementa cum materia | Heaven, without matter
the elements, with matter

21–24 | sine accidente   deus
sine mutatione   angel[us]
sine quantitate   anima
sine materia   cel[um] | without accident   God
without change   Angel
without quantity   soul
without matter   heaven

26–29 | lumen, claritas, gaudium
clarum gaudium et glaudiosa [sic] claritas
in celo risus. | light, clarity, joy
clear joy and joyous clarity

foot (cf. ll. 24–25) | In numinibus illis est claritas mirum in modum gladiosa [sic] et clarum gaudium cuius in celo lux illius imago est et quasi risus. | In heaven there is laughter.
In those divine beings is joyous clarity of a wonderful kind and a clear joy, of which the light in heaven is the image and, as it were, the laughter.

[lxx^v] **48 Amicitia vera est quam religio vera concilliavit** | **48 Friendship based upon true piety is true friendship**

38–41 | Ex religione vera amicitia. Ex amore Dei hominum amor. Conjuncti deo inter se facile et firmissime conjunguntur. | True friendship comes from piety. From love of God comes love of man. Men who are joined by God are joined together readily yet firmly.

---

[1] Colet appears to have derived his etymology of this unfamiliar term from Niccolò Perotti's *Cornucopiae*. Cf. (Venice, 1496), ed. fols. 156^r and 196^v (misnumbered cxcix).

MARGINALIA

[xcv^v]	**49 Matrimonii laus**	**49 In praise of marriage**
8–9	probat matrimonium gratum nature; sculpit filios[1]	[Ficino] approves of marriage as acceptable to nature; it creates sons.
17	Socrates ab uxore	Socrates [learned moral discipline] from his wife.
22–23	matrimonium non impedire litteras	Marriage does not prevent scholarship.
29	sapientie dediti	those who are dedicated to wisdom [are exceptions to Hermes Trismegistus's statement that unmarried men are no better than dead trees in the eyes of God.]
34	cum musis miscere Venus	Venus mixes with the muses.
42–44	Homo maxime sociabile est. Huc sermo, huc leges. Nemo extra societatem nisi aut super hominem aut infra.	Man is the most sociable [of all animals. It was] for this [reason that nature provided him alone with the faculty of] speech [and the faculty of making] laws. No one lives outside of society unless he is either above man or below man.

[xcvi^r]	**50 Philosophia sapientiam gignit**	**50 Philosophy produces wisdom**
head (cf. ll. 40–44)	Nemo bene utitur omnibus nisi bonitate, nisique ipse scit bonum. Bono usu bona sunt bona et etiam etiam [sic] mala; malo usu mala peiora sunt et bona mala. Cumque est quodque uti ipse est, bonis beneque utentibus bona omnia, malis maleque ute[n]tibus mala omnia. Sapiens est qui se suasque vires cognoscit et ex viribus agit nec plus attemptet [sic] quam possit vincere ad bonumque traducere. Hec sapientia, ut cognoscas te ipsum, a sapientia querenda est et perdiscenda, que scit omnia et sapienter utitur omnibus. Dicati sapientiae, igitur, soli felices sunt, quibus nihil malum quia sciunt uti bene omnibus etiam malis et in miseria beati esse, qui sunt in tenebris sapientes et in malis bon[i], qui non coniugem et filios neminem et, ut inquid Paulus, in bono vincunt malum. Alii mali; sua malicia bonum devorat, et in malum versat et pro sua malicia omnia illis sunt	No one makes good use of anything except by goodness, and unless he himself knows the good. It is by good usage that goods are goods; and the same argument applies to evil things: by bad usage evils become worse and goods evil. The quality of the action is determined by the quality of the doer: to good men and men who use things in the right way, all things are good; to evil men and men who use things in the wrong way, all things are evil. The wise man is the man who knows himself and his own strength and acts according to his powers, not attempting more than he can control and turn to the good. This wisdom, that you know yourself, must be sought and learned from wisdom, which knows all things and always acts wisely. Only those dedicated to Wisdom, therefore, are happy, those to whom nothing is evil because they know how to use everything well, even evil things, and how to be happy in misery, those who are wise in the midst of darkness and good in the midst of evil, who have no wife or children, and who, as St. Paul says, by goodness overcome evil.[2] The

[1] In line 10 of this page, where Ficino's text reads *soluptor*, Colet has corrected it to *sculptor*.

[2] Rom. xii. 21.

	mala. Hinc vide dignitatem et sapientie et philosofie.	rest are evil; their wickedness destroys good and turns it into evil, and because of their own evil everything is evil to them. From this you may see the value of wisdom and philosophy.
26–foot (cf. ll. 26–39)	Christus dei virtus et dei sapientia. Dives et potens Juno non audit. Experiamur quid numen sit, quia viget ubique, quiaque omnibus adest qui ei volunt adesse. Immo audit non vocatus; rite precantem quemlibet exaud[it]. Ab illo omne auxilium petendum quo tollamus nos humo et superas auras evadamus. Potest ille solus ad caput rerum qui ex capite natus. Illum rite precemur i.e. sapienter. Nam sapientie nihil rectum nisi sapienter precatur. Sapienter [precatur] qui poscit sapientiam ap[ud] ipsam sapientiam, rite et sapienter petendam sapientiam [sic?]. Hinc Salomon sapientiam poposcit ut cognoscat quid bonum, quid malum, quia nihil bonum nisi sapienti et bono; insipientibus habita bona vulgo mala sunt quia eis nequitur sine sapientia sapienter uti nec sine bonitate bene. Bonus autem pro bonitate etiam malis bene utitur, bonoque usu mala sibi saltem facit bona. Omnia quae facit sibi bene succedent ad imitationem dei, cui bene omnia succedunt quia illius providentia utitur bene. Hec felicitas.	'Christ is the power of God and the wisdom of God.'[1] Rich and mighty Juno does not hear us. Let us try the power of God, because He is powerful everywhere and because He is present to all who wish to be in His presence; indeed Christ hears even when He is not called; He listens to anyone who prays properly. It is from Christ that we must seek the aid we need to raise ourselves from the earth and escape to Heaven. He alone has influence over the head of things Who was born from the head of things. Let us pray to Him properly, that is, wisely. For there is no rightness in wisdom unless one prays for it wisely. [A man prays] wisely who asks for wisdom from Wisdom Itself, [and only for such] wisdom as ought wisely and properly to be sought. Hence Solomon asked for wisdom in order that he might distinguish between good and evil, because nothing is good except to the wise and good man. [Conversely,] to unwise men what is normally thought good is evil, because it is impossible to use them [i.e. good and evil] wisely without wisdom, or well without goodness. But the good man, because of his goodness, uses even evils well, and by good use makes evils good, for himself at least. Everything he does will turn out well for him with a view to imitation of God; everything turns out well for him because he makes the right use of God's providence. This [is] happiness.
[xcvi^v] head (cf. fol. xcvi^r, l. 44–fol. xcvi, l. 11)	In philosophia ergo desiderioque sapientie et petitione et expectatione et amore perfectum sacerdotium et quae ipsa sapientia est consistit: ut votis, sacrificii[s], precibus assequatur; ut sciat quid bonum et malum; ut malis quae fugere nequit bene	Thus the perfect priesthood,[2] which is wisdom itself, consists in philosophy, in the desire for wisdom, in prayer, hope, and love, so that by vows, sacrifices, and prayers it may obtain knowledge of good and evil, so that it may use well those evils which cannot be avoided; and so that because of its goodness no evil can

---

[1] I Cor. i. 24.
[2] Colet's view of the priesthood seems to derive mainly from the Pseudo-Dionysius; see Frederic Seebohm, *The Oxford Reformers* (London, 1913), pp. 65–70. See also Colet's *De Sacramentis*, trans. Lupton, pp. 46–49.

MARGINALIA

uti; ut pro sua bonitate nihil ei malum accidat, nec ipsa quidem mala quae sua bonitate decoquit ad bonum. Hii vere sacerdotes Christi qui sapiunt soli faciuntque ut alii sapiant. Ut dolendum est eos ita indigne impieque a vulgo tractari, ut qui ii [i.e. ii qui] sal terre sint et sapientia, a vulgo soli desipere iudicentur. Iudei Christum desipisse existimaverunt et Agrippa Paulum. Sed ut malis omnia mala, ita stultis omnia stulta. Ut quum a vulgo insano quis rideatur, vero laudi sibi esse putet et rideat insanum vulgus, quod admirari nequidum est ei. Eorum flebilis risus et deflendus quem luget Heraclitus et ridiculus fletus quem risit Democritus.

befall it—not even those evils which because of its goodness it converts to good. They are truly ministers of Christ who are possessed of a unique wisdom, and try to bring it about that others become wise [also]. How grievous it is that they are treated so shamefully and irreverently by the masses, that they, who are the salt[1] and wisdom of the earth are thought to be the only mad ones by the masses. The Jews thought Christ was insane, and Agrippa thought the same of Paul. But just as to the wicked everything is wicked, so to fools everything is folly. The result is that anyone who is ridiculed by the senseless masses should actually regard this as something to be proud of and should himself ridicule them in return, for it is impossible for him to admire them. Their laughter, which Heraclitus weeps over, is pathetic and pitiable, and their tears, which Democritus laughed at, are ludicrous.

[xcvi^v]

51 Disputatio contra iudicium astrologorum

35-foot

Vana sunt et fallacia astrologorum iudicia ex stellarum viribus collecta et perniciosorum errorum causae. Nam providentiam auferunt et imperium dei quum asserunt vi astrorum necessario evenire omnia. Ubi tum summi dei [providentia] et imperium liberimum [sic] absolutum si a subiectis astris fiant omnia? Angeli.

51 A treatise against the views of astrologers

The pronouncements of astrologers, based on the influence of the stars, are false and worthless and are the the cause of pernicious error. For they take away the providence and omnipotence of God when they say that all events occur necessarily as a result of the compulsion of the stars. Where is the providence of the supreme God, and where is His absolute and free authority if everything is caused by the inferior stars? [What about the free will of] angels . . .[2]

[xcvii^v]

52 Montes non seperant [sic] animos montibus altiores

22–29

Coniu[n]cti conspirant in unum vi animorum montibus altiorum et amantes semper sunt juncti ob amplitudinem animorum et coitum.

52 Mountains cannot separate souls which are higher than mountains

Joined together, [Ficino and his friend are able to] unite by virtue of their souls, which are loftier than the mountains [separating them], and lovers always are joined because of the greatness and union of their souls.

---

[1] Colet uses *salt* in the sense of astringent; thus the Apostles were the 'salt' of the earth for their work of purifying. Cf. *Exposition of Romans*, p. 114 and *Lectures on Romans*, p. 75.

[2] Colet was here apparently going on with his paraphrase of Ficino's attack on astrology, but then thought better of it and stopped here.

[xcviiiʳ] **53 Leges divinae fides scientia confirmatur [sic]**

53 Divine law and faith are confirmed by knowledge

head (cf. ll. 4–16) — Christiane legi et voluptas et vis et ratio adversata est. Hinc patet nec humanam nec fatalem a celique dispositione pendentem sed a quadam supracelesti potentia perfectam.

Desire and will and reason are all opposed to Christian law. Hence it is clear that law is not human, nor is it fated, as though deriving from the disposition of the heavens; rather it is laid down by some supra-celestial power.

4–7
$$\left.\begin{array}{l}\text{ratione}\\ \text{autoritate}\\ \text{vi}\\ \text{voluptate}\end{array}\right\} \text{leges inducuntur}$$

$$\left.\begin{array}{l}\text{reason}\\ \text{authority}\\ \text{power}\\ \text{desire}\end{array}\right\} \text{Laws are brought about by these}$$

2–11 syderum dispositio

[Law is not laid down by] the disposition of the stars.

Requirit vel voluptatem vel vim vel rationem vel autoritatem.

[Law] needs [some reason for existing, such as] desire, power, reason, or authority.

13–15 Argumentationes probabiles: arma potentum, voluptatum usus.

Probable deterrents [i.e. which would have prevented the establishment of law if it were merely a human institution]:
    the arms of the mighty
    the pursuit of pleasure

17–33 Cum scientia firmatur credulilitas [sic] illa, divina fides certior. Divine credere quam humane scire humana sapientia. Sapientia sine credulitate vacilla[t]. Veritati credendum, bono sperandum. Bonum non frustratur, non derelinquit amantes quia ipsum bonum illuminavit ut sperare[n]t et ut amarent inflammavit.

When belief is confirmed by knowledge, divine faith is more certain. Believing in the divine way is superior to knowing in the human way; without divine faith, human wisdom wavers. We should believe the truth and hope for the good. The good does not disappoint or fail those who love it because the good itself enlightened them to hope for it and inflamed them to love it.

[xcviiiᵛ] **54 Nullum in malis refugium est nisi ad summum bonum**

54 There is no refuge in [the midst of] evils except to the highest good

17–foot (cf. ll. 20–41) — Tragedia vita humana est. Re enim fabulam agit, miseriamque ostendit; sive enim contempleris, sive agas, sive voluptate fruaris. Nam hiis tribus felicitas censetur, sapientia, potestas, voluptas. Verum hii meserimi [i.e. miserrimi]. In contemplatione ambiguitas et quum velint omnia in singulis cognoscere, de omnibus in singulis dubitant. Illuc aspiraverint ut videant se nescire et sine consilio sint. In amaritudinem et confusionem versentur [sic] qui

Human life is a tragedy, for indeed it does perform a play, and it exhibits unhappiness, whether one lives the life of contemplation, action, or pleasure. For happiness is thought to consist of one of these three: wisdom, power, or pleasure. In fact, they are [all] most wretched. In contemplation there is [always] dubiety, and although contemplatives seek to understand the whole through its parts, all they learn from the parts is doubt about the whole. They have concentrated on that goal, with the result that they realize they do not know [anything] and are devoid of

MARGINALIA

non quaerunt veritatem in veritate ipsa et lumen in lumine.

       laborosum Sa[lomon][1]
       insipientiam Pa[u]l[u]s
       vanitatem Esa[ias]

Hinc vagantur in temebris [sic] misere, quia non credunt veritati ipsi in quo non est falsitas. Confidunt sibi ipsis, non Deo. Confidunt falsitate, non veritate; querunt ceci colores non in solis splendore, sed in oculis [i.e. oculi] radio inspicere. Maxime agentes maxime passiuntur, maxime domini, maxime servi, maxime alti, humiles maxime; miseririores [sic] qui didicerunt deforme quam qui nihil didicerunt. Querunt lumen confisi ipsis et non inveniunt.

understanding. Those who do not seek truth in itself, and light in the light, live in bitterness and confusion.

[descriptions of human wisdom]   Solomon: full of labour [and grief][2]
                      Paul: foolishness [before God]
                      Isaiah: vanity [before God]

Hence they wander wretchedly in darkness because they do not believe in the truth itself, in which there is no falsehood. They trust in themselves rather than in God. They trust in falsehood rather than in truth; they are blind and attempt to look at colours not by the light of the sun, but in the ray of the eye. They do much and suffer much. The most powerful lords become the most abject slaves; the highest become the humblest; for they are more wretched who have learned badly than they who have learned nothing at all. They seek the light, trusting in themselves, but do not find it.

[xcix^r] head (cf. fol. xcviii^v, l. 43–fol. xcix^r, l. 3)

Profectio ad actionem est incidere in passionem.

Proficisci ad dominationem est incidere ad servitutem.

Proficisci ad voluptatem est incidere ad dolores.

To aim for action is to fall into suffering.

To aim at domination is to fall into servitude.

To aim at pleasure is to fall into pain.

head (cf. fol. xcviii^v, l. 43–fol. xcix^r, l. 27)

Quam frustratur hominis propositum et omnem eventum preter intentum et res habet alias; rerum voluptas dolorem, potestas impotentiam, scientia stulticiam. Letandum [sic] in Deo, confisus in Deo, . . .[3] in Dei potestate, possit remedium decedere a nobis qui falisi [i.e. falsi], qui varii . . .[4] stulti simus; ad quod verum et stabile est ei confidamus. Adest omnibus; in eo sumus et vivimus; distracti a plurimis ad veritatem eamus i.e. spem. Spes est veritas. Speremus uniti et stabiles ut unum et statum ipsum consequamur.

How man's aims are frustrated, become altered, and have every outcome except the one planned. Pleasure is changed to pain, power to weakness, wisdom to foolishness. But, to find our pleasure in God, our strength upon God, and our . . . in the power of God can be the means of escaping from ourselves, for we are false, changeable, stupid . . .; let us put our trust in what is true and stable. He is with us all; in Him we live and have our being. Let us withdraw from multiplicity and seek only truth, that is hope. Hope is truth. Let us hope that [by being] unified and stable we may reach the one and the stable itself. Let us not lose hope through being

---

[1] This indented section was apparently written first, as a summary of a passage underlined in the text (see underlined passage No. 23); the main body of the note runs consecutively past it and is on another subject.

[2] These views of wisdom are stated respectively in Eccles. i. 18, 1 Cor. iii. 19, and Isa. xl. 17.
[3] Word illegible.
[4] Word illegible.

Non desperemus, distracti ad plurimum, sed speremus vero ad unum. Hoc ipsum bonum est cui sperandum est, quod spem non frustratur, quod sperantes facit, quod unum quod appetunt omnia, quia est in omnibus. Illi adherere est perfici. Hec adhesio est amor et desiderium quia bonum est desiderabile. Hoc desiderium comitatur lux sicuti flammam et emicat clarius ubi fervet flamma ardentius.

distracted to multiplicity; let us hope with a view to the one. This itself is the good for which we must hope, the good which does not frustrate but encourages hope, the one which all things seek because it is in all things. To cleave unto that [i.e. the good] is to be made whole. This devotion [to the good] is love and desire, because the good is desirable. The light [of God] accompanies this desire as light accompanies a flame, and it shines most brightly where the flame burns hottest.

16–18   Amor flamma boni.

foot (contin. of above)   Deus { ipse amor charitas / ipsa lux fides / ipsum bonum spes }   lux benigna, bonum lucidum

Love is the flame of the Good.

God is { true love   charity / true light   faith / true good   hope }   a kindly light, a shining good.

[xcix^v]   55 **Nullus incontinens potest sapiens esse**

55 **No intemperate person can be wise**

head (cf. ll. 7–17)   Suprema ratio et intellectus est anime virium.[1] Infime gustus et tactus; hec in corporea natura versantur. Ille ascendunt ad naturam divinam; hec deorsum, ille sursum. Non potest quisquam utrisque servire, simulque ascendere et descendere; aut ascendas aut descendas oportet. Aut in lucem aut in temebris [i.e. tenebras] vergat [sic]. Illa bona si gustaris ab hiis ridiculis illecebris malorum abhorrebis. Illa separata sunt quare oportet te hinc separes et purgatis moribus et intenta speculatione, illuc te conferas ut eternas rerum rationes videas, ut transgressus temporalia eterna metiaris, ut degustatis eternis temporalia contemnas. Vide quam animus degenerare potest et evadere corporea ut nihil sentia[t] nisi corporeum.

Reason and intellect are the highest powers of the soul. The lowest are taste and touch. These latter [senses] operate in corporeal nature; the former rise toward the divine nature. [Taste and touch] point downward, [reason and intellect] point upward. No man can serve both masters and go up and down at the same time; you have either to go up or go down, either toward the light or toward the dark. If you once experience those goods, [of reason and intellect] you will be repelled by the absurd blandishments of the evils [of taste and touch]. Those goods [of reason and intellect] have been set apart; hence it is necessary for you to set yourself apart; by purging your moral life and by extending your contemplative life, you may bring yourself thither [i.e. into the presence of the Good] in order to see the eternal principles of things, so that having passed over the temporal, you may pass through the eternal, and

[1] Ficino's text reads: Inter omnes animae vires quae in cognoscendo versantur, supremae sunt intellectus et ratio.

so that having tasted the eternal, you will scorn the temporal. See how the soul can degenerate, and become so physical that it is unaware of anything except the physical.

[cix^r]¹	**56 Patientia sine religione haberi non potest**	**56 It is impossible to be patient without religion**
22–	Verte necessitatem in voluntatem et esto liber, liber ne servus sis. Hac sola ratione semper eris liber: si volueris quaequumque fiunt ita fieri, et omnia in bonam partem verte. Hoc est tua bonitate malum in bonitatem coquere; bona voluntas bonusque amor cogit omnia. Hic sanus est; huc amor et caritas. In quo [?] Christi caritas, in eo sanitas. In quo caritas, in eo spiritus sanctus, qui omnia in bonum vertit.	Turn necessity into will and be free,⁴ free lest you be enslaved. By this one principle you may always be free; simply desire everything to happen as it does happen; and so make the best of everything. This means refining evil into goodness by means of your own goodness. Good will and good love compel everything. This is the healthy man; hither [come] love and charity. A man of Christian charity is a healthy man. A man who has charity is a man in whom the Holy Spirit [abides], which turns everything to good.
[cx^r]	**57 Non ex humanis divina: sed ex divinis humana sunt iudicanda**	**57 Divinity is not measured by humanity**
foot (cf. ll. 27–28)	Non altitudo divinorum ex hominis ingenio metienda. Divina ex humanis pendent.²	The loftiness of things divine cannot be measured by human standards; divinity does not derive from humanity, but humanity from divinity.
[cix^r]³	**58 De salute philosophorum ante Christi adventum**	**58 On the deliverance [from Hell] of the pre-Christian philosophers**
20–23	naturale morale judicia ceremoniae	natural } [law] moral } [law] } [classes of Mosaic law judgments } [rules] } 'according to the theo- rites } [rules] } logians']
27	unius dei cultores	worshippers of one God [i.e., among the pagans, specifically Pythagoras, Socrates, and Plato]
30	mereri superna non	Heaven could not be merited [without Christ's grace.]
31	in Lymbo unius dei cultores	Those [among the pagan philosophers] who believed in one God [are] in limbo.
32	vitare inferos sic	Thus they escape Hell.

¹ There are two folios cix; this is the first.
² Colet has inadvertently reversed Ficino's statement: Non ab humanis divina, sed a divinis humana dependent.

³ There are two folios numbered cix; this is the second, an error for cxi.
⁴ Epictetus, *Discourses* IV, x.

[cxxi^v]	59 Orphica comparatio Solis ad Deum	59 The Orphic comparison of the sun to God
foot (cf. ll. 35–39)	celestis glauci viridis cerulei flavum fuscum nigrum	heavenly grey[1] green blue dull yellow brown black
[cxxii^r] 1–18 (cf. fol. cxxi^v, ll. 35–39)	splendor limpiditas nititidas albedo croceitas rubedo clarior rubedo plenior celeste glaucum viridis ceruleum flavum fuscum nigrum	radiance clarity, brilliance whiteness bright yellow bright red dark red heavenly grey green blue dull yellow brown black
[cxxxv^v]	60 Divina lex fieri a coelo non potest	60 Divine law cannot be prescribed by the stars
23–24 34–36 38–39	Signa non cause stelle. Signa illa sunt quasi vultus animorum celestium. quod provident illi indicant facie celi	The stars are signs, not causes [of events]. Those signs are the faces, as it were, of celestial spirits. What they foresee they indicate on the face of heaven.
[cxxxvi^r] 2	celum animal	The sky is an animal [which obeys God's commands].
12 14 15–18 21 22 27 34	divinitatem Calcidius stella Balaham Messias Herodis porcum Si[billa] Cumea	divinity Calcidius[2] the star [which heralded the birth of Christ] Balaham[3] Messiah Herod's pig[4] the Cumaean Sibyl

[1] In this section Ficino is discussing the nature of light and listing all the colours that are included in 'pure' light. Colet abandoned his first list, possibly because he saw that he had not left himself room at the bottom of the page for the entire list. In the second list, he changes the colours from adjectives to nouns.

[2] Author of Latin translation of and commentary on first part of Plato's *Timaeus*; fl. A.D. 350[?]

[3] Presumably Balaam, the soothsayer of Num. 22–31.

[4] Reference to an aphorism, attributed to Augustus, that it was better to be Herod's pig than Herod's son (because of the wholesale executions of members of Herod's family which grew out of the quarrels between Herod's wife Mariamne, and Herod's sister and son).

MARGINALIA

[cxxxvi^v]

6–7	defectus solis passionis Christi	The eclipse of the sun at the passion of Christ.
13–14	exorto lux, morienti tenebre	With his birth came light, with his death, darkness.
19–21	disposito bene celo et terra, Deus hominem salutavit	By his ordering of the heavens and the earth God has spoken to man [on various occasions].

[cxlviii^r] **61 Platonici deo et animae mundi nihil praeter contemplationem sacrificant**

61 The Platonists worship God and the World Soul by contemplation only

25-foot (cf. ll. 25–44)

Deus ⎫ supra corpora sunt
Mundi anima ⎭ omnino
Anima mundi complexum corpus sustinet. Que intus anima sunt composita ex corporibus et animis, lucibus, vitis, viribus, ex mundi anima perfluentibus. Aliqua composita sunt media inter animam serenam et crassum corpus huc atque illuc volantia qui spiritus sunt et demones vocantur. Sunt internuncii et mundi magnis menbris [sic] ex animi sententia ministrant. In quibus multum est spiritus certe illi facile inserviunt bone anime ad bonumque ubique contendunt. Contra, in quibus vicit corporea labefactati viribus et judiciis mala machinantur, malas opiniones et falsas de se habent, sibi honores arrogant, se deos putant colique oportere. Atque in illorum pabulo quo vescuntur incontenentes [sic] sunt et intemperati et ebrei [sic], invidiosi, pigri, lascivi, libidinem quaerentes, et ob id cause [sic] cum talibus hominibus libenter vi[v]unt. Tales facile talibus agitantur.

God ⎫ these are entirely supra-corporeal
World Soul ⎭
The World Soul sustains the world body with which it is united. Things within the World Soul are composed of bodies and of souls, with light, life, and strength flowing through them from the World Soul. There are some composite beings, halfway between pure soul and the material body, which fly hither and thither; they are spirits and are called demons.[1] They are messengers and they minister to the vast spaces of the world as they wish. Demons in whom the spirit [element] is strong of course readily serve the good soul and everywhere work for the good. On the other hand, demons in whom the bodily element predominates, weakened in strength and judgement, plot evils: they hold evil and false opinions about themselves, arrogate honours to themselves, think they are gods and should be worshipped and, in the nourishment of these [opinions] on which they feed, they become incontinent and intemperate, drunken, envious, slothful, lascivious, and lustful, and on that account they live by preference with men of the same character. Such men are readily roused by such demons.

[cxlviii^v]

head (cf. ll. 4–6)

Est in demonibus ut in hominibus quod qui homines suo corpori dominantur boni sunt, qui vero corporis

It is the same with demons as with men; men who are masters over their bodies are good, but those who are slaves of their bodily

---

[1] This paragraph is a note on the next page of the text (i.e. cxlviii^v). For general background on theories of demons, see especially R. H. West, *The Invisible World* (Athens, Ga., 1939), pp. 65–109, and Julius Tambornini, *De antiquorum daemonismo* (Giessen, 1909). Colet is apparently interested in Ficino's theory of demons primarily as a means of explicating 1 Cor. x. 20 and Rom. viii. 1–15.

appeticionibus subjiciuntur, hii necessario mali malificique sunt. Sic quoque in demonibus qui animis et tenuibus corporibus constant ut in illa contentione[1] se habet victoria, ita boni malique evadent. Nam radii anime mundi infirmantes se tenuibus corporibus spiritus componunt mundi; hii a christianis angeli vocantur, a paganes [sic] demones. Partito mundo mundi partibus preficiuntur et rerum generibus et hominum artibus et quicquid quod magnum sit in mundo habet aliquid ei destinatum ex spiritibus quo sustiniatur [sic] et proficiat in bono. Ex superbia corporis nascitur nascitur[2] malum. Demones mali sunt.

appetites are necessarily evil and wicked. So also in the case of demons, for they are composed of both soul and airy body; so that they will turn out good or evil according to which [body or soul] conquers in that struggle. For rays of the World Soul dissipating themselves into airy bodies constitute the spirits of the world; they are called 'angels' by the Christians and 'demons' by the pagans. The world is divided, and they are put in charge of parts of the world, classes of things, and arts of men. Everything of importance in the world derives something of its nature from the spirits by which it is supported and advanced in goodness. All evil is born in pride of body; demons [which are dominated by the bodily element] are evil.

[cxlix^r] head (cf. fol. cxlviii^v, l. 31–fol. cxlix^r, l. 13)

In crassis corporibus vita infusa ab anima evadit crassa et petulans; sensus cecus, appetitus effrenatus, anima inserviens, auctorem malorum facit. Tales sunt mali demones, victi a crassis corporibus. Eorum machinatores malorum hominibus, tamen, bonorum effectores se predicantes, dicentes mala illata quando irascuntur, quum placantur, bona. Placari sacrificiis supplicationebusque [sic] oportere. Nam ex ex[2] cecitate arrogare sibi a stultis hominibus divinos honores. Dicunt se deos esse colendos quum sunt animalia longioris vite quam homines perspicatiorisque imperii, providentiores in bonis, artificiosiores in m[ala]; mala inferre ut homines ut homines [sic] moneantur ad supplicat[iones] quibus adducuntur ut desinant male age[re]. Nihil ergo faciunt b[ene] sed male agere des[inere]. Etiam nos in malas cogitationes impellunt et cupiditates honooris, divitiarum, libidinum, dicentes in diis tal[a] fieri. Boni laborant

In thick bodies, the life infused by the soul becomes gross and reckless. Blind sensuality, unbridled desire, a slavish soul; all this makes [a person] a doer of evil. So it is with evil demons who are dominated by gross bodies. The doers of these evils, however, represent themselves to men as doers of good, saying that they do evil deeds when they are angered but good ones when they are pleased. They claim that they ought to be worshipped with prayers and sacrifices, for from blindness they claim for themselves divine honours from stupid humanity. They say that they are gods to be worshipped, since they are animals of longer life than man, and of more far-sighted rule, and are more powerful in good things and cleverer in evil than men are; they say that they cause evil so that men may be warned to make prayers by which they [i.e. the demons] may be dissuaded from committing evil. Thus they do nothing good except to desist from evil. Moreover, they impel us to evil thoughts, and to desire for honour and riches and lust, saying that there are such things among the gods. The good [demons] strive to purify us even by dreams; but we do not know how to read their writing.

---

[1] Colet seems to have written *consternatione* and then corrected it.

[2] Another erroneous repetition; omitted in the translation.

MARGINALIA

u[t] nos emendent, [sic] admo[dum] somniis, sed nescimus litteratas legere.

[cxlix^v] 37–foot (cf. fol. cxlix^v, l. 39– fol. cl^r, l. 1)

Divinus vir cuius anima Deo dedita et divina est, pura, sancta, complectens sibi corpus imperviens [i.e. impervium] i.e. corpus castum et abstinens, a demonibus vexari non potest quidem. Nam demones materiales qui habent corpora fundunt ex se quam [i.e. quae] influunt in corpora sensibilia, maxime in ea corpora a quibus alliciuntur et trahuntur tamquam esca. Quapropter demones qui nidore carnium delectantur illuc attracti ipsas carnes faciunt multum demonicas, quod qui eas degl[utiunt] non nihil commovebuntur demonica ratione, appetitiones demonicas habebunt composito et i[m]mixto nutrimento. Amica et pellecta est potestas demonica. Nam simile simile trahit. Igitur dum vescuntur odoribus vaporibusque tenuibus. Nam ex anima et corporibus tenuibus constant, cuius defectio odoribus maxime calore et igne concitatas [sic] reficitur; ad quos quum accedit potestatem a se demonicam fundit, quos defluxus deglutientes cibos intus in nos admittimus. Quapropter recte a theologis admonemur ut abstineamus nec sine causa qui sanctissimi [?] esse [bottom cropped] . . . vesci voluerunt.

The saintly man, whose soul is dedicated to God and is divine, pure, and holy, clasping to itself a body impenetrable [by demons], (that is, a body that is chaste and pure), cannot even be harassed by demons. For the corporeal demons, who have [airy] bodies, pour from themselves sensory effluences which flow into bodies, especially into those bodies to which they are attracted and drawn, as it were by bait. For this reason demons which are pleased by the smell of flesh are attracted there and make that flesh itself demonic to a great extent, for a man who gulps down the flesh will be much affected by the demonic principle and will acquire demonic desires from the adulterated and tainted food he has eaten. The demonic power is seductive and alluring, for like attracts like. Therefore demons feed on odours and airy vapours, for demons consist partly of soul and partly of airy body, and their exhausted strength is restored by odours, especially those produced by heat and fire. When a demon comes upon the odours [of hot] food, it pours into the odours some of its own demonic power, and when we swallow the food, we take the infected odours into ourselves. Therefore, we are rightly warned by theologians to abstain, and not without cause . . . they wished to eat.

[cl^r] head (cf. ll. 1–4)

Theologi cavere debeant a calidis et fumantibus epulis, contenti frigidis et simplicibus; fugienda etiam illa loca in quibus corpori et sensibus sunt iucundiores fumi ut sunt deorum templa et popine. Offer deo puram mentem perturbationibus vacuam, quod si feceris, illustraberis divina sapientia et divino amore incenderis.

Theologians ought to beware of warm and steaming foods and be happy with cold and simple ones; moreover they ought to avoid places where the odours are especially pleasing to the body and the senses, such as restaurants and pagan temples. Present to God a pure and unperturbed mind[1]; if you do this, you will be enlightened by the divine wisdom, and you will be inflamed with divine love.

[1] cf. Rom. xii. 1.

[clxxiv^r]	**62 Heroicorum virorum laboriosa ... vita ...**	**62 The toilsome life of heroic men**
14	proclivi sumus ad libidinem	We are prone to lust.

[clxxxii^v]	**63 Excerpta ex Proculo in rem publicam Platonis**	**63 Excerpts from Proclus's commentary on Plato's Republic**[1]
16–18	bonitas pura potentia expedita cognitio certa	[God's] goodness is pure [God's] power is ready [God's] knowledge is certain
32–35	unde malum mali non Idea materia prima materia necessaria	Whence evil [comes].[2] There is no Platonic Idea of evil. prime matter Matter is necessary
40–44	dispersa ⎱ causa mali particularia ⎰	plural ⎱ and ⎰ as the cause of evil particular
	inordinatio particularium causa malorum	disordering of particulars as a cause of evil
[clxxxiii^r]		
9	nihil purum malum	Nothing is purely evil.
14	apparentia spirituum	the appearance of spirits
20	visa	things seen
37	de responsis	about replies [of oracles]
[clxxxiii^v]		
26–27	apparent dii pro modo suscipientis	The appearance of the gods varies according to the form of the thing which receives them [i.e. in which they appear].

[clxxxvii^r]	**64 Nullus mala poenitus et curas extirpare potest**	**64 No one can completely eradicate evil and care**
15–17	scandala ⎱ offensiones ⎰ impedimenta mala ⎱ adversa ⎰ contraria	scandals ⎱ offences ⎰ hindrances evils ⎱ adverse ⎰ contrary
26–27	contemplativos agitari	Contemplatives are harassed.
28–30	contemplantes ve[l] ⎱ s[ancti] ⎰ phi[losophici]	contemplatives ⎱ religious [are either] ⎰ or philosophical

[1] Ficino published (Venice, 1497, &c.) translations of some other works of Proclus (see P. O. Kristeller, *Supplementum Ficinianum*, I, pp. lxix–lxx), but his translation of Proclus's commentary on *Republic* I–VII seems never to have been published except in the form of these excerpts, which he sent on 3 August, 1492, to Martin Uranius.

[2] In this section Ficino begins by stating three principles of Plato (in the *Republic*) about the nature of God. The first is that God is entirely good; on this point Ficino raises the question, 'whence, then, comes evil?' and answers it at length in the section so marked by Colet. The second point is that God is immutable; on this point Ficino raises the question, 'Why then does He take so many forms?' (e.g. in apparitions). Ficino's answer to this question begins at Colet's note 'the appearance of spirits'. The third point is that God never lies; on this point Ficino raises the question whether false prophecies and oracles do not disprove God's veracity. He answers this question in the section marked by Colet, 'about replies'.

31	sancti deli[ramenta]	Religious contemplatives [escape] absurdities, [but they fall victim] to daemons. God rouses up the religious contemplative, and daemons harass him.
32	sancti in demones	
33–34	Deus sanctos excitat, demones vexant.	
40	religiosus demon	The religious contemplative [suffers from] the daemon.
41	philosophus atrabilis	The philosophical contemplative [suffers from] melancholy.
foot (cf. ll. 15–34)	In regione malorum sumus. Scandala, offensiones, impedimenta, mala necesse. Extirpare [sic] non possunt. Fato, natura, fortuna, ab hominibus ipsis, a bestiis, a nobis ipsis, vel negotiosis vel libidinosis. At ociosi temperatique etiam perturbantur; solicitudines vitates [i.e. vitantes] solicitantur. Nam spretis hiis vel religiosi vel philosophici a demonibus temptantur; trahit Deus, revocat demon; exercet Deus, vexat demon. Negotia et oblectamenta vi[r]tutes in atram bilem. Ita vitantes mala, in mala incidunt, et incidunt in scyllam cupientes vitare carybdym. Ita undeque [sic] obstrepit malum et vexat. Si mergaris, in malis es; si emargas [sic] spiritualia mala invenis. Victo carne et sanguine, restant demones; numquam vitabimus. Huc illuc semper adest.	We live in the region of evils. Scandals, offences, frustrations and evils are necessary and cannot be eliminated. [We are troubled by] fate, nature, fortune, men, animals, and ourselves, whether in business or in pleasure. Even those who are at rest and are moderate are disturbed; even though they avoid anxiety, they are anxious. For even when religious and philosophical men despise these [ordinary] troubles, they are tempted by demons. God calls them and the demon calls them back; God tests them, the demon harrasses them. The virtues of business and pleasure turn to melancholy. So in avoiding one evil they fall into another; they run into Scylla in trying to avoid Charybdis. Thus evil threatens and torments us on every side. If you sink down [into the flesh] you are [involved] in physical evil, but if you rise [above the flesh] you run into spiritual evil. Even if we master flesh and blood, the demons remain; we can never avoid them. Here, there, [and everywhere] evil is always with us.
clxxxvii^v head (cf.fol. clxxxvii^r, l. 34– fol. clxxxvii^v, l. 1)	Hec M[arsilio] Mala religiosi et philosophici providentes et constantes ac fortes reluctante [sic] et tandem vincentes, gloriosam victoriam reportabunt autore Deo et promittente Deo. Mala negotiosi et voluptiosi [sic] paulatim in pessima.	Marsilio says: When the religious and philosophical person, being provident, faithful, and brave, finally and with difficulty conquers evil, he will win a glorious victory with God's help and permission. The worldly and lustful person [merely turns] bad things gradually into worse things.

[clxxxvii^v] **65 Solem non esse adorandum tanquam rerum omnium auctorem**

65 The sun is not to be worshipped as if it were the creator of everything

15–17 Socrates attonitus ad solem ex oriente donec resurgeret.

Socrates remained rapt turned towards the sun from the dawn until the sun rose again.

21–23	demo[ne] ⎫ genio ⎬ hominis angelo ⎭	a man's ⎧ demon ⎨ genius ⎩ angel
26–28 foot (cf. ll. 25–28)	Deus Dei filius primus intel[lectus] secundus visibilis	God the first offspring of God, the angelic mind the second, the visible world
34–36 foot	Jacobus Apostolus Deus Dei filius intellectu contemplabilis sol visu spectabilis	the apostle James God the Son of God, knowable by the intellect the sun, visible to the sight

[clxxxviii^r]

3	veritas	truth [the sun]
4	imago	its image
5	umbra	its shadow
7–8	status ipse qui principium est luminum	[God is] stability which is the fount of light.

[clxxxviii^r] **66 Copula philosophiae cum legibus**   **66 The relation between philosophy and law**

27–34	Sapientia cum legibus
	    Saturnus
	    Juppiter
	    △ leges △
	Ex sapientia leges
		[the connexion between] wisdom and law
		Saturn
		Jupiter
		△ Laws △
		Laws come from wisdom.

[clxxxviii^v]

head (cf. fol. clxxxviii^r, l. 43–fol. clxxxviii^v, l. 11)	Sapientie studium capescite, sive te ipse [i.e. ipsum] inspicias, sive deum suspicias, sive homines circumspicias, necessaria sapientia. Hec animum felicem facit; hanc possedentem philosophum, genus hominum nobilissimum.	Pursue the desire for wisdom; whether you look in, to yourself, or look up, to God, or look around, to your fellow men, in any case wisdom is necessary. This [i.e. wisdom] makes the soul happy. Those who possess this [i.e. wisdom] are philosophers, the highest class of men.
11	philosophi	philosophers
13	Daniel	Daniel
17	firmamentum	the firmament

19–21	tenuis lux ⎧ rara ⎧ spissa
	          ⎨ sparsa ⎨ unita
	          ⎩ candida ⎩ turbida
		clear light thin dense
		              scattered unified
		              clear hazy

[clxxxix^r] **67 Similitudo Mercurii cum Saturno**   **67 A comparison between Mercury and Saturn**[1]

head (cf. ll. 19–27)	Querentes sapientiam eandem religiosi; mercuriales saturnei. Mercurium [sic] ad sapientiam provocat,	Religious persons seek the same wisdom [which philosophers seek]; they are both mercurial and saturnine.

[1] cf. marginalia 1.

MARGINALIA

	Saturnus ad religionem; edibus aspectuque Mercurius cum Saturno.	Mercury arouses us to wisdom, Saturn to religion; Mercury and Saturn have the same houses and the same aspect.
17	Saturnus Deus	Saturn: God
18	Mercurius sapientia	Mercury: wisdom
25	a Mercurio	[one goes] from Mercury to Saturn
26	in Saturnum	
foot (cf. ll. 19–27)	Deus Saturnus religio Mercurius sapientia	religio legislatio sapientia

God	Saturn	religion	religion
			law
Mercury	wisdom	wisdom

[clxxxix^r] **68 Apologia in librum suum de Sole & lumine**

68 In defence of his book *On the Sun and Light*

foot (cf. ll. 38–44)

Suborte nebule offendunt solem.

noctuas
vespertilione[m] ⎫ offendit sol

Hii [i.e. His] caligantibus cecatientibus consulendum est, si sibi consuli volunt, ut non incusent lucem quam sibi molestam tam ceteris salutarem; se [i.e. sed?] indagni [i.e. indigni] lumine delitescant.

The rising mist offends the sun.

The sun offends the owl and the bat.

These blind and groping creatures should be considerate, if they wish to be considered themselves, and instead of finding fault with light, which is as annoying to them as it is beneficial to others, they ought to hide themselves away, being unworthy of the light.

[clxxxix^v] **69 Sepe in coelestibus gemini sunt**

69 There are several pairs of twins among the heavenly bodies

Dioscori [sic]

Saturnus ⎫
Mercurius ⎦

Mars

14–22

Iupiter ⎫
Venus ⎦

Phebus ⎫
Phebe ⎦

The Dioscuri [are not the only pair of twins in the heavens]

Saturn ⎫ [related but not twins; Mercury
Mercury ⎦ is a younger brother, as it were, to Saturn.]

Mars [has no brother or sister.]

Jupiter ⎫
Venus ⎦

Apollo ⎫
Diana ⎦

31–32 de divinitate mysterium

The mystery about divinity [may be understood through the analogy of light].

foot (cf. ll. 29–42)

Parum lucentia proprius [i.e. propius] quaeruntur et solicitius [sic] cum anxietate quadam, disquisitione scrupelosa [sic]. Que vero clarissima luceque abundant, suapte natura patent; [?] modo oculus se

Things which have very little [visible] light are investigated [by getting] closer [to them], by taking greater care and a certain amount of pains, by scrupulous inquiry. The brightest things, however, and those which have an abundance of light are open for us to see of

parat [i.e. paret] ut lucem recipiat; hoc est [?] si se purgatos convertant. Sic qui parum habent lucis invisibilis i.e. veritatis, disquitisione [sic] argumentorumque discusione [sic] ac propius accedendo intusque inspiciendo acrius cernunt. Contra, plenitudo invisi[bi]lis lucis deus. Contrarium propius accedendo non paramur ut perscrutemur.

their own nature; only let the eye prepare itself to receive the light; that is, let them [the eyes] purify themselves and turn themselves [towards the light]. Similarly, those who have too little of the invisible light, i.e. truth, behold it by inquiry and by the assessment of arguments and by approaching more closely and by looking within. But the plenitude of invisible light is God. That opposite [kind of light] we are not fitted to examine merely by approaching closer.

[cxc^r] **70 In librum de sole**

4   sors
5   sol
7   non lunam sed solem

70 On my book *On the Sun*

fate
the sun
not the moon, but the sun

[cxcv^r] **71 De Jove amicabili et Apolline**

26   Jovem[1]
27   Jovis est [lux]
29   Jovis est [calor]
30   Jovis fons [harmoniae]

71 On Jove the Friendly and Apollo

Jove
Jove is light
Jove is heat
Jove is the source of harmony

[cxcvi^r] **72 Cur providentia permittat adversa**

31   demon
33   callidus serpens

72 Why Providence permits adversity

the demon
the subtle serpent

[flyleaf^v] **73**

foot   Divi Pauli epistolam quae est prima ad Corinthios Jo[annes] Colet die lune proxime sequente quam melius poterit deo aspirante conabitur expl[an]are, loco et hora solita.

73

Next Monday, at the usual time and place, John Colet will try to expound, as best he can with God's help, St. Paul's first epistle to the Corinthians.

[flyleaf^v] **74**

head   Deus ———→ unio major   Deus maius nobis . . .[2]

         nos ———→ unio media   secundo nos nobis

         proximus →unitio minor   mos [i.e. nos] proximo[3]

99 li li 98 pro Epistola ad Corynthios

---

[1] These notes appear to be in the same seventeenth-century hand as that of **75** below.
[2] Word illegible.   [3] cf. Marginalia **25**.

MARGINALIA

74 No title

God ———→ greater union¹   God is our greatest [obligation]

we ———→ mean union   We are our second [obligation]

neighbour →lesser union   [Third is] our [obligation] to neighbours.

[Use folios] 99 and 98 of the book for [the Commentary on] the Epistle to the Corinthians.²

[flyleaf ᵛ] **75 Dr. Kinge³**

middle   Juno, Minerva, Venus, nemorosae in vallibus Idae
discrimen formae cum subiecit suae
Inter formosas si tu dea quarta fuisses vicisses reliquas, o dea sola, deas.
Quam Juno jeiuna foret, quam pallida Pallas,
quam dea vana Venus, quam dea sola fores.
Pallas, Juno, Venus, Sophia, diademate, forma,
corda, caput, vultus, imbuit, ornat, alit.

75 Dr. Kinge⁵

When Juno, Minerva, and Venus met in the valleys of wooded Ida for their beauty contest,
If you [Sophia] had been the fourth goddess among those beautiful creatures, you would have defeated the others, O goddess without peer.
How jejune Juno would have seemed, how pale Pallas, how vain Venus; how godlike you only.
Yes, Pallas, Juno, and Venus; but Sophia would have taken the prize, for she instructs the mind, sustains the heart, and makes the face more lovely.

[flyleaf ᵛ] **76 Lib[ri] Log[ici]⁴**

Sotus de Praedicabil [ibus]

76 Logic Books

Sotus⁶ on the 'predicables'⁷

---

¹ Mr. J. B. Trapp has pointed out to me the parallel with a passage in Colet's *Catechism*, reprinted Lupton, *Life* (1887), App. B. 'Charyte' is here divided into 'the love of God', 'The love of thyne owne selfe' and 'the love of thy neyghbour'. The lines in the diagram show that 'we' must love not only God and our neighbours but ourselves. The right hand column is apparently a confused restatement of the same idea.

² Colet's notes to himself in preparing his lectures on First Corinthians. See Introduction, p. 31.

³ This section is not in Colet's hand, but in a hand of the early seventeenth century, apparently the same as that in 71 above.

⁴ This section is not in Colet's hand; it presumably dates from the early seventeenth century. The character of the list, which contains no Ramist works, suggests a rather conservative logician.

⁵ The 'Dr. Kinge' referred to may be any one of the following:
(a) Dr. John King, of Christ Church, Oxford, D.D., 1601, d. 1621.
(b) Dr. John King, Vice-Chancellor of Oxford, D.D. 1625, d. 1639.
(c) Dr. Robert King, Bishop of Oxford, D.D. 1519, d. 1557.

⁶ Dominicus Sotus [Domingo (de) Soto] O.P. (1494–1560).

⁷ The *praedicabilia* or *universalia* are the *quinque voces*, *the five common words* (species, genus, accident, property and difference). That is, the five predicates of propositions, which make those propositions scientifically true. The actual work here referred to is Soto's *In librum praedicabilium Porphyrii* . . . printed with his *In Dialecticam Aristotelis* . . . Salamanca, 1544, &c.

Hispanus de eisdem
Aemilius Acerbus de variis quaestionibus logic[is] et Phy[sicis]
Arsenius de 5 Praedicabil[ibus]
Regius
Scotus

Peter the Spaniard on the same subject[1]
Aemilius Acerbus on various questions in logic and physics[2]
Arsenius on the 5 'predicables'[3]
[Johann] Regius[4]
[Duns] Scotus[5]

[1] Petrus Hispanus [Pope John XXI] (c. 1215–77). An edition of his *Summulae Logicales*.

[2] Aemilius Acerbus [Emilio Acerbi] of Bergamo, Benedictine of Vallombrosa (c. 1560–1625). Either or both of his *Logicarum quaestionum libri IV*, Venice, 1596 and *Quaestionum peripateticarum libri V*, Venice, 1602 are probably meant here.

[3] Arsenius Crudelius [Arsenio Crudeli] of Poppi, Benedictine of Vallombrosa (c. 1556–1615). The work is his *In Porphyrii V universalia ... dilucidationes*, Florence, 1599.

[4] Johann Regius of Danzig (1567–1605) ... *Commentariorum ac disputationum logicarum libri V* ... Mülhausen, 1603.

[5] Perhaps *Quaestiones Johannis Duns Scoti super Universalibus Porphyrii et super libris Praedicamentorum et Perihermeneias Aristotelis* ... Venice, 1483, &c.

APPENDIXES

A. The identification of Colet's hand.

B. Passages marked for reading in Ficino's table of contents.

C. Passages underlined in Ficino's text.

D. Colet and Ficino's 'De raptu Pauli'.

HAND OF JOHN COLET
(Cambridge University Library MS Gg. IV. 26.)

APPENDIX A: THE IDENTIFICATION OF COLET'S HAND

THE extant manuscripts of most of Colet's major works are in one of two hands.[1] One is the clear book hand of Colet's one-eyed amanuensis, Peter Meghen, exemplified in Emmanuel College, Cambridge MS. III.3.12. The other is the English secretary hand of Colet himself, exemplified in Cambridge University Library MS Gg. IV. 26 (Plate I). The hand of the All Souls marginalia edited herein (Plate II) is the same as that in the Cambridge University Library MS. and is therefore the hand of Colet himself.

This relatively simple case for the identity of the hand in the All Souls volume is unfortunately complicated by the fact that no one has actually proved that the hand in the Cambridge University Library MS. is Colet's. The catalogue says the hand is Colet's, and Colet's sole editor and greatest biographer, J. H. Lupton, says the hand is Colet's, but neither Lupton nor anyone else has published photographs to prove it. The purpose of this appendix is to publish the visual evidence upon which Lupton's assertion rests.

The evidence consists of a known holograph manuscript of Colet's. Of the several such manuscripts in existence, Lupton mentions particularly one at Lambeth Palace called the 'Admission Book of Doctors' Commons'.[2] This is presumably the volume now listed in the Lambeth Palace Library as 'Register of the entries of Doctors of Law in the College of Advocates in Doctors Commons'. On fol. 8r of that manuscript appears the following entry: 'Et ego quoque Jo. Colet polliceor me facturum quod alii faciunt videlicet soluturum singulis quibusque annis venerando Collegio doctorum vi^s viii^d'. The hand in this entry (Plate III) is the same as that in the Cambridge University MS. and in the All Souls volume. Since the Lambeth hand is Colet's, the Cambridge and All Souls hands must be Colet's also. Among the distinctive features of the hand in all three examples are these:

1. The tendency to break off between i and any following letter except n.
2. The flat, often closed a.
3. The open e.

---

[1] The manuscripts are described by J. H. Lupton in his *Life of Colet* (London, 1887), pp. 62–63. His designation of the Emmanuel College MS. as III.3.16 is incorrect; it is III.3.12. [2] *Life*, p. 63.

4. The straggling *que* suspension.
5. The irregularity of the slant.
6. The light touch of the hand as a whole.

There are, however, two further complications which must be taken into account. First, not all the manuscript notes in the All Souls volume are written in the same hand; there are, in fact, three different hands involved, which I have called hands A, B, and C.

Hand A: The light English secretary hand of Colet which we have been discussing (Plate II). In this hand are written:
1. All three of the letters on the flyleaves of the volume.
2. Notes written across the title page of the volume (listed as item 1 of the marginalia in my text).
3. All of the marginalia in the volume from the last part of item 5 through item 72, except item 71.
4. Notes written on the back flyleaves (items 73 and 74 in my text).

In different conditions of time and space Colet's hand varies a good deal throughout the book. But examples of all but two of the seemingly different hands can be shown to run into and become each other within individual passages.

Hand B: A fifteenth-century English humanistic hand (Plate IV). In this hand are written only:

Marginalia items 2–4, and the first part of 5.

The marginalia in the volume actually begin in this hand. (The notes on the title page are not really marginalia.) But almost immediately, on the fourth page of the text, in the middle of one of Ficino's letters, the marginalia shift from Hand B into the faster and less formal Hand A of Colet. It is possible, I think, that Hand B may also be Colet's, but it is certainly very different from hand A.

Hand C: An early seventeenth-century English secretary hand. In this hand are written only: item 71, item 75, and possibly item 76. Items 75 and 76 are scribbled on a back flyleaf under a line which separates them from the item in Colet's own hand at the top of the leaf, but item 76 may be in a fourth hand (D?), of about the same period as C.

Whose hand this is I do not know; the 'Dr. Kinge' referred to in the heading of item 75 is probably one of the Oxford men cited in the notes, and the poem therefore probably dates from about 1620.

PRIMVS XXVIII

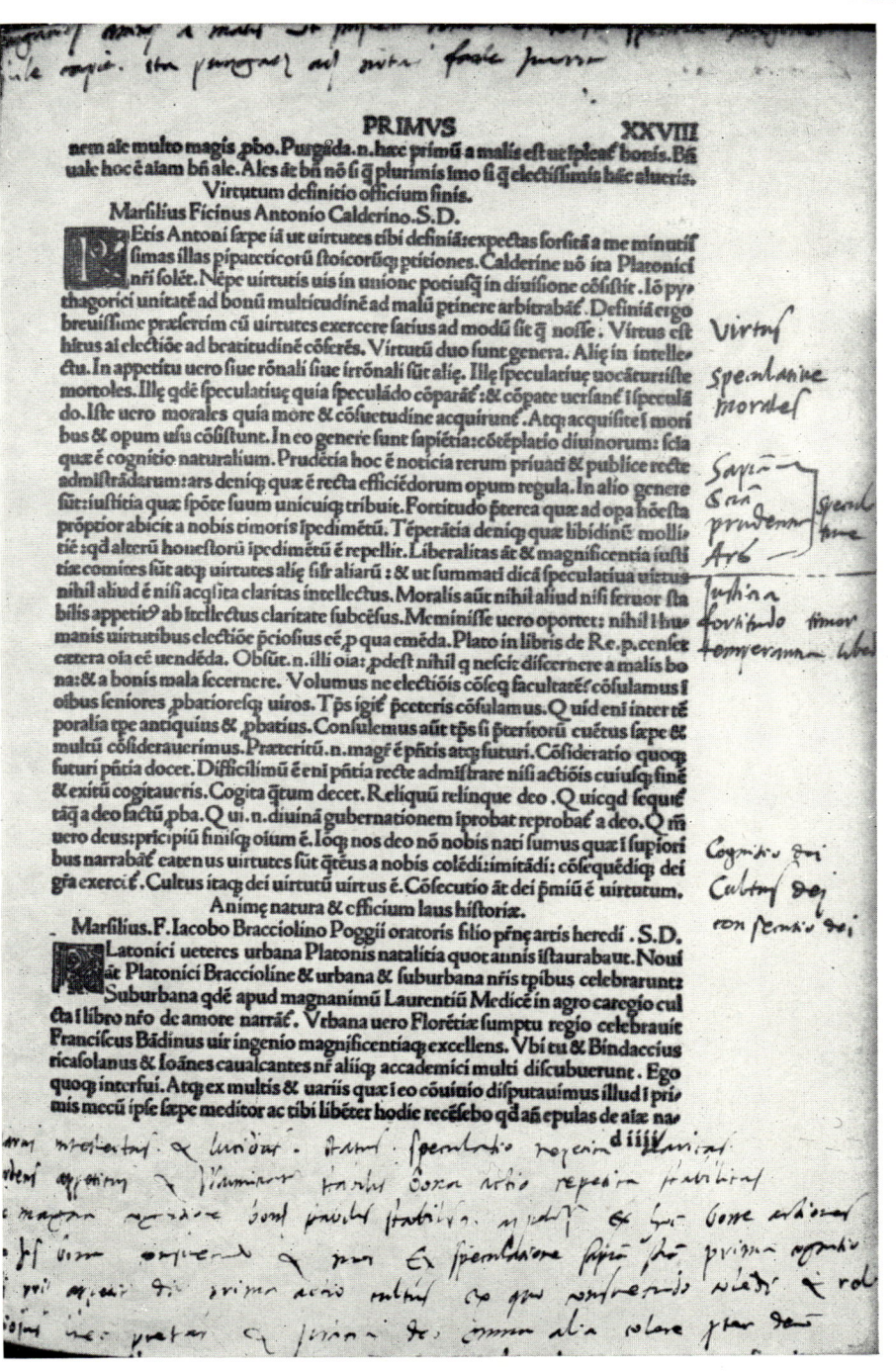

nem alę multo magis pbo. Purgāda .n. hęc primū a malis est ut spleat bonis. Bn̄ uale hoc ē aiam bn̄ ale. Ales āt bn̄ nō si q̄ plurimis imo si q̄ electissimis hęc aluerit.

Virtutum definitio officium finis.

Marsilius Ficinus Antonio Calderino. S.D.

Exis Antoni sępe iā ut uirtutes tibi definiā: expectas forsitā a me minutissimas illas pipateticorū stoicorūq̄ pticiones. Calderine nō ita Platonici n̄ri solet. Nępe uirtutis uis in unione potiusq̄ in diuisione cōsistit. Iō pythagorici unitatē ad bonū multitudinē ad malū ptinere arbitrabāt. Definiā ergo breuissime pręsertim cū uirtutes exercere satius ad modū sit q̄ nosse. Virtus est hītus ai electiōe ad bratitudinē cōserēs. Virtuti duo sunt genera. Alię in intellectu. In appetitu uero rōnali siue irrōnali sūt alię. Illę speculatiuę uocaturistę mortoles. Illę q̄dē speculatiuę quia speculādo cōparāt: & cōpate uersant ī speculado. Iste uero morales quia more & cōsuetudine acquirunt. Atq̄ acquisitę ī moribus & opum usu cōsistunt. In eo genere sunt sapiētia: cōtēplatio diuinorum: scia quę ē cognitio naturalium. Prudētia hoc ē noticia rerum priuati & publice recte admīstradarum: ars deniq̄: quę ē recta efficiēdorum opum regula. In alio genere sūt: iustitia quę spōte suum unicuiq̄ tribuit. Fortitudo ptera quę ad opa hōesta propior abicit a nobis timoris īpedimētū. Tēperātia deniq̄ quę libidinis mollitię: q̄d alterū honestorū īpedimētū ē repellit. Liberalitas āt & magnificentia iustitię comites sūt atq̄ uirtutes alię sūt aliarū: & ut summati dicā speculatiua uirtus nihil abiud ē nisi acq̄sita claritas intellectus. Moralis aūt nihil aliud nisi feruor stabilis appetit9 ab ītellectus claritate subcēsus. Meminisse uero oportet: nihil humanis uirtutibus electiōe pciosius ē: p qua emēda. Plato in libris de Re.p. censet cętera oia ē uendēda. Obsūt .n. illi oia: pdest nihil q̄ nesciī discernere a malis bona: & a bonis mala secernere. Volumus ne electiōis cōseq̄ facultatē: cōsulamus ī oibus senioribus pbatioresq̄ uiros. Tp̄s igī p̄ceteris cōsulamus. Quid eni inter tēporalia tpe antiquius & p̄batius. Consulamus aūt tp̄s si p̄teriorū cuetus sępe & multū cōsiderauerimus. Pręteritū .n. magī ē p̄ntis atq̄ futuri. Cōsideratio quoq̄ futuri p̄ntia docet. Difficilimū ē eni p̄ntia recte admīstrare nisi actiōis cuiusq̄ finē & exitū cogitaueris. Cogita q̄tum decet. Reliquū relinque deo. Quicq̄d sequit tāq̄ a deo factū pba. Q ui .n. diuinā gubernationem īprobat reprobat a deo. Q m̄ uero deus: principiū finisq̄ oium ē. Ioq̄ nos deo nō nobis nati sumus quę ī supiori bus narrabāt catenus uirtutes sūt q̄teus a nobis colēdi: imitādi: cōsequēdiq̄ dei gr̄a exercē. Cultus itaq̄ dei uirtutū uirtus ē. Cōsecutio āt dei p̄miū ē uirtutum.

Animę natura & efficium laus historię.

Marsilius. F. Iacobo Bracciolino Poggii oratoris filio p̄rnę artis heredi. S.D.

Latonici ueteres urbana Platonis natalitia quot annis istaurabaūt. Noui p̄āt Platonici Braccioline & urbana & suburbana n̄ris tpibus celebrarunt: Suburbana q̄dē apud magnanimū Laurentiū Medice in agro caregio culcta ī libro n̄o de amore narrāt. Vrbana uero Florētię sumptu regio celebrauit Franciscus Bādinus uir ingenio magnificentiaq̄ excellens. Vbi tu & Bindaccius ricasolanus & Ioānes caualcantes n̄r aliiq̄ accademici multi discubuerunt. Ego quoq̄ interfui. Atq̄ ex multis & uariis quę ī eo couinio disputauimus illud ī primis mecū ipse sępe meditor ac tibi libēter hodie recēsebo q̄d ası epulas de alę natu

HAND OF JOHN COLET
(All Souls College, Oxford L. infra l. 5. fol. xxviii^r.)

PLATE III

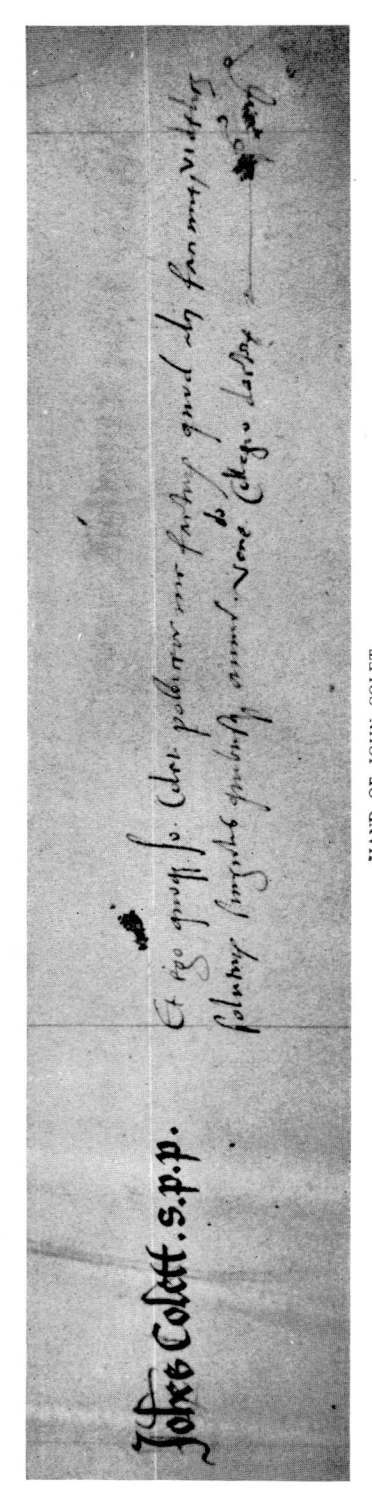

HAND OF JOHN COLET
Lambeth Palace Library, 'Register of . . . Doctors Commons', fol. 8r.

Quae sit ad foelicitatem uia.

Marsilius Ficinus Magno Cosmo. S.D.

Eniá ad te cū primum potero q̄ libētissime. Quid. n. gratius q̄ in chare gio hoc ē gratiaru̅ agro una cū cosmo gratiaru̅ patre uersari. Interi accipe paucis q̄ apud Platonicos uia sit ad foelicitate̅ accōmodatissima. Et quis existime̅ non opportere ei uiā mo̅strari qui ppē ia pueni̅t ad calce; desiderio tame̅ tuo & iusbe̅ntia & in p̄sentia obsequendū cē censui: Omnes ho̅ies bene agere; hoc est bene uiuere uolūt. Bene aute̅ uiue̅t si bona illis adsint q̄ plurima. Bona uero hæc dicu̅t. Diuitiæ: sanitas: forma: fortitudo: tēperantia: & p̄cæteris oibus sapientia: quæ q̄de̅ dentia: p̄terea iustitia: fortitudo: cōplectie. Foelicitas quippe in p̄sp̄era optati finis cōsecutione uim o̅m foelicitatis cōplectie. Foelicitas quippe in p̄sp̄era optati finis cōsecutione consistit. Id aute̅ in singulis facultatibus sapie̅tia præbet. Siquide̅ p̄titi tibicines q̄c q̄d tibiarum usus reqrit optime co̅secunt. Et eruditi grānatici q̄d ad litteras tum legendas tū scribe̅ndas p̄tinet. Sapīetes quoq̄; gubernatoresd p̄lperum nauigatio nis portu̅ p̄cæteris assecu̅nt. Necnō belli dux sapiens q̄d ad militia̅ attinet tutius expedit. Et lapicīs medicus melius adoptata̅ p̄ducit corporis ualitudine̅. Quaob,

HAND B

(All Souls College, Oxford L. infra l. 5. fol. 1r.)

PLATE V

Statuta paulinæ scholæ

Hunc Libellum ego Joannes Colet tradidi in manibus
Magistri Lilij xvij die Junij a° x° m°ccccc°
xvij ut eum in scola servet et observet

Of halydayes and halfe halydayes all Nombred
togyder in whiche ys no techinge there be yn the
hole yere lxxvii and viij

Joannes Colet fundator scole manu sua propria

Sm lxxxv li

MUSEUM BRITANNICUM

To Pyttis to the reparations sute and casuelte
and all other chargis extra ordynary

lxxxviij li xij s̄ in toto

Joannes Colet fundator Noue scole
manu mea propria

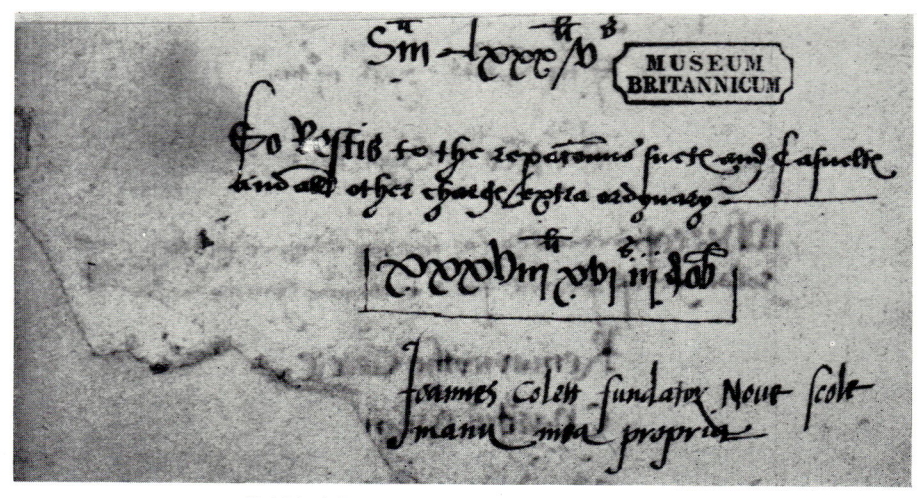

British Museum, Additional MS. 6274.

APPENDIX A

The second and final complication in identifying Colet's hand concerns Colet's *Ordinances* for St. Paul's School. In his *History of St. Paul's School*,[1] Michael McDonnell refers to two extant copies of these Ordinances. The original draft of the Ordinances, which was presumably in Colet's own hand, seems to have disappeared, but two sixteenth-century copies still survive, one in the Library of Mercers' Hall, London,[2] and the other in the British Museum.[3] Both copies are in an English secretary hand of the sixteenth century, different from the hand usually attributed to Colet. Yet in three different places on the document appear subscriptions presumably by Colet. (I illustrate from the British Museum copy only):

1. Hunc libellum ego Joannes Colet tradidi in manubus Magistri Lilii xviii° die Junii anno Christi MCCCCCXVIII ut eum in scola servet et observet [title page].
2. Joannes Colet fundator scole manu sua propria [fol. iv].
3. Joannes Colett fundator Nove scole manu mea propria [p. 20].

Although the spelling of the name Colet shifts, and the pronoun *sua* shifts to *mea*, all three subscriptions are in the same hand. The fact that this hand describes itself as Colet's 'own hand' and yet is so different in appearance (see Plate V) from Colet's entry in the Lambeth Register might be explained by the fact that the two copies of the Ordinances were made not by Colet himself, but by a scribe working from Colet's original and copying everything he saw, including Colet's subscriptions. Unfortunately, the hand of the subscriptions is evidently a different hand from that of the text of the Ordinances, suggesting that the subscriptions are actually Colet's additions, as they seem to be. If they are in Colet's hand, it is a much later, heavier, and less cursive hand than that in the Lambeth Register. In any case the British Museum and Mercers' Hall copies of Colet's Ordinances for St. Paul's School certainly do not invalidate Lupton's identification of the hand in the Lambeth Register as also Colet's. If Lupton was right in regarding the hands at Lambeth and in the Cambridge University Library manuscript as Colet's, then we, too, are right in regarding Hand A in the All Souls copy of Ficino's *Epistolae* as Colet's.

---

[1] (London, 1959), pp. 33-34.
[2] In that library the manuscript is designated only by its title.
[3] Additional MS. 6274.

APPENDIX B: PASSAGES MARKED FOR READING IN FICINO'S TABLE OF CONTENTS[1]

1. Causa peccandi spes remedium
2. Quos Deus coniunxit moribus coniunget foelicitate
3. Neque amor sine religione neque religio sine amore laudatur
4. Stultitia et miseria hominum
5. Liberalitas laus: helemosine laus
6. Verus amicus non eget absentia ut magis desideretur
7. Jurisconsulti bonitas et dignitas
8. Dignitas sacerdotis   NB
9. Non cuilibet dandi sunt sacri ordines   NB
10. Quid est bene vivere   NB
11. Vota non sunt spernenda   NB
12. Nobilitas utilitas et usus medicine
13. Tempus parce expendendum
14. Homo sine religione bestiis est infoelicior   NB
15. De lege et justitia
16. Consolatio in amici obitu

[1] Marked with hands and also, where indicated, with NB; marks appear on first page only of table of contents (sig. AAii^r), but one other 'Nota' in the same hand appears in the margin opposite a letter on the cause of sin, *Epistolae*, fol. xiii^r. This later "Nota" and the fact that several of the passages marked above are annotated by Colet are the only evidence that the marks on this part of the table are Colet's. In another part of the table (Books IV through X), there is another set of marginal marks (lower case v and x) which someone has used to point out letters on the subjects of love and friendship. There is no evidence that these later marks are Colet's.

APPENDIX C: PASSAGES UNDERLINED IN FICINO'S TEXT

No.	folio	Title of letter
1.	AAvi^v	Prohemium
2.	i^r	Prologus
3.	i^r	De foelicitatis desiderio
4.	i^{r-v}	Quae sit ad foelicitatem via
5.	i^v	Imitatio utilior est quam lectio
6.	i^v–ii^r	Dialogus inter Deum et animam theologicus
7.	iii^r	Lex et justitia
8.	iii^v	De divino furore
9.	v^r	Excusatio prolixitatis
10.	v^v	Solitariae vitae utilitas
11.	xiii^r	Causa peccandi. Spes. Remedium
12.	xiii^v	Praestantior est legum conditor quam sophista
13.	xvi^r	De humanitate
14.	xxii^v	Homo sine religione bestiis est infoelicior
15.	xxviii^v	Animae natura et officium. Laus historiae
16.	xxix^v	Cognitio et reverentia sui ipsius omnium optima
17.	xxxi^r–xxxii^v	Quid est foelicitas
18.	liv^v	De raptu Pauli ad tertium coelum
19.	lxi^v	Qualis est amor talis amicitia
20.	lxxiii^r	Omnia mundi bona illi mala sunt qui immundus vivit in mundo
21.	lxxvii^r	Sicut pulchritudo natura gignit amorem . . .
22.	xcviii^v	Nullum in malis refugium est nisi ad summum bonum
23.	cxxxvi^r	Divina lex fieri a coelo non potest: sed forte significari

No.	folio	Title of letter
24.	clxxii^v	Pallas: Juno: Venus: Vita contemplativa: activa: voluptuosa
25.	clxxiv^r	Apologus de voluptate
26.	clxxxvii^{r-v}	Nullus mala poenitus et curas extirpare potest
27.	clxxxvii^v	Solem non esse adorandum tanquam rerum omnium auctorem
28.	clxxxviii^v	Copula philosophiae cum legibus
29.	clxxxix^r	Apologia in librum suum de sole et lumine
30.	clxxxix^v	Saepe in coelestibus gemini sunt
31.	clxxxxv^v	Pro libro de religione
32.	clxxxxv^v	Oratio . . . ad Carolum Magnum
33.	clxxxxvii^r	Pia Platonis sententia
34.	clxxxxvii^v	Pro libro de sole
35.	clxxxxvii^v	Pro libro de sole

[AAvi^v] **1 Prohemium**

Quotiens aepistolae [sic] meae amicis meis (me jubente) salutem dicitis: totiens amicissimo vestro Hieronymo Rossio[1] immortales salutes dicite.

[i^r] **2 Prologus**

Magnus Cosmus[2] magnanime Juliane[3] avus tuus patronus saepe Platonicum illud habebat in ore: nihil ad aegregias res agendas accommodatius esse quam prudentium doctorumque virorum benivolentiam:... Aureum hoc Platonis nostri praeceptum . . . Longe ditior hominum; prudentie justitieque ditissimus.

3 De foelicitatis desiderio [i^r]

Contuli heri me in agrum Charegium:[4]

4 Quae sit ad foelicitatem via [i^r]

Quid enim gratius quam in Charegio hoc est gratiarum agro una cum Cosmo gratiarum patre versari . . .

---

[1] Girolamo Rossi, of Pistoia, a friend of Ficino to whom he dedicated Book XII and the whole of the *Epistolae*; see references to Rossi in Ficino's *Opera*, pp. 607, 804, 825, 936, 945, 954, and 958 (references cited from Kristeller, *Supplementum*, II, p. 362).

[2] Cosimo de'Medici (1389–1464), Ficino's patron.
[3] Giuliano de'Medici (1453–78), grandson of Cosimo and son of Piero.
[4] Careggi, the villa above Florence where Ficino lived and the Platonic Academy met.

APPENDIX C

[iv] Omnes homines bene agere, hoc est bene vivere volunt ...
Praeterea ii duntaxat quibus bona plurima assunt beati dicuntur ... Neque prosunt unquam nisi illis utantur ... In quibus illis duntaxat: qui artis periti sunt tam materia quam instrumentis recte utuntur ... Minus autem male agens minus est miser. Agit certe minus, si pauper sit quam si dives, si debilis quam si robustus ... Itaque nulla eorum quae in superioribus bona nuncupabantur; per se bona sunt ... rectum vero rerum usum scientia praebeat: caeteris omnibus praetermissis omni cum [philosophiae] plenitudine tum pietatis studio niti quisque debet, ut quam sapientissimus fiat. sic enim animus noster Deo qui sapientia ipsa est evadit similimus.

[iv] **5 Imitatio utilior est quam lectio**

... is enim superioribus diebus bibliothecam meam graeco ornavit Platone. Domum [i.e. Donum] Amerige[1] tuum laudo ... Accommodatior namque ad virtutem via est imitatio quam lectio.

[iv] **6 Dialogus inter Deum et animam theologicus**

... moralia usu comparanda esse, naturalia ratione quaerenda ...

[iir] Legi etiam apud Platonem nostrum[2] divina ob vitae puritatem revelari potiusquam doctrina verbisque doceri. Haec igitur atque similia cum sedulo cogitarem, coepi quandoque lugere animo. ...
DEUS: Misera quid tantum luges anima mea? Pone iam finem o filia lachrymis. En assum tibi pater tuus. Assum medicina salusque tua.
ANIMA: O utinam meus mihi pater aspiret. Ha! si putarem posse tantum mihi munus obtingere, ha! quantum laetitia insanirem. ...
DEUS: Pone finem o filia lachrymis ne te afflictes o filia. ... Assum equidem tibi simul et insum. Adsum equidem tibi quia insum.
[Part of fol. iiv is bracketed in margin.]

7 Lex et Justitia [iiir]

Maumethes[3] rex Arabum ab angelo Gabriele, noster Plato Legum libros exhorditur[4] a Deo; quem esse ait communem legum omnium conditorem. Quod etiam in dialogo qui Protagoras inscribitur[5] confirmavit, dicens artes illas quae ad victum pertinent a Prometheo, hoc est humana providentia, nobis traditas esse. Legem vero bene foeliciterque vivendi ab Jove, id est divina providentia, per Mercurium, hoc est inspirationem angelicam, fuisse concessam.

8 De divino furore [iiiv]

Itaque Paulus ac Dionysius,[6] christianorum theologorum sapientissimi, invisibilia Dei asserunt, per ea quae facta sunt; quaeque hic cernuntur intelligi. Divinae vero sapientiae

---

[1] Amerigo Benci, friend of Ficino; see Ficino's *Opera*, pp. 609, 936; (references cited from Kristeller, *Supplementum*, II, p. 358).
[2] Probably *Laws*, 716C–17A.
[3] See marginalia **6**, n. 9.
[4] *Laws*, 624A. [5] *Protagoras*, 320C2–C.
[6] See Rom. i. 20; the passage is discussed by the Pseudo-Dionysius in the first two chapters of the

[v^r] **9 Excusatio prolixitatis**

Si miraris Cosme quod tam prolixe loquatur Laurentius cum Salomon[1] tam breviter sit loqutus [sic] respondeo ob hoc ipsum cogi Laurentium fore prolixum quia Salomon brevissimus fuit. Quanto enim magis Salamonis nodus implicatus est, tanto pluribus ad explicandum opus est machinis ... sed ne ego quoque dum prolixitatem excuso sim prolixior, vale

[v^v] **10 Solitariae vitae utilitas**

Audisti proverbium illud: nullius boni possessionem absque socio jucundam esse.

[xiii^r] **11 Causa peccandi. Spes. Remedium**

[First six lines of letter bracketed in margin]

[xiii^v] **12 Praestantior est legum conditor quam sophista**

Carneades[2] disputando lites introduxit; Lycurgus[3] vero dissolvit. Carneadis argutiae saepius inutiles quam utiles. Utiles autem paucis raro alicubi. Lycurgi disciplina semper utilis; ubique et omnibus necessaria.

13 De humanitate [xvi^r]

... non homo, ut ita loquar, fuit Nero sed monstrum quoddam pelle homini simile. Si enim revera fuisset homo caeteros homines tanquam membra quaedam eiusdem corporis dilexisset.... Nihil Deo gratius quam charitas. Nullum certius aut dementiae inditium aut miseriae portentum quam crudelitas.

14 Homo sine religione bestiis est infoelicior [xxii^v]

Reor equidem genus humanum cultu divino sublato fore cunctis animalibus infoelicius: micto [i.e. mitto] continuam multiplicemque inermis et imbecillis [sic]....

15 Animae natura et officium. Laus historiae [xxviii^v] (first fol. of this no.)

Iudicantur ut plurimum satis belle, sed ut plurimum turpiter diliguntur profecto iudex rei iudicandae formam in se transfert. Amator vero se transfert in amati formam. Satius est inferiora ad nos adtollere iudicando quam nos ad illa amando dejicere.

16 Cognitio et reverentia ipsius omnium optima [xxix^v]

Minuisti cum Paulo minus ab angelis[4] et quae sequuntur: rursus ego dixi dii estis et filii excelsi omnes.

Celestial Hierarchy. In the 1495 ed. the sentence ending *intelligi* is run on into the next sentence. Colet realized that the sense stopped after *intelligi* and put a vertical stop mark there to indicate the proper end of his under-linings. He often uses the same mark (ψ) to show the beginning or end of a passage which interests him.

[1] The reference here must be to some comment on Ecclesiastes by Lorenzo de' Medici delivered at the Careggian Academy.
[2] Carneades (c. 213–129 B.C.), Greek philosopher who delivered a series of lectures on *Justice* in Rome, shocking Cato the Elder by his scepticism.
[3] See marginalia 6, no. 9.   [4] Heb. ii. 7.

APPENDIX C

[xxxi^r] **17 Quid est foelicitas**
Negociamur enim ut otiemur et bellum gerimus ut in pace vivamus. . . . Atque beatitudo sit summus actus summae potentiae circa obiectum summum.

[xxxii^v] . . . ideo, ut Plato inquit, livor abest a divino choro.[1]

[liv^v] **18 De raptu Pauli ad tertium coelum**
Nox illuminatio mea in delitiis meis.[2]

[lxi^v] **19 Qualis est amor talis amicitia**
Res una eademque contraria quaedam aut agere aut pati eodem tempore secundum idem et ad idem numquam potest.

[lxxiii^r] **20 Omnia mundi bona illi mala sunt qui immundus vivit in mundo**
[Most of letter bracketed in margin.]

[lxxvii^r] **21 Sicut pulchritudo natura gignit amorem sic amor opinione regenerat pulchritudinem**
[Entire letter bracketed in margin.]
Ut nihil mirum sit si que [i.e. quae] celerrime scripsimus levissima videantur . . . non consilii filiam, sed amoris.

[xcviii^v] **22 Nullum in malis refugium est nisi ad summum bonum**
Hanc Salomon omnium divino iudicio sapientissimus affere laborem inquit[3] atque dolorem. Hanc apud deum insipientiam existimari Paulus Apostolus asserit.[4] Huius cogitationes apud Deum vanas haberi propheta Isaias exclamat.[5]

[cxxxvi^r] **23 Divina lex fieri a coelo non potest: sed forte significari**
[see fol. cxxxiv^r for beginning of this letter]
praesertim cum stella quadam ducerentur miraculosa potiusquam naturali Calcidius Platonicus[6] varias adducit hystorias de stellis, quae, cum raro videantur, ingentes portendunt calamitates. Deinde subdit. Est quoque alia sanctior et venerabilior hystoria quae perhibet ortu stelle cuiusdam non morbos mortesque denunciatas. Sed descensum Dei venerabilem ad humane servationis rerumque mortalium gratiam quam a Caldeis observatam fuisse testatur, qui Deum nuper natum muneribus venerati sunt. Haec Calcidius. . . . Orietur stella ex Jacob: et consurget virga ex Israel. . . . Cum audisset Augustus, inter pueros, quos in Syria Herodes rex Iudeorum intra bimatum iussit interfici, filium quoque eius occisum, ait: praestat Herodis porcum esse quam filium. . . .[7] Qum [sic] iam et Sibilla Cumea tempore eadem descripsisse videtur: quibus magnus ab integro saeclorum nasceretur [sic] ordo.

[clxxii^v] **24 Pallas: Juno: Venus: Vita contemplativa: activa: voluptuosa**
. . . merito imprudenter foelicitatem

---

[1] *Phaedrus* 247A. [2] Ps. cxxxix. 11–12.
[3] Eccles. i. 18.   [4] 1. Cor. iii. 19–20.
[5] Isa. xxix. 14.

[6] See marginalia **60**, n. 2.
[7] See marginalia **60**, n. 4.

sperans incidit in miseriam. Due tantum occurrisse traduntur Herculi, Venus scilicet, atque Juno.

[clxxiv^r]

25 Apologus de voluptate

Tunc temeritas, dialecticas, ait, mittamus argutias. Voluptas utpote simplex et innocens eiusmodi se non munit aculeis ... una haec uno quodam nutu foeliciter implet, nullum trahens, omnes volentes ducens, retinensque libentes.

[clxxxvii^r]

26 Nullus mala poenitus et curas extirpare potest

Necesse est ut veniant scandala. Idem profecto quod et Platonicum illud: mala poenitus extirpari non possunt.... Non enim his est certamen adversus carnem et sanguinem Paulus inquit Apostolus,[1] sed adversus maleficos quosdam spiritus aeris caliginosi tyrannos....

[clxxxvii^v]

qui seminant in lachrimis in exultatione mettent [sic]. Euntes ibant et flebant, mittentes semina sua, venientes autem venient cum exultatione, portantes manipulos suos.

[clxxxvii^v]

27 Solem non esse adorandum tanquam rerum omnium auctorem

Hunc Jacobus Apostolus[2] patrem luminum apellavit. [sic].... Apud quem non sit transmutatio, neque vicissitudinis obumbratio.... Quamobrem omne datum optimum scilicet menti naturaliter insitum, et omne donum perfectum videlicet post naturales dotes adhibitum, non a sole hoc stellisque mundanis, sed altius ab ipso patre luminum descendere censet.

[clxxxviii^v]

28 Copula philosophiae cum legibus

Fulgebunt (inquit ille)[3] docti, sicut splendor firmamenti. Et qui multos erudierint ad justitiam tanquam stelle in perpetuas aeternitates.

[clxxxix^r]

29 Apologia in librum suum de sole et lumine

Nebulas quidem aut venti protinus dissipabunt, aut sol ipse cum ascenderit altius, extenuabit atque dissolvet. Vespertilionibus autem sub lumine caligantibus cecutientibusque consulito si modo consilii sint capaces ne lucem quidem incusent caeteris salutarem. Sed ipsi splendorem hunc effugiant, suo more potius, atque (ut par est) indigni lumine assidue delitescant.

[clxxxix^v]

30 Saepe in coelestibus gemini sunt

[Marginal brackets by last part.]

31 Pro libro de religione [clxxxxv^v]

Praeterea duo potissimum amor, ut sit perfectus, desiderare videtur: ardorem, inquam, atque firmitatem.

---

[1] Eph. vi. 12. [2] Jas. i. 17. [3] Dan. xii. 3.

APPENDIX C

[clxxxxv^v] **32 Oratio . . . ad Carolum Magnum**[1]

. . . populus Florentinus tuus proculdubio credit, firmiter sperat, vehementes congratulatur.

[clxxxxvii^v]
33 Pia Platonis sententia

Interiores enim sermones quidam sunt in uno quoque nostrum. Quos et opiniones et spes nominare solemus, sunt quinetiam phantasmata picta . . . Bonus vir a Platone censetur . . . ad Deum aut pius est, ad homines vero iustus . . . Semper ergo solicitatur intus atque languent eorumque voluptates similes sunt falsis voluptatibus egrotantium, somniantium insanorum.

[clxxxxvii^v]
34 Pro libro de sole [to Joannes Ganay]

Quem denique nondum salutavi praesentem hunc absentem munere quodam Phoebeo saluto. Siquidem ipse Phoebus qui forte non tangit globo, radiis interim attingit ubique splendor quin et tuus suis hucusque radiis, me contingit. Per ipsum luminis Phoebei calorem te obsecro splendidissime mi Joannes.

[clxxxxvii^v]
35 Pro libro de sole

Quanquam si vos invicem ea (ut arbitror) charitate devincti estis, ut sit alter in altero, cum primum aspexi Paulum in Paulo introspexi Joannem. . . .

[1] Charles VIII, King of France, 1483–98.

APPENDIX D: COLET AND FICINO'S 'DE RAPTU PAULI'

J. H. LUPTON, in his translation of Colet's abstract of the *Ecclesiastical Hierarchy* of the Pseudo-Dionysius (London, 1869), pp. xviii and 36, was the first to suggest that Colet knew the *Epistolae* of Ficino. His argument was that one passage in Colet's abstract paraphrased part of a work by Ficino called 'De raptu Pauli ad tertium caelum' which was first published in Ficino's *Epistolae*. The two passages concerned are printed in parallel below.

If we agree with Lupton that this passage from the *Hierarchies* does paraphrase Ficino's 'De raptu Pauli ad tertium caelum', then Colet must have written the supplement to his abstract of the *Hierarchies* of Dionysius after his reading of the *Epistolae*, for Ficino's tract (*Epistolae*, fols. li^v–liii^r; *Opera*, pp. 609–12) is not known to exist in any manuscript which Colet could have seen (see P. O. Kristeller, *Supplementum Ficinianum*, I, pp. v–lv) and was never published elsewhere in Colet's lifetime. Apart from its obvious debt to the Pseudo-Dionysius, the passage is primarily concerned with John I. 5.

The following text of the Colet passage is taken from Lupton's edition (pp. 187–9). The text of the Ficino passage is from the All Souls volume (fol. lii^v); Colet has not marked or annotated the passage. There is a modern edition of the Ficino passage in Eugenio Garin, *Prosatori Latini del Quattrocento* (Milan, 1952), pp. 940, 942.

Ficino, 'De raptu Pauli':

Et si nihil usquam reperio extra immensum bonum quod universum et omnino intrinsecus imbuit et infinite extrinsecus ambit; tamen quicquid reperio quod non sit ipsum bonum: video ex lucidis quibusdam tenebris et tenebrosa quadam luce componi. Scio neque tenebras posse seipsas illuminare neque lucem a tenebris comprehensam ex seipsa lucere: alioquin in se vigeret ac purissime plenissimeque luceret. Lucere ergo eam animadverto ex ipsa luce in qua tenebrae non sunt ullae. Ideoque quando lucet in tenebris tenebre ipsam non compraehendunt. . . . Hoc cum ex se et sui gratia efficiat omnia et perficiat certe ad sui ipsius exemplar tanquam medium cuncta disponit. Est ergo principium medium finisque cunctorum. Et quia omnino indivisibile est in quolibet trium continentur et reliqua. Finis autem actionis movet quodammodo principium ad agendum. Principium movet exemplar operis atque formam. Huc omnes beati spiritus assidue oculus mentis intendunt. Singuli tria haec intuentur: sed diversa ratione diversi. Atque in his inspiciunt veras rerum omnium quae in universo sunt rationes. Seraphini finem ipsum proprius attentiusque quam reliqua contemplantur. Cherubini in fine principium. Throni in fine medium speculantur. Dominationes autem ipsum principium. Virtutes in principio finem. Potestates medium in principio. Principatus et si mirantur omnia tamen medium proprius et ut ita dicam libentius intuentur. Archangeli in medio finem. Angeli principium in medio contemplantur. . . .

Colet, *Hierarchies*:

Deus, immensum bonum, intrinsecus imbuens omnino, extrinsecus infinite ambiens, lux ipsa est, in quo tenebrae non sunt ullae. Quapropter, quando lucet in tenebris, tenebrae eum non comprehenderunt. . . . In his non est fas homini aliter loqui quam tres personas, et unum Deum, principium, medium et finem omnium. . . . Seraphici quidem qui in finem propius et attencius intendunt, omnia amanter et suaviter in fine speculantur, et principium et medium, et potenciam Dei et sapientiam. . . . Cherubici in fine medium et ordinem et pulchritudinem dicuntur scientes; throni in fine maxime principium et potenciam et stabilitatem, stantes nominantur. . . .

BIBLIOGRAPHY OF JOHN COLET

I. Colet's Own Writings

Note: Lupton prints a list of twenty-eight known works of Colet, including letters, in an appendix to his translation of Colet's *Letters to Radulphus*, trans. J. H. Lupton (London, 1876), pp. 307–14. Lupton's list is based on an earlier list by John Pits in *Relationum historicarum de rebus Anglicis tomus unus* (Paris, 1619), 692. The fullest list since Lupton's has been that of E. W. Hunt, *Dean Colet and His Theology* (London, 1956), pp. 131–3. Within each group in the following list works are listed in approximately chronological order.

A. Biblical commentaries.

1. Commentary on Genesis (*Letters to Radulphus*).
MS.: Corpus Christi College, Cambridge, MS. Parker CCCLV.
Edition: J. H. Lupton, in *Opuscula* (London, 1876) [Latin and English].

2. First Commentary on Romans (the 'Exposition').
MS.: Corpus Christi College, Cambridge, MS. Parker CCCLV.
Edition: J. H. Lupton, in *Opuscula* (including *Letters to Radulphus*) (London, 1876) [Latin and English].

3. Commentary on First Corinthians.
MSS.: Cambridge University Library MS. Gg. iv. 26.
  Emmanuel College, Cambridge MS. III.3.12 (incorrectly numbered 3.3.16 by Lupton and Hunt).
Editions: J. H. Lupton, *Enarratio in Epistolam Primam S. Pauli ad Corinthios* (London, 1874) [Latin and English].
P. B. O'Kelly, *A Commentary on First Corinthians by John Colet* (Harvard MS. Diss., 1960) [Latin and English].

4. Second and third Commentaries on Romans (the 'Lectures').
MSS.: Cambridge University Library MS. Gg. iv. 26.
  Corpus Christi College, Cambridge, MS. Parker CCCLV.
Edition: J. H. Lupton, *Enarratio in Epistolam B. Pauli ad Romanos* (London, 1873) [Latin and English].

B. Sermon: the sermon to the Convocation at St. Paul's, 1511:

LATIN VERSIONS
1. *Oratio habita ad Clerum in Convocatione* (London, [1511–12] STC 5545).
2. Reprinted by Samuel Knight, in *Life of Dr. John Colet* (London, 1724), pp. 273–85.

ENGLISH VERSIONS
1. *The Sermone of Doctor Colete.*
MSS.: Lambeth Palace MS. 30.9.22.
Editions: (London, [1530]) (STC 5550); (London, 1661) (Wing C 5096); London, 1701).
2. Edited by Thomas Smith as *A Sermon of Conforming and Reforming* (Cambridge, 1661, 1701); reprinted in *The Phoenix*, II (1708); reprinted separately (London, 1724), (Oxford, 1823); extract printed separately (London, 1831).
3. Edited by Samuel Knight in *Life of Dr. John Colet* (London, 1724), pp. pp. 289–308.
4. Edited by J. H. Lupton, *Life of John Colet* (London, 1887), pp. 293–304.

C. *Grammar (c. 1509), i.e. his* Aeditio *of the Latin Grammar of William Lily including as prefatory material a catechism (the* Cathecyzon), *articles of admission to St. Paul's School, and a proheme to the catechism. STC 5546, entitled* Paules Accidence, *is an edition of this same work.*

Editions: London, 1527, 1534 (STC 5542–3) (*DNB.* lists a London, 1539, ed. which I cannot verify). Antwerp, 1527, 1533, 1534, 1535, 1536, 1537, and 1539. See Nijhoff and Kronenberg, *Nederlandsche Bibliographie 1500–40* (Hague, 1940), II, Nos. 2683–9; also listed (No. 2690) is a possible Antwerp, 1530, ed. of the *Aeditio* entitled *De nominibus heteroclitis, &c.* Parts are printed in Samuel Knight, *Life of Dr. John Colet* (London, 1724), pp. 442–6 and 451–3.
Parts are also printed in J. H. Lupton, *Life of John Colet* (London, 1887), pp. 285–92.
Parts are also printed in Samuel Blach, *Die Schriftsprache in der Londoner Paulsschule* . . . (Halberstadt, 1905).

D. *Statutes.*
1. St. Paul's School London (June 18, 1518); called 'Ordinances'.
MSS.: British Museum MS. Addit. 6274. Mercers' Company, London.
Editions:
   (*a*) Samuel Knight, *Life of Dr. John Colet* (London, 1724), pp. 356–69 [English].
   (*b*) R. B. Gardiner, *Admissions Register of St. Paul's School* (London, 1884), pp. 375–88.

(c) J. H. Lupton, *Life of John Colet* (London, 1887), pp. 271–84 [English].

(d) Samuel Blach, *Die Schriftsprache in der Londoner Paulsschule* . . . (Halberstadt, 1905).

2. The Fraternity of Jesus (a London Guild).

MS.: Bodleian Library MS. Tanner 221.

Editions: W. Sparrow Simpson in *Registrum Statutorum . . . Cathedralis Sancti Pauli* . . . (London, 1873), pp. 446–52.

Samuel Blach, *Die Schriftsprache in der Londoner Paulsschule* . . . (Halberstadt, 1905).

3. St. Paul's Cathedral, London.

Versions

(a) (1505).

W. Sparrow Simpson, *Registrum Statutorum . . . Cathedralis Sancti Pauli* (London, 1873), pp. 217–36.

(b) (1518) proposed to Wolsey as 'Exhibita'.

(i) William Dugdale, *A History of St. Paul's Cathedral* (London, 1658, 1716, 1818).

(ii) W. Sparrow Simpson, *Registrum Statutorum . . . Cathedralis Sancti Pauli* (London, 1873), pp. 237–49.

E. Miscellaneous Works.

1. Paraphrase of the Lord's Prayer.

Editions:

(a) *Horae beate Marie Virgini ad usum Sarum ad longum*, ed. Erasmus (Paris, 1532).

(b) *Prymer of Salisbury Use* (Paris, 1532).

(c) *Horae . . . ad usum Sarum*, ed. Robert Wyer (London, 1533).

(d) *Prymer of Salisbury Use* (London, 1536).

(e) *The VII Petycions of the Pater Noster* (Netherlands, c. 1533). Cited by Nijhoff and Kronenberg, II, 2691.

(f) Samuel Knight, *Life of Dr. John Colet* (London, 1724), p. 450.

2. *Disputation with Erasmus* (A quoted fragment in Erasmus's *Disputatiuncula de taedio . . . Christi*).

(a) Erasmus, *Lucubratiunculae* (Antwerp, 1503). [Latin only].

(b) Erasmus, *Enchiridion Militis Christiani* (Basle, 1518, 1519, &c.) [Latin only].

(c) Erasmus, *Opera* (numerous editions).

3. *On Christ's Mystical Body.*
MS.: Cambridge University Library MS. Gg. iv. 26.
Edition: J. H. Lupton, *De compositione sancti corporis Christi mystici* (London, 1876) [Latin and English].

4. *On the Sacraments.*
MS.: St. Paul's School (London) MS.
Editions: J. H. Lupton, *De Sacramentis Ecclesiae* (London, 1867) [Latin only].
John G. Rowe, (unpublished) [English].

F. Works noted by Pits and now presumably lost.
Note: See John Pits, *De Rebus Anglicis* . . . (Paris, 1619), 692.
All of the works noted by Pits are accounted for elsewhere in this bibliography except for the following:

In proverbia Salomonis
In Evangelium S. Matthaei
Breviloquium dictorum Christi
Excerptiones Doctorum
Conciones Ordinariae
Conciones Extraordinariae
Epistolae ad Tailerum
Ortolanus[1]
Abbreviationes[1]

G. Correspondence.
1. With Erasmus: see section IV below.
2. With Thomas More; no letters of Colet survive. Letters of More to Colet survive as follows:
   (*a*) Letter dated 23 October [1504].
Editions:
   (1) Thomas Stapleton, *Tres Thomae* (London, 1689), p. 7 [Latin only]; English trans. of *Tres Thomae*, including this letter, by Philip E. Hallett (London, 1938).
   (2) John Jortin, *Life of Erasmus* (London, 1758–60), ii. 623.
   (3) J. H. Lupton, *Life of John Colet* (London, 1887), 145–6 [English only].
   (4) Elizabeth F. Rogers, *Correspondence of Sir Thomas More* (Princeton, 1947), 5–9 [Latin only].

[1] *DNB* suggests that these two works may be respectively the apophthegms and abstracts of St. Paul's *Epistles* in Trinity College, Cambridge, MS. 0.4.44.

(b) Letter dated [c. March 1512?].
Editions:
  (1) Thomas Stapleton, *Tres Thomae* as above.
  (2) Elizabeth F. Rogers, in *Correspondence of Sir Thomas More* (Princeton, 1947), p. 15 [Latin only].
3. With Wolsey: one letter, dated 18 December [1517?].
Editions: Henry Ellis, *Original Letters*, Third Series (London, 1846), i. 190 [Latin only].
  J. H. Lupton, *Life of John Colet* (London, 1887), pp. 226–7 [English only].
4. With Christopher Urswick: one letter, dated 1 April 1493.
MS.: Princeton University MS. 89.
Edition: W. K. Ferguson, 'An Unpublished Letter of John Colet', *AHR*, xxxiv (1934), 696–9.
5. With William Lily: one letter prefixed to Lily's *Libellus de constructione* (London, 1513, 1533, 1535) [STC 5544, 15602–15605].
6. With Richard Kidderminster, Abbot of Winchcombe: one letter, dated winter [1467?].
MS.: Cambridge University Library MS. Gg. iv. 26.
Editions: Samuel Knight, *Life of Dr. John Colet* (London, 1724), pp. 311–14 [Latin only]; J. H. Lupton, *Life of John Colet* (London, 1887), pp. 90–93 [English only].
7. With Marsilio Ficino: three letters.
MS.: All Souls College, Oxford MS. h. infra 1–5.
Edition: herein (all); part in R. Marcel, 'Les découvertes d'Erasme en Angleterre', *Bibliothèque d'Humanisme et Renaissance*, xiv (1952), 117–23.

H. Wills.

1. Testament of Endowment of St. Paul's School, dated 1511.
Edition: Samuel Knight, *Life of Dr. John Colet* (London, 1724), pp. 334–8.
2. Last will (dated 22 August, 1519).
MS.: Chapter House MS. at St. Paul's Cathedral, London.
Editions: Samuel Knight, *Life of Dr. John Colet* (London, 1724), pp. 464–74.
  N. H. Nicolas, *Testamenta Vetusta* (London, 1826), ii. 568–73 (reprinted from Knight).

I. Marginalia.

In his copy of Marsilio Ficino's *Epistolae* (Venice, 1495), now All Souls College, Oxford h. infra 1–5. Edited herein.

II. Biographies of Colet

Erasmus, Latin life of Colet included in letter (Allen 1211) to Jodocus Jonas written 13 June 1521. Latin text in all editions of *Epistolae* of Erasmus (see section IV below). English translations have appeared as follows:

1. Thomas Smith, *A Sermon of Conforming and Reforming* (Cambridge, 1661, 1701); reprinted in *The Phoenix*, II (1707).
2. Christopher Wordsworth, *Ecclesiastical Biography*, 3rd ed. (London, 1839), vol. I; and 4th ed. (London, 1853), vol. I.
3. J. G. Nichols, in *Pilgrimages to St. Mary of Walsingham, &c.* (London, 1849), 1875).
4. William Palmer, *A Compendious Ecclesiastical History* (New York, 1841). (*DNB*'s reference to a translation by W. Palmer, 1851, unverified, is presumably this.)
5. J. H. Lupton, *Lives of Jehan Vitrier and John Colet* (London, 1883).

John Foxe, *Actes and Monuments . . .* (London, 1837), iv. 246–8.
Polydore Vergil, *Anglicae Historiae* (Basle, 1534, 1546, 1555, &c.), Lib. XXVI.
John Bale, *Illustrium Maioris Britanniae Scriptorum Summarium* ('Ipswich', 1548; Wesalia, 1549; Basle, 1557, 1559, &c.).
John Leland, *De Rebus Britannicis Collectanea* (Oxford, 1715, 1770, 1774).
John Pits, *Relationum historicarum de rebus Anglicis Tomus unus* (Paris, 1619), i. 692.
Henry Holland, *Hieroologia Anglica* (London, 1620); see especially B.M. copy G. 1435, p. 146.
Thomas Fuller, *Abel Redivivus* (London, 1651 and 1867).
Thomas Fuller, *Daily Devotions . . . 19th edition, with a brief account of the author's life* [i.e. Colet's] *by Dr. Fuller* (London, 1684).
Henry Wharton, *Historia de Episcopis et Decanis Londinensibus* (London, 1695), 233–237.
White Kennett, Collection of notes for a life of Colet (*c.* 1720), British Museum MS. Lansdowne 1030.
Samuel Knight, *Life of Dr. John Colet* (London, 1724; Oxford, 1823). German translation by T. Arnold (Leipzig, 1735). N. H. Nicolas, *Testamenta Vetusta* (London, 1826), ii. 568, mentions a reprint of Knight in Oxford, 1825; I suspect this is a ghost. The manuscript versions of the book are in the Cambridge University Library, Patrick MSS. 22 and 46.
Thomas Tanner, *Bibliotheca Britannico-hibernica* (London, 1748).
Andrew Kippis, *Biographia Britannica* (London, 1778). Includes an abstract of Knight's *Life of Dr. John Colet*.

Daniel Bellamy, *On Benevolence; with a Summary of the Life of Dean Colet* (London, 1756).
Anthony à Wood, *Athenae Oxonienses*, ed. Philip Bliss (London, 1813, 1820), I, Col. 22.
Frederic Seebohm, *The Oxford Reformers* (London, 1867, 1869, 1887, 1914).
Sir Sidney Lee, 'John Colet' in the *DNB* (1887).
J. H. Lupton, *A Life of John Colet* (London, 1887, 1909. Reprint Hamden, Conn. 1961.)
Sidney Dark, *Five Deans* (New York, 1928).
Sir J. A. R. Marriott, *The Life of John Colet* (London, 1933).
A. B. Emden, 'John Colet' in *A Biographical Register of the University of Oxford to A.D. 1500* (Oxford, 1957), i. 462–4.

III. Other Secondary Works

Erasmus, *Colloquy* entitled *Peregrinatio religionis ergo* (contains an account of a pilgrimage to Canterbury with Colet). For numerous Latin versions, see B.M. catalogue under Erasmus - Colloquies. English translations have appeared as follows:

(*a*) Erasmus, *A Dialogue of Communication With Other Persons* (London, [1540?]) (STC 10454).

(*b*) J. G. Nichols, *Pilgrimages to St. Mary of Walsingham, etc.* (London, 1849, 1875).

(*c*) J. H. Lupton, *Life of John Colet* (London, 1887), 207–213 (abridged).

Christoph Wirsung, *General Practice of Physicke* (London, 1617), p. 120. (An anecdote on Colet's phenomenal memory.)
Sir William Dugdale, *History of St. Paul's Cathedral* (London, 1658, 1716, 1818).
Herbert Kynaston, *Commemoration Address in Praise of Dean Colet* (London, 1852).
Herbert Kynaston, *Commemorative Verses* (London, 1853).
Herbert Kynaston, *Rete Coletinum* (London, 1861).
J. H. Lupton, *John Colet, A Lecture* (London, 1886).
W. H. Shaw, *Introductory Lectures on the Oxford Reformers* (Oxford, 1889); negligible.
W. S. Simpson, 'On a Newly Discovered MS. Containing Statutes Compiled by Dean Colet for the Government of the Clergy in St. Paul's Cathedral', *Archaeologia*, lii (1890), 145–74.

J. H. Lupton, *The Influence of Dean Colet Upon the Reformation of the English Church* (London, 1893).

Arthur J. Mason, *Lectures on Colet, Fisher, and More* (London, 1895).

F. W. Farrer, *History of Interpretation* (London, 1896).

P. S. Allen, 'Dean Colet and Archbishop Warham', *EHR*, xvii (1902), 303–6.

Samuel Blach, *Die Schriftsprache in der Londoner Paulsschule zu Anfang des XVI Jahrhunderts (bei Colet, Lily, Linacre, Grocyn)* (Halberstadt, 1905).

G. F. Bridges, *The Oxford Reformers* (London, 1908); negligible.

A. F. Leach, 'St. Paul's School Before Colet', *Archaeologia*, lxii (1910), i. 121–238.

Kurt Schroeder, *Platonismus in der englischen Renaissance vor und bei Thomas Eliot* (Berlin, 1920) (*Palaestra*, LXXXIII).

M. L. Mackenzie, *Dame Christian Colet* (Cambridge, 1923).

W. R. Inge, *The Platonic Tradition in English Religious Thought*, (London, 1926); negligible on Colet.

Karl Bauer, 'John Colet und Erasmus von Rotterdam', *Archiv für Reformationsgeschichte*, Ergänzungsband, v (1929), 155–87.

Walter F. Schirmer, *Der englische Frühhumanismus* (Leipzig, 1931).

Friedrich Dannenberg, *Das Erbe Platons in England bis zur Bildung Lylys* (Berlin, 1932).

Albert Hyma, 'Erasmus and the Oxford Reformers', *Nederlandsch Archief voor Kerkgeschiedenis*, N.S., xxv (1932), 69–92, 97–134.

W. Nelson, 'The Friendship of More and Colet; an Early Document', *MLQ* i (1940), 459–60.

N. D. Hurnard, *Studies in Intellectual Life in England* (D.Phil. thesis, Oxford, 1936).

Albert Hyma, 'The Continental Origins of English Humanism', *HLQ*, iv (1940–1), 1–25.

K. D. MacKenzie, 'John Colet of Oxford', *Dalhousie Review*, xxi (1941), 15–28.

W. E. Campbell, 'John Colet, Dean of St. Paul's', *Dublin Review*, 218 (1946), 97–107.

H. W. Garrod, 'Erasmus and His English Patrons', *Library*, 5th ser., iv (1949), 1–13.

F. Grossmann, 'Holbein, Torrigiano and Some Portraits of John Colet', *Journal of the Warburg and Courtauld Institutes*, xiii (1950), 202–36.

Leland Miles, *Plato and The Early Reformation* (Ph.D. dissertation, University of North Carolina, 1950).

E. L. Surtz, 'The "Oxford Reformers" and Scholasticism', *SP*, xlvii (1950), 547–56.

Leland Miles, 'Protestant Colet and Catholic More', *Anglican Theological Review*, xxxiii (1951), 30–42.
R. Marcel, 'Les découvertes d'Erasme en Angleterre', *Humanisme et Renaissance*, xiv (1952), (*Mélanges Augustin Renaudet*), 117–23.
E. F. Rice, Jr., 'John Colet and the Annihilation of the Natural', *Harvard Theological Review*, xlv (1952), 141–63.
Ernst Cassirer, *The Platonic Renaissance in England*, trans. J. P. Pettegrove (Edinburgh and Austin, 1953). (Originally published in German as *Studien der Bibliothek Warburg* 24, Leipzig, 1932.)
P. A. Duhamel, 'The Oxford Lectures of John Colet', *JHI*, xiv (1953), 493–510.
W. A. Clebsch, 'John Colet and the Reformation', *Anglican Theological Review*, xxxvii (1955), 167–77.
E. W. Hunt, *Dean Colet and His Theology* (London, 1956).
George B. Parks, *The English Traveler to Italy* (Stanford, Calif., 1954), i. 357–82, 466–7.
L. Miles, review of E. W. Hunt, *Dean Colet and His Theology*, in *RN*, xi (1958), 134, 136.
D. J. Parsons, 'John Colet's Stature as an Exegete', *Anglican Theological Review*, xl (1958), 36–42.
Pearl Hogrefe, *The Sir Thomas More Circle* (Urbana 1959).
Sir Michael McDonnell, *The Annals of St. Paul's School* (London, 1959).
Leland Miles, *John Colet and the Platonic Tradition* (La Salle, Ill. 1961; London, 1962).
Robert P. Adams, *The Better Part of Valor* (Seattle 1962).

IV. *Colet in the Correspondence of Erasmus*

The standard edition of the letters of Erasmus is P. S. Allen *Opus Epistolarum D. Erasmi* (Oxford, 1906–58), 12 vols. The letters are also printed, of course, in the standard edition of the *Opera* of Erasmus by J. LeClerc (Leyden, 1703–6), 10 vols., and in many early editions of the *Epistolae* alone (see B.M. and B.N. catalogues for references).

An English translation of some of the letters is available in F. M. Nichols, *Epistles of Erasmus* (London, 1901), 3 vols. For convenience I give both the Allen and the Nichols references to all of the correspondence of Erasmus which pertains to Colet; my numbering of the letters from Nichols does not correspond to Nichols's index, which is erratic, but to the letters themselves. All references to the letters of Erasmus in my footnotes are to volume and page of the Allen edition. Samuel Knight's English translation of some of the Colet-Erasmus correspondence is in Cambridge University Library Patrick MS. 21.

A. *Letters from Colet to Erasmus:*

Allen	Nichols
106	99
110	[107]
230	223
258	246
314	305
423	411
593	586

Four of these letters are reprinted in Samuel Knight, *Life of Dr. John Colet* (London, 1724), pp. 315–22 [Latin only].

B. *Letters from Erasmus to Colet:*

Allen	Nichols
107	100
108	108
109	[106]
111	[ ]
181	180
195	195
225	219
227	221
231	224
237	231
260	248
270	252
278	271
786	757
825	787
891	[ ]

One of these letters from Colet to Erasmus is reprinted in Samuel Knight, *Life of Dr. John Colet* (London, 1724) pp. 323–4 [Latin only].

BIBLIOGRAPHY

C. *Letters from Erasmus to other correspondents, in which Colet is mentioned:*

Allen	Nichols	Allen	Nichols
I (I, 6, 9, 20, 21, 44)		468 (II, 347)	457
III (I, 55)		471 (II, 350, 351)	
IV (I, 59, 62, 63)		474 (II, 354)	
113 (I, 261)	105	480 (II, 368)	
115 (I, 267)		491 (II, 385)	435
116 (I, 268)		494 (II, 405)	
118 (I, 273)		535 (II, 481)	
120 (I, 283)		543 (II, 495)	
159 (I, 368)	155	706 (III, 131)	
218 (I, 456)		855 (III, 357)	
244 (I, 489)		966 (III, 585)	
245 (I, 492)		976 (III, 602)	
248 (I, 495)		999 (IV, 21, 22)	
291 (I, 557)		1025 (IV, 87)	
296 (I, 570)		1026 (IV, 88)	
298 (II, 2)		1027 (IV, 89)	
300 (II, 4)		1028 (IV, 90)	
341 (II, 119)		1029 (IV, 92)	
373 (II, 166)		1030 (IV, 94)	
414 (II, 246)		1075 (IV, 202)	
455 (II, 320)		1110 (IV, 279)	
457 (II, 330)		1211 [*Life*] (IV, 507–27)[1]	
467 (II, 346)	[?]	1229 (IV, 569)	
		1347 (V, 239, 247)	
		2209 (VIII, 267)	

[1] For English translation of this letter, see section II above.

INDEX

Academy, Platonic, at Florence, *see* Careggi.
Acerbus, Aemilius, 132 n.
action, and contemplation, 50, 56, 59, 65, 68–78, 93, 101, 118, 140, 143; corresponding to justice, 89; emphasis on moral, in Colet, 52, 64, 68, 72, 73, 78, 91, 93, 101; leads to suffering, 119; objects of, 111.
actuality and potentiality, 113.
Adam, 46, 53.
Adams, Robert P., 157.
Advocates, College of, 135.
agape, 45 n.
Agrippa II, 51, 117.
Alexandra, 92 n.
Alexandrian 'Platonists', 43 n.
All Souls College, *see* Oxford University.
allegory, Ficino's use of, 71.
Allen, P. S., 16 n., 32 n., 48 n., 156, 157.
aloe, 100.
Ambrose, St., 49.
ambrosia (allegorical meaning), 47, 89, 90, 102.
Anaxagoras, Clazomenius, 102.
angels, 41, 45, 64, 86, 88, 105, 107–9, 124, 128, 141–2; eyes, as, 106; free will of, 117; hierarchies of, 8, 63, 107–9, 146–7; represented by stars, 104.
Anichini, Giuseppe, 56 n.
animals, 7, 54, 115, 122, 124, 127, 138, 139, 142.
Apollo, 19 n., 50 n., 51, 92, 129, 130, 145.
Apostles, 41, 117 n.
apparitions, 126 n.
appetitive passions, 111–12, 123–4.
Apuleius Madaurensis, Lucius, 88 n.
Aquinas, St. Thomas, *see* Thomas Aquinas, St.
Aristippus, 102.
Aristotle, 7, 9 n., 100, 102, 131 n., 132 n.
Arnold, T., 154.
art, as a speculative virtue, 100.
Arthur, Prince of Wales, 29.
ascent, of Paul to Heaven, 106; of the soul to Heaven, 8, 39, 40, 44–47, 50, 52, 56, 58, 78, 85, 89, 90, 93, 94 n., 101, 108 n., 111, 114, 120.

astrology and astrologers, 9, 19, 53, 59, 85, 117, 118, 122.
Athene, Pallas, *see* Minerva.
Athenagoras, 36.
Athens, 42.
Augustine, St., Bishop of Hippo, 38, 40, 52, 52 n., 59, 70, 71 n., 73, 75, 77, 78, 83 n.
Augustus, Emperor, 102, 122 n., 143.
authority, 41, 44; importance of, 101; as source of law, 118.
aversive passions, 111 n.
Avicenna, 102.

Bacon, Francis, 76.
Balaam, 122.
Bale, John, 154.
Ball, Hugo, 43 n.
baptism, 43 n.
Barbaro, Hermolao, 16.
Barlow, C. W., 42 n.
Baron, Hans, 75.
Basil, St., The Great, 72 n.
Basle, 13.
Battenhouse, R. W., 52 n., 71 n., 83 n.
Bauer, Karl, 38 n., 44 n., 156.
Beaufort, Lady Margaret, 22, 24.
beauty, 99; divine, soul's pursuit of, 60, 90, 91; as a human good, 57, 61 n., 87; love of, 139, 143; physical and divine, 90.
being, as attribute of God, 64, 103; as attribute of man, 57; chain of, 108 n.; concept of, 103; relation of to becoming, 57; soul as monad of, in Ficino, 57; the soul's, 93; third function of the soul, 64–68.
Bellamy, Daniel, 155.
Benedictines, 58.
Bennett, Josephine, 29 n.
Bergamo, 132 n.
Bible, The, 22 n., 40 n., 43, 44, 45, 47, 54; Colet's lectures on, 21–23, 43, 64 n., 68, 77; 1 Corinthians, 20, 25, 41 n., 45, 51, 52, 53 n., 60, 63, 64, 71 n., 72 n., 110 n., 119 n., 123 n., 130, 143 n.; Daniel, 144 n.; Ecclesiastes, 119 n., 142 n., 143 n.; Ephesians, 144 n.; Galatians, 25 n.; Genesis, 27, 28,

INDEX

Bible, The—*contd.*
   44, 49, 62; Hebrews, 142 n.; Isaiah, 109 n., 119 n., 143 n.; James, 62, 72 n., 144 n.; John, 74 n., 146; New Testament, 41 n.; Numbers, 122 n.; Peter, 25 n.; Psalms, 109 n., 143 n.; Romans, 19–20, 20 n., 23, 25, 25 n., 26, 26 n., 31, 34, 41 n., 45, 52, 53, 61, 61 n., 64, 65, 69, 72 n., 75, 89 n., 97 n., 99 n., 115 n., 123 n.; *see also* exegesis, biblical.
Blach, Samuel, 150, 151, 156.
Bloomfield, M. W., 45 n.
Bloxham, J. R., 14 n.
Boase, C. W., 14 n., 15 n.
Bodleian Library (Oxford), 151.
body, the, 8, 88; as the church, 32; concept of in Colet, 58, 58 n., 69, 89–90, 93–95, 106 n., 123–6; concept of, in Ficino, 57; created by the world, 95; and demons, 123–5; and light, 112–13; relation to the soul, 57, 89, 93, 103–4, 110, 111; as reminder of divine beauty, 90; to be scorned, 101, 120–1, 123–5; soul's love for, 46, 89; source of evil, 124.
Bohemian heretics, 17.
Bologna, 16 n.
Botevant, Prebend of, at York, 17.
Brandt, W. J., 41 n.
Bridges, G. F., 156.
British Museum, 137, 150, 155, 157.
Bruges, 29.
Bruni, Leonardo, 48.
Burckhardt, Jakob, 38.
Burrows, Montagu, 15 n., 16 n., 24 n., 42 n.
Bush, Douglas, 38.

Cabala, 59.
Caesar, Julius, 102.
Cambridge University, 9, 98; library of, 30 n., 135, 149, 152–4, 157; Corpus Christi College, 149; Emmanuel College, 135; Trinity College, 25 n., 152 n.
Campbell, T. L., 43 n.
Campbell, William, 15 n.
Campanella, Tommaso, 19 n.
candle, soul as, 61.
canon law, degrees in, 16 n.
Canterbury, pilgrimage to, 19.

Careggi, Academy at, 5, 5 n., 17, 18, 19 n., 44, 50, 68 n., 71, 87, 142 n.
Carneades, 142 n.
Cassirer, Ernst, 157.
Castor and Pollux, 129.
Catherine of Aragon, 29.
Cato, the Elder, 142 n.
celibacy, 53–54, 115.
Chalcidius (or Calcidius), 122, 143.
charity, 59, 60–68, 99, 101, 109, 121, 131 n., 142; *see also* faith, hope and charity.
Charles VIII, King of France, 140, 145.
Chastel, André, 59 n., 71 n.
chastity, 125.
Cheiney, Edward, 17 n.
cherubim, *see* angels.
Chevalier, Dom. P., 29 n.
Christ, Jesus, 10, 32, 38, 41, 45, 46, 51, 53, 54, 54 n., 59, 61, 61 n., 64, 64 n., 75, 75 n., 85, 103, 112, 116, 117, 121, 122, 123; birth of, 143.
Christianity, 39–41; and Hellenism, 78; and Platonism, 43–47; 78.
Christian(s), 41, 56, 64, 112, 124.
chromatic scale, 8, 122.
Church, concept of the, 32, 112 n.
Cicero, 48, 53 n., 100 n.
cinnamon, 100.
clarity, 101, 105, 113, 114.
Clebsch, W. A., 157.
Clement of Alexandria, 45, 52, 72 n.
Coleridge, Samuel T., 40, 78.
Colet, Dame Christian, 156.
Colet, John: *Abbreviations* [?], 152; *Apophthegms* [?], 152 n.; *Breviloquium dictorum Christi* [?], 152; *Commentary on First Corinthians*, 12 n., 20, 20 n., 25, 31–34, 38 n., 53 n., 54 n., 62 n., 63 n., 64 n., 65, 67, 72, 99 n., 149; *Commentary on Genesis*, 27–28, 49, 62, 149; *Commentary on Peter*, 25 n.; *Commentary on Romans*, 12 n., 25–34, 49, 52, 53, 61, 64, 65, 67, 149; *Conciones Extraordinariae* [?], 152; *Conciones Ordinariae* [?], 152; *Convocation Sermon*, 36, 149–50; *De compositione sancti corporis Christi mystici*, 25 n., 32 n., 33, 152; *De Sacramentis Ecclesiae*, 33–34, 112 n., 116 n., 152; *Disputation with Erasmus*, 151; *Ecclesiastical Hierarchy* (of Dionysius), abstract of, 4 n., 30–32, 43 n., 63 n., 64,

INDEX

Colet, John—*contd.*
96 n., 99 n., 146–7; *Epistles,* Pauline: abstracts of [?], 152; Colet's lectures on, 20, 25–27; *Epistolae ad Tailerum* [?], 152; *Excerptiones Doctorum* [?], 152; *Exposition of Romans,* 12 n., 25–34, 44 n., 49 n., 58 n., 61 n., 62 n., 65 n., 66 n., 68 n., 69 n., 99 n., 117 n., 149; *In Evangelium S. Matthaei* [?], 152; *In Proverbia Salamonis* [?], 152; Letters, 67–68, 82–83, 152–3, 157–8; *Letters to Radulphus,* 3 n., 25 n., 26 n., 27 n., 49 n., 52 n., 62 n., 149; *Lord's Prayer,* paraphrase of, 151; *Ordinances* (for St. Paul's School), 137, 150–1; *Ortolanus* [?], 152; *Statutes* (for St Paul's Cathedral), 151, 156; Academic degrees, 15, 21, 22, 35–36, 48; attitude towards Ficino, 50–55, 81; biographical table, 36; biography of, 3–37, 154–5; Christianity of, 39–40; correspondence with Ficino, 4, 18–21, 81–83; family of, 39; ecclesiastical preferments, 14, 15, 17, 17 n., 23, 23 n., 35, 35 n.; Greek, knowledge of, 48; hand identified, 135–7; Latin style, 12–13; memory, 30, 32, 32 n.; modern interpretations of, 38–39; Oxford writings, chronology of, 21–34, 36; portraits of, 156; religious zeal, 40; in Rome, 3 n., 17; theology of, 38–55, 58; wills, 153; works of, 3, 3 n., 37, 77, 149–53.
Coletus, Joannes (French scholar), 21 n.
Collingwood, Ralph, Dean of Lichfield, 27, 27 n.
Collins, J. B., 43 n.
colour, 8, 113, 119, 122.
concupiscible passions, 111–12.
contemplation, and action, 50, 56, 59, 65, 68–78, 93, 101, 118, 140, 143; corresponding to wisdom, 89, 120; three kinds, 102; as worship of God, 123.
contemplative life, Ficino advocates, 59; limitations of, 69, 126–7; kinds of, 69, 126–7.
Convocation Sermon, see Colet.
correspondence, Colet-Ficino, 4, 18–21, 81–83.
1 Corinthians, *see* Bible.
creation, of the world, 44, 97, 104.
Crudelius, Arsenius, 132 n.
Cudworth, Ralph, 76.
cynics, 102.
Cyprian, Saint, 49.
Cyril, Saint, 72 n.

Daemons, 19 n., 45, 47, 69, 92 n., 108, 123–5, 127, 128, 130, 144.
Daniel, *see* Bible.
Daniel, the prophet, 128.
Dannenberg, Friedrich, 38 n., 156.
Danzig, 132 n.
Dark, Sidney, 38 n., 155.
darkness, 107, 112, 113, 115, 119, 123.
David, King of Israel, 109 n.
Davies, John, 76.
Deism, 40.
Deissner, Kurt, 42 n.
Della Torre, Arnaldo, 5 n.
Democritus, 31 n., 51–52, 102, 117.
demons, *see* daemons.
Dennington, Suffolk, 15.
desire, as source of evil, 124–6; for God, 101, 111, 120; and reason, 111–12; as reason for law, 118.
devils, 38; *see also* daemons.
DeWitt, N. W., 41 n.
Diana, 129.
Dionysius the Areopagite (Pseudo-Dionysius), 8, 28–34, 36, 42–43, 43 n., 45, 49, 52, 53 n., 55, 62–64, 69, 141–2 n., 146; as Christian theologian, 7, 71 n., 141; as Platonist, 19 n.; *Celestial hierarchy,* 28–34, 43 n., 45 n., 62–64 n., 142 n.; *De divinis nominibus,* 36, 72 n.; *Ecclesiastical hierarchy,* 28–34, 43 n., 63, 69 n., 96 n., 146–7; *Mystic theology,* 36, *see also* Colet, abstract of Dionysius.
Dionysus, 92.
Dioscuri, 129.
divination, 84, 92.
Dix, Dom Gregory, 42 n.
Doctors' Commons, 135.
Dodds, E. R., 43 n.
Doget, John, 48.
Donatus, Aelius, 46, 47.
dreams, 7, 96; used by daemons, 124.
Dress, Walter, 58 n.
Dugdale, William, 14 n., 151, 155.
Duhamel, P. A., 38, 157.
Duns Scotus, John, 22, 58, 76, 132, 132 n.
Durnford, England, 55 n.

Ecclesiastes, *see* Bible.
'Edmund', *see* Knevet, Edmund.
Egerton, A. F., 4.
Egidi, Pietro, 17 n.
elements, the four, 9, 84, 104, 114.
Elijah, 107.
Ellis, Henry, 153.
Ellrodt, Robert, 55 n.
Elsee, C., 43 n.
emanation, 47, 52 n., 112.
Emden, A. B., 14 n., 155.
Empyrean, the, 104, 108.
England, 17–21, 54, 75, 157.
Epictetus, 42, 121 n.
Epicureans, 41 n.
epistles, Pauline, 20, 25, 25 n., 27, 34 n., 52, 152; Colet's lectures on, *see* Colet and Bible.
Erasmus, Desiderius, 3, 3 n., 12, 15, 16, 17, 18, 19 n., 21, 21 n., 22, 23 n., 25, 25 n., 36. 38 n., 40, 41 n., 44 n., 47, 48, 49, 70, 71 n., 103 n., 151, 152, 153, 154–8.
Eriugena, Joannes Scotus, 43 n.
Eros, 45 n.
essence, divine, 89.
eternity, 109, 120–1.
Everyman, 58.
evil, absence of Platonic idea of, 126; as motion and multiplicity, 85, 92; caused by demons, 69, 123–5; causes of, 126; causes unhappiness, 87; elimination, of, 7, 56, 73, 95, 126–7, 140, 144; escape from, 95, 118, 139, 143, 144; nothing is purely, 126; obstacle to good, 72, 99–100; prior to evil actions, 115–16; source of, 126—in disorder, 126, in ignorance (Ficino), 69, in ignoring Heaven, 46, 89, in irreligion, 69, in multiplicity, 69, in pride of body, 124; the world as naturally, 56, 126–7.
evolutionism, 40.
exegesis, techniques of Biblical, 26, 26 n., 27, 27 n., 28, 38, 40, 44, 45, 47, 49, 54, 64 n., 68, 157.

Faith, and knowledge, 118; and law, 85; and works, 74–75; as intellectual virtue, 60–68; as virtue, 127; Colet's reordering, 62–68; hope, and charity (triad), 30 n., 31, 33, 52, 60–68, 107, 120; necessary to read Bible, 54.

fall of man, the, 29 n., 45–47, 89.
Farrer, F. W., 156.
fate, 127, 130.
Fathers, Church, 16, 43 n., 61, 72 n.
Ferguson, W. K., 1 n., 17 n., 71 n., 153.
Ficino, Marsilio, 4–13, 14, 27, 28, 34, 36, 38, 43 n., 47, 70, 81, 94, 95, 117, 126 n., 127, 136, 140 n; library of, 141; *Athenagorae de resurrectione*, 36; *Commentary on Romans*, 26 n., 27 n., 34; *Commentary on the Gospels*, 44 n., 94; *Commentary on the Symposium*, 60, 71 n.; *Contro la pestilenza*, 36; *De Christiana religione (Della religione cristiana)*, 36; *De raptu Pauli ad tertium caelum*, 85, 106–11, 139, 143, 146–7; *De sole et lumine*, 19, 19 n., 36, 72 n., 85, 129, 130; *De vita*, 18 n., 36; *Dialogue between God and the Soul*, 84, 87; *Dialogue between Paul and the Soul*, 74; Dionysius Areopagite (trans.), 36; *Epistolae*, 4, 11, 18, 25 n., 28–34, 43, 44, 45, 49–50, 51, 52, 53, 53 n., 54, 59, 60, 62, 64, 67, 69 n., 71, 71 n., 72 n., 74 n., 81 n., 83 n., 90 n., 102 n., 137, 146–7, 153; Hermetic *Pimander* (trans.), 36; Jamblichus (trans.), 36; Plato (trans.), 18 n., 36; Plotinus (trans.), 18 n., 27 n., 36, 48; *Theologia Platonica*, 12, 18 n., 27 n., 28, 29, 31 n., 36, 43, 43 n., 49, 52, 57, 59, 61, 67, 68, 96 n., 105 n.; *Theological address to God*, 84; biographical table, 36; books written by, 44 n., 94; charges of heresy against, 43; Colet's attitude toward, 50–55, 66–68; Colet's biographical relations with, 17–20; Colet's reading of, 43–44, 49; concept of wisdom, 71–72; correspondence with Colet, 4, 18–21, 81–83, 153; daemons, theory of, 123–5; Latin style, 12; letter-writing habits of, 5–6, 37 n.
fire, 83, 125; heat and light of, 90, 111.
Fisher, John, St., Bishop of Rochester, 156.
flesh, and spirit, 52, 57, 64, 69, 127; as imprisoning the soul, 58, 73, 89, 93; goodness as aversion to, 69, 89–90, 123–5; *see also* body.
Florence, 5, 16, 16 n., 17, 68 n., 78, 81, 140 n., 145.
Flynn, V. J., 17 n.
food, as source of evil, 125.
form, 29 n., 62, 85, 104, 109, 111.
fortitude as a human good, 84, 87, 100, 127.

INDEX

fortune, 84, 95, 127.
Foxe, John, 154.
France, 21, 70.
Franciscans, 58.
Fraternity of Jesus (London Guild), 151.
friendship, 84, 85, 96, 111, 114, 117, 138, 139, 140, 143.
Fuller, Thomas, 154.
Fulwood, William, 5.

Gabriel, the Archangel, 88 n., 141.
Gabriel, A. L., 21 n.
Gaguin, Robert, 21 n.
Galatians, *see* Bible.
Gale, Thomas, 25 n.
Galli, Ettore, 5 n.
Ganay, Germain de, Bishop of Orleans, *see* Orleans.
Ganay, Joannes, 145.
Gandillac, Maurice de, 43 n.
Gardiner, R. B., 150.
Garin, Eugenio, 146.
Garrod, H. W., 156.
Gasquet, F. A., Cardinal, 17 n.
generosity, 138.
Genesis, *see* Bible.
genius, 128.
Gentiles, 26 n., 41, 64, 75.
Germany, 70.
Gibson, Strickland, 15 n., 16 n., 22 n., 24 n., 48.
gifts, the seven, of the Holy Ghost, 109.
Gloucestershire, 4 n.
Gnostics, 45.
Gods, 124, 126.
good, concept of, 47, 51–52, 62–66, 72–73, 90, 99–100, 103, 116, 118, 120, 124.
Goodeaster, London, 23 n.
Goodness, 42, 57, 62–66, 90, 121; and Truth, 118; as attribute of God, 64, 103, 105, 106, 126; as heroism, 92; prior to good actions, 51, 68, 101, 115, 116, 139, 143.
goods, human, 86, 87, 120, 141.
Grace, law of, 53; necessary for justification, 54, 73–75, 85, 89, 107, 119, 121; necessary for knowledge of God, 63, 72, 74, 95, 107, 109, 143.
Graces, the, 87.
grammar-book, Colet's, 40, 150.
grammar, moralized Latin, 46.

Grant, F. C., 40 n.
Greek: Colet's knowledge of, 42, 48; language and literature, 71 n., 87; Plato in, 141; religion, 45, 71 n., 92 n.; studies, 40, 41, 41 n., 42.
Gregory I, Saint, Pope, 72 n.
Grocyn, William, 14, 15 n., 16, 16 n., 24, 24 n., 25, 29, 36, 40, 42 n.
Grosseteste, Robert, 43 n.
Grossmann, F., 156.
Guthrie, W. K. C., 92 n.

Habit, 68, 101.
Hallett, Philip E., 152.
happiness, 29 n., 84, 87, 89, 93, 94–95, 102, 116, 128, 139, 140, 143.
Harding, Thomas, 3.
harmony, divine, 91; Jove as source of, 130; soul's desire for, 91.
Harvard University, 149.
Harvey, Gabriel, 5.
Hatch, Edwin, 40 n.
Hawkins, R. M., 25 n.
health, as a human good, 87, 102.
heat, 107, 120, 125, 130; and fire, 83, 90, 111; as force of will in soul-ray, 62–65; of the sun, 90, 105, 145.
Heaven and heavens, 8, 9, 47, 74, 85, 89–90, 104, 106, 107, 108, 109 n., 111, 114, 116, 118, 122, 123, 139, 140, 143, 144, 146.
Hebrews, *see* Bible.
Hell, 121.
Hellenism, 16, 40, 40 n., 75, 78.
Hennessy, George, 35 n.
Henry VII, King of England, 15 n., 17.
Heraclitus, 31 n., 51–52, 96 n., 102 n., 117.
Hercules, 144.
Herillus, 102.
Hermelink, Heinrich, 44.
Hermes, *see* Mercury.
Hermes Trismegistus, 36, 44, 115.
Herod, King of Judea, 122, 143.
Herodotus, 88 n.
heroism, as goodness, 92.
Hilberworth, 15 n.
Hilduin (translator of Dionysius), 43 n.
Hippocrates, 51.
Hispanus, Petrus, *see* Peter the Spaniard.
Holbein, Hans, 156.

Holiness, 95–96; *see also* Piety, Righteousness.
Holland, Henry, 154.
Holy Spirit, 103, 107, 109, 121; *see also* Trinity, doctrine of.
honour, as a human good, 87, 102.
Hoopes, Robert, 76 n.
hope, 60–68, 95, 107, 116, 118; as Truth, 119; *see also* Faith, hope and charity.
Humanism, 4, 8 n., 38, 39, 48, 56, 56 n., 70, 156.
humanity, 139, 142.
Hurnard, N. D., 156.
Hunt, E. W., 38 n., 43 n., 58 n., 61 n., 75 n., 149, 157.
Hyma, Albert, 23 n., 34 n., 38, 38 n., 156.
hypostases, Neoplatonic, 44, 104 n.

Ida, Mount, 131.
ideas in the mind of God, 71 n., 89, 93, 141.
identification (third stage of mystic's ascent to God), 60.
Idolum in Ficino, 57.
ignorance of Heaven as cause of evil (Ficino), 89.
illumination, doctrine of, in Colet, 62–65, 104–7, 109, 143; second stage of mystic's ascent to God, 60, 64, 70.
imitation, 84, 87, 97, 99, 139, 141.
immortality, *see* soul.
intellect, and love in Ficino, 49–50, 60, 82–83; correspondence to faith, 60–68; faculty of, 57, 120, 128; *mens* as, 105, 105 n.; -will duality, 56–78, 101, 102, 103 n., 105, 106, 109.
invisibilia and visibilia, 7, 26 n., 27 n., 71 n., 89, 105, 110, 128, 129–30, 141.
Isaiah, 119, 143.
Israel, 143.
Italy, English scholars in, 16, 16 n., 20, 24, 37 n., 38, 157.

Jack, C. D., 10.
Jacob, 143.
Jamblichus, 36, 43.
James, the Apostle, 128, 144.
Jerome, Saint, 49.
Jewel, John, *see* Salisbury.
Jews, 41, 51, 64, 75, 78, 117.
John, Pope XXI, *see* Peter the Spaniard.
Jonas, Jodocus, 154.
Jortin, John, 152.
joy, 94–95, 99, 111, 114.
Juno, 50, 51, 59, 116, 131, 140, 143, 144.
Jupiter, as divine providence, 141; (the god), 44, 50, 71, 86, 88, 91, 92, 128, 130; the planet, 129.
justice, correspondence to action, 89; as human good, 87; and law, 84, 97, 138, 139, 141; as form of prudence, 95–96; as road to self-knowledge, 91; as virtue, 100, 110.

Kennett, Bishop White, 3 n., 154.
Ker, N. R., 4.
King, John, 131 n.
King, Robert, *see* Oxford.
Kinge, Dr., 86, 131 n., 136.
Kippis, Andrew, 155.
Knevet, Edmund, 26.
Knevet, Sir William, 15.
Knight, Samuel, 1 n., 14 n., 22 n., 149, 150, 151, 153, 154, 155, 157, 158.
knowledge, 99–100, 119, 139, 142; Augustine's theory of, 83 n.; character in *Everyman*, 58; and faith, 118; Ficino's emphasis on, 84; as a good, 141; of good and evil, 116; and love, 30 n., 49, 102, 108, 108 n., 109; of God, 47, 63, 74, 90, 99, 113, 126; the object of, 87; of self, 71–72, 91, 98, 101, 115; as virtue, 65, 69.
Koch, H., 72 n.
Kristeller, Paul O., 4 n., 5 n., 8 n., 26 n., 34 n., 36 n., 38, 43 n., 52 n., 57, 57 n., 58 n., 59, 68 n., 94 n., 105 n., 126 n., 146.
Kynaston, Herbert, 155.

Lady Margaret professorship of divinity, 22–24.
Lambeth Palace Library, 135–7, 150.
Lambourne, Berks, 35 n.
Latimer, Hugh, 16 n.
Latin, studies, 41, 46; style, Colet's, 12–13.
laughter in Heaven, 114.
law, and faith, 29 n., 53, 85, 97, 118; and justice, 84, 138, 139, 141; and love, 97; and philosophy, 85, 128, 129, 140, 144; and

INDEX

law, and faith—*contd.*
    wisdom, 53, 128; and works, 75; as having supra-celestial sanction, 118; canon, degrees in, 16 n.; divine, 122, 139, 143; faculty of making, 54, 115; founder of, 53, 139, 142; Mosaic, 121; profession of, 8, 88.
lawyer, the parts of a, 53, 84, 98, 138.
Leach, A. F., 40 n., 156.
Le Clerc, J., 157.
Lee, Sir Sidney, 155.
Le Fèvre d'Étaples, Jacques, 70.
Le Neve, John, 17 n.
Leland, John, 154.
Lethe, 47, 89, 90.
liberal arts, the seven, 48.
Lichfield, 27 n.
Liddell, J. R., 5 n.
light, 26 n., 107, 111, 122; as figure for personal influence, 81; as force of intellect in soul-ray, 63–65, 93; as Jupiter, 130; as object of soul's search, 119, 120; equivalent to intellect-faith, 61–65, 120; Ficino's book on, 85, 129, 130, 140, 144; God as, 88, 89, 106, 109, 110, 112–14, 118–20, 123, 128–30, 146; nature of, 53, 72, 85, 93, 112–14, 128–30; of fire, 83, 90, 111; of the sun, 72 n., 105, 109–10, 112, 145; renaissance theory of, 72 n.
Lily, William, 16, 137, 150, 153.
limbo, 121.
Linacre, Thomas, 16, 40.
Little, A. G., 48 n.
logic books, 86, 131–2.
logoi spermatikoi, 42 n.
London, 14, 35, 78.
Lord's Prayer, Colet's paraphrase of, 151.
Love, 12, 57–58, 90, 97–99, 107, 116, 142; and intellect, 28, 49–50, 60–68, 78, 82–83; as desire for beauty, 139, 143; as friendship, 81, 85, 114, 139, 143; divine, 60, 72, 75, 90, 107, 125; and knowledge, 30 n., 49, 102, 108, 109; of God, 99, 107, 109, 120, 131 n.; of Good, 118, 120, 121.
lust, 56, 100, 126, 127.
Lupton, J. H., 3, 3 n., 4 n., 12, 12 n., 17 n., 23 n., 25 n., 26 n., 27 n., 29 n., 30 n., 31 n., 34, 34 n., 38 n., 44 n., 52 n., 135, 137, 146, 149–56.
Luther, Martin, 70.

Lycurgus, 88, 142.
Lyons, 21 n.
Lyte, H. C. M., 22 n., 24 n.

McDonnell, Michael, 137, 157.
Macchioro, V. D., 42 n., 53 n., 92 n., 96 n.
Mackenzie, M. L., 156.
MacKenzie, K. D., 156.
Macray, W. D., 14 n.
madness, divine, 5, 84, 89–92, 139, 141.
magic, 19, 19 n., 92 n.
Mahomet, 88, 141.
majorana, 100.
Mallet, C. E., 15 n., 25 n., 46 n.
Mancini, G., 29 n.
Marcel, Abbé Raymond, 4, 4 n., 5 n., 153, 157.
Margaret, Lady, *see* Beaufort, Lady Margaret.
Mariamne (wife of Herod), 122 n.
marriage, 38, 53–54, 85, 112 n., 115, 138.
Marriott, Sir J. A. R., 17 n., 38 n., 155.
Mars (the god), 72, 86, 129; the planet, 129.
Martha, 50.
Mary Magdalen, 50.
Mary, the Virgin, 10, 103, 151.
Mason, Arthur J., 156.
masses, the, 44, 51, 85, 92–93, 95, 114, 117.
matter, 8, 9, 104, 109, 111, 114, 126.
Maumethes, *see* Mahomet.
Medici, Cosimo de', 7, 36, 140, 142.
Medici, Giuliano de', 140.
Medici, Lorenzo de', 7, 19 n., 84, 93 n., 94, 142, 142 n.
Medici, Pietro de', 19 n.
Meghen, Peter (Colet's amanuensis), 135.
melancholy, 127.
memory, 30, 32 and n., 90 n., 98, 99, 100 n.
Mens (concept in Ficino), 57, 105, 105 n.
Mercer's Hall, London, 137.
Mercury (the god), 85, 88, 128–9; as angelic inspiration, 141.
Mercury (planet), 129.
Messiah, 122.
Midas, 102.
Miles, Leland W., 38 n., 47, 52 n., 55, 90 n., 156–7.
Mills, Laurens J., 96 n.
Milo, 102.
Milton, John, 72 n., 76.

mind, 8, 9, 57, 84, 94, 101, 103–5, 109, 114, 128; music of the eternal, 90; of God, 103, 109
Minerva, 50, 59, 71, 131, 140, 143.
Minos, King of Crete, 88.
Mitchell, R. J., 16 n.
Monnier, M. L., 21 n.
moon, the, 19, 19 n., 81, 112, 130; as soul, 104, 107.
Moore Smith, G. C., 5 n.
Mora, Prebend of, 35.
More, Sir Thomas, 29, 38 n., 40, 41 n., 47, 52 n., 90 n., 152–3, 156–7.
mortification, doctrine of, 96 n.
Mosaic law, 121.
Moses, 53, 88.
motion, 8, 92, 101, 104, 111.
multiplicity as evil, 69–70, 92, 99, 99 n., 119–20; of form, 113.
muses, 19 n., 54, 91, 92, 115.
music in Ficino, 19 n.; of the spheres, 90, 91.
mystery religions, 45, 71 n., 92.
Mysticism, 41 n., 43 n., 60, 64.

'Nation', German, at Paris, 21 n.; at Orléans, 21 n.
nature, 7, 38 n., 99, 104; law of, 53, 97.
nectar (allegorical meaning), 47, 89, 90, 102.
Nelson, William, 3 n., 156.
Neoplatonism, 46, 52 n., 55 n., 72 n., 104 n.
Nero, 7, 142.
Nicolas, N. H., Sir, 153, 154.
Nietzsche, Friedrich Wilhelm, 78.
night and night-creatures, 109, 129, 143.
Nijhoff and Kronenberg, 150.
nobility, 101; of birth as human good, 87.
nous, 44; *see also* mind.
Numa, Pompilius, 88.
Numbers, *see* Bible.
Nygren, Anders, 45 n.

O'Brien, Gordon W., 110 n.
Oes, Fifteen, 10, 103.
O'Kelly, P. B., 149.
Oliver, R. P., 42 n.
One, the (Plotinus), 44, 120.
opacity, 113.

oracles, 126, 126 n.
order, soul's desire for, 91, 100, 126.
Origen, 45, 49, 52.
Orléans, France, 16, 21, 21 n., 34, 36; Bishop of: Ganay, Germain de, 34.
Orpheus, 19 n., 44, 53 n., 92, 92 n., 104 n.
Orphism, 85, 92 n., 122.
Osiris, 88.
Ovid, 46.
Oxford University, 4, 5, 14–37, 136, 156; All Souls College, 4, 5, 10, 14, 14 n., 16, 153.
Oxford, England, 78; Bible, study of, 22–23; Bishop of (Robert King), 131 n.; Colet's career at, 14–37, 48–49, 77; Lady Margaret Professorship at, 24.
'Oxford Hellenists', 40–41.
'Oxford Humanists', 41.
'Oxford Reformers', 23 n., 38 n., 40 n., 41, 116 n., 155, 156.

Padua, 16 n.
Palinode, 10, 114.
Pallas Athena, *see* Minerva.
Palmer, William, 154.
Panofsky, Erwin, 71 n.
Paris, 16, 21, 21 n., 22, 29, 36.
Parker, J., 43 n.
Parks, G. B., 16 n., 157.
Parsons, D. J., 157.
passion and reason, 105 n., 111–12; concupiscible and irascible, 111–12, 123–24.
Paternoster, 151.
patience, 84, 85, 95, 121.
Paul, St., 7, 20, 25, 25 n., 26, 26 n., 27 n., 30–32, 40–45, 50, 51, 52, 53 n., 59, 60, 64, 67, 69, 70, 71 n., 74, 78, 85, 109 n., 115, 117, 119, 130, 139, 141, 142, 143, 144, 145, 152; ascent to Heaven, 106, 108 n.; Colet's vocation of being a new, 39, 40; Ficino's conception of, 52; triad of (i.e. faith, hope, charity), 31, 33, 52, 60–68.
Pauline Epistles, *see* Epistles, Pauline; *see also* individual epistles listed under 'Bible'.
Pelagianism, 46.
Pelster, F., 48 n.
Perotti, Niccolò, 42 n., 114 n.
Peter Lombard, 22, 35.
Peter the Spaniard, 132.
Petrarch, 70.

INDEX

Philo Judaeus, 52 n.
Philopompi, 9, 98.
philosophers, pre-Christian, 121; pseudo-, as 'philopompi', 98; the highest class of men, 51, 128.
philosophies, the three (moral, natural, divine), 48.
philosophy, and philosophers, 26 n., and law, 85, 128, 129, 140, 144; Colet's views of, 38, 39, 41, 54, 54 n., 72, 90, 115–16, 141; Ficino's views of, 72, 85, 115–16, 127–9; moral, natural and divine, 141.
Phoebus Apollo, *see* Apollo.
physician, Christ as, 10, 103; Ficino as, 59; Hippocrates as, 51.
Piccolomini, Aeneas Sylvius, 17.
Pico della Mirandola, Giovanni, 27, 28, 31 n., 38, 44, 49, 105; *Heptaplus*, 27, 44, 49.
Piety, 87, 110, 125, 141; and friendship, 114; habitual, 101; towards God and man, 86; *see also* Holiness, Righteousness.
pig, Herod's, 122, 143.
Pimander, Hermetic, *see* Hermes.
Pits, John, 3, 3 n., 149, 152, 154.
planets, 72, 111, 129.
Plato, *Charmides*, 88 n.; Colet's reading of, at Oxford, 48–49; eloquence of, 48; *Laws*, 141; *Meno*, 48; *Parmenides*, 48; *Phaedo*, 46, 48; *Phaedrus*, 89 n., 143 n.; *Philebus*, 59; *Protagoras*, 141; *Republic*, 47, 85, 126, 126 n.; *Symposium*, 46, 60; *Theatetus*, 95 n.; *Timaeus*, 29 n., 46, 48, 122 n.; *summum bonum* in, 57; general references to, 43, 44, 46, 50, 52, 53, 57, 71 n., 86–88 n., 92–93, 102, 121, 140–2, 145.
Platonic Academy at Florence, *see* Careggi, Academy at.
Platonic theology, 85, 105, 111.
Platonism, 17, 27, 28, 38, 38 n., 42, 43, 46 n., 48; and Christianity, 43–47, 52, 55, 56, 60, 72 n.; and Neoplatonism, 46; and the Reformation, 66; Augustinian 55; Clementine, 55; Ficinian, 55 n.; Florentine, 43, 55; in Colet's thought, 70, 73, 77–78; *see also* Neoplatonism.
Platonists, 7, 19 n., 28, 30, 31, 40, 84, 85, 92 n., 103, 123, 144.
pleasure, 7, 41 n., 47 n., 56, 61 n., 86, 102, 109, 118, 119, 127, 142.

Plotinus, 43, 44, 46, 50, 53 n., 59; as key to Colet's thought, 47; Colet's reading of, at Oxford, 48–49; *Enneads*, 46.
Plutarch, 102 n.
poetry, and divine madness, 91; as imitation of divine harmony, 91; poetic madness, 91; renaissance, 71.
Poliziano, Angelo, 16.
polyp, 95.
Poppi, 132 n.
Porphyry, 131 n., 132 n.
power, 102, 110 n., 119; and wisdom of God, 51, 64, 116, 126, 146; as a human good, 64–65, 87; relation to law, 118.
Prat, Fernand, 42 n.
prayer, 7, 10, 26 n., 54, 87, 103, 116, 124, 138.
preaching and sermons, 39, 40, 40 n.
predicables, 131, 132.
pride, 124.
priesthood, Colet's view of the, 6, 12, 51, 92, 116, 117, 138.
primitivism, in Colet, 39.
Princeton University Library, 17 n., 153.
Proclus Diadochus, 85, 126.
Prometheus, 71, 88, 103, 141.
prophets, 32, 41.
Protestantism, 38, 38 n., 66.
providence, divine, 8, 9, 88, 103 n., 116, 117, 141; *divine* permitting adversity, 86, 130.
prudence, 87, 95–96, 99–100, 101, 127.
Pseudo-Dionysius, *see* Dionysius the Areopagite.
Pullus, Gratianus, 19 n.
punctuation, Colet's, 13.
purgation, 60, 64, 70; of sin, 63, 75, 94, 100, 120.
purification, Colet's doctrine of, 72, 75.
purity, 105.
Pythagoras, 121.

Quantity, 101, 111, 114.
Quintilian, 100 n.

Ralph, *see* Collingwood, Ralph.
Ramus, P., 131 n.
Rashdall, Hastings, 22 n.
ratio, concept in Ficino, 57.
reason, 68, 78, 87, 97, 99, 100, 101, 105, 105 n.; and natural truth, 87; and passion,

reason—*contd.*
    105 n., 111, 112; as centre of circle, 112 n.; as choice, 76; as faculty of soul, 111, 120; and law, 118.
Reformation, English, 66, 156, 157.
Regius, Johann, 132 n.
relics, Colet's view of, 19.
religion, 97, 99, 121, 129, 138, 139, 140, 142, 144; fostered by Saturn, 128–9.
revelation, 41, 44, 88 n.
Rice, E. F., Jr., 38 n., 70, 73 n., 75, 157.
Righteousness, 8, 97; *see also* Piety, Holiness.
Robb, Nesca, 5 n.
Rogers, Elizabeth F., 152–3.
Rome, 3 n., 17, 36, 37 n., 88 n., 102 n.
Rossi, Girolamo, 140.
Rowe, John G., 152.
Rufinus, 100 n.

Sacraments, Colet's views of, 90 n.
St. Martin's-le-Grand (London), 23, 23 n., 35.
St. Mary's, Walsingham, 154.
St Paul's Cathedral, 3, 14, 14 n., 16, 35, 36, 149, 151, 153, 155, 156.
St. Paul's School, 16, 30 n., 36, 38–40, 40 n., 137, 150–3, 156.
Salisbury, 35 n., 151; Bishop of (John Jewel), 3 n.
salvation, 7, 39, 40, 46, 56 n., 58, 62, 70, 73–76.
Salvinus (Salvini, Sebastiano: friend of Ficino), 50.
Sapientia, 70–73, 84, 115–16, 129, 141; *see also* wisdom.
Saturn (the god), 44, 59 n., 71, 85, 86, 128–9; the planet, 129.
Savonarola, Girolamo, 70.
Schirmer, Walter F., 156.
Scholasticism, 8, 8 n., 22, 26, 39, 40, 40 n., 48, 58, 156.
Schopenhauer, Arthur, 78.
Schroeder, Kurt, 38 n., 156.
Schweitzer, Albert, 25 n., 41 n.
Scotus, *see* Duns Scotus and Eriugena, Joannes.
Scylla and Charybdis, 127.
secularization, of Christianity, 41, 47, 70, 75; of concept of wisdom, 70, 75.

Seebohm, Frederic, 17 n., 23 n., 116 n., 155.
Seneca, Lucius Annaeus, 42.
senses, the five, 112, 120.
seraphim, *see* angels, ranks of.
Serrazin, Jean le (translator of Pseudo-Dionysius), 43 n.
shadows, 90, 110.
Shaw, W. H., 155.
Sibyl, Cumaean, 45, 122, 143.
sight (analogy to understanding), 128; *see also* sun.
Simonides, 100.
simplicity, 63, 69–70, 88, 99, 99 n., 105.
Simpson, W. S., 151, 156.
sins, 84, 95, 100, 118, 123–5, 138, 139, 142; the seven deadly, 45 n., 109, 123.
siren, the, 91.
sky, the, as an animal, 122.
Smith, Thomas, 150, 154.
Socrates, 45, 50, 51, 54, 69, 73, 89, 96 n., 115, 121, 127.
Solomon, King, 7, 51, 73, 116, 119, 142, 143.
Solon, 88.
Sophia (divine wisdom), 131.
Sophist, 139, 142.
Soteriology, 39, 40, 56 n., 58, 73–78.
Sotus, Dominicus, 131 n.
soul, the, 8, 71, 84, 88, 95, 97, 98, 110, 141; ascent to God of, 8, 39, 40, 45–47, 50, 52, 56, 58–75, 84, 89, 90, 93, 98, 107, 108, 111, 114, 120; as immortal, 98, 103 n., 109; as intellect, 106 n.; as life, 105; as moon, 104, 107; as ray of sun, 61, 65, 110; depraved condition of, 56, 71, 84, 96; Dialogue between Paul and the, 74; Dialogue between God and the, 84, 88, 139, 141; faculties of, 57, 58, 61, 73, 91, 111–12; descent of, 44–47, 52, 89, 120–1; nature of, 56–58, 139, 142; parts of, in Ficino, 57; wings of, 47, 89, 90; world, 8, 44, 58, 85, 91, 104, 114, 123–4; *see also* ascent.
Souter, A., 25 n.
Spenser, Edmund, 55 n., 76.
spheres, Muses as souls of, 91; music of the, 90, 91; the nine, 91, 108.
spirit, 8, 52, 64, 88, 98, 108, 111; and daemons, 123–5.
spirits, the appearance of, 126; nine orders of evil, 108.

INDEX

spiritus, Ficino's concept of, 19 n., 61, 64.
Stapleton, Thomas, 152–3.
stars, the, 111, 144; in astrology, 9, 117; representing angels, 104; signs not causes of events, 53, 118, 122, 139, 143.
Stegmüller, Friedrich, 25 n.
Stewart, H. L., 5 n.
Stoicism, 42, 42 n., 102.
strength as human good, 87, 102.
substance, 8; and the motion of the heavens, 104; four grades of, 105 n., soul as, 98.
Summa Theologica, see Thomas Aquinas, St.
summum bonum, 57, 118, 139, 143.
sun, and the moon, 81, 130; as alive, 104 n.; as father of lights, 144; as God, 19 n., 104–10, 112, 113, 119, 122; as Elijah, 107; as light, 105; as object of worship, 85, as peace, 86; as Truth, 105, 128; as Venus, 107; eclipse of, during the passion of Christ, 123; Ficino's book on the, 85, 129, 130, 140, 144, 145; metaphor, 19, 52, 61, 72 n.; Orphic comparison of, to God, 85; representing God, 19 n., 104; soul as ray of, 61, 65; worship of, 127, 140, 144.
Surtz, E. L., 40 n., 41 n., 47, 156.
Svendsen, Kester, 72 n.
Sybarites, 102 n.
Syria, 143.

Tables, Colet's interest in, 8.
Tambornini, Julius, 123 n.
Tanner, Thomas, 155.
temperance, 87, 100, 120.
Theanthropon, 33.
theocentric theology, 39, 52.
theology, Christian and Platonic, 43–50; Colet's study of abroad, 49; course in at Oxford, 15–37; Platonic, 85, 105, 111.
Théry, D., 43 n.
Thomas Aquinas, St., 29 n., 58, 59, 70, 76.
Thomism, 56 n., 61.
Thurning, Hampshire, 15, 17 n.
Torrigiano, Pietro (Florentine sculptor), 156.
Toul, France, 21 n.
Trapp, J. B., 10, 12, 91 n., 92 n., 131 n.
Traversari, Ambrosia, 29, 43 n.
Trinity, doctrine of the, 44, 109.
Trismegistus, Hermes, see Hermes Trismegistus.

Truth, 41, 44, 45, 47, 52, 57, 59, 78, 90, 100, 109–11, 119; and goodness, 72, 118; as arcane, 71, 87; as attribute of God, 64, 105, 106; and mythology, 71; the sun of, 105, 128; three classes of, 87.
twins, in the heavens, 85, 129, 140, 144.

Unity, and simplicity as goods, 92, 119–20; as attribute of God, 62–65, 105, 109; of form, 113; *see also* One, the.
Uranius, Martin, 126 n.
Urswick, Christopher, Dean of York, 17, 153.

Valla, Lorenzo, 29, 29 n.
Vallombrosa, 132 n.
Venice, 4, 13.
Venus (the goddess), 44, 45, 54, 59, 71, 86, 92, 107, 115, 131, 140, 143, 144; (the planet), 72, 129.
Vergil, Polydore, 154.
Vieri, Francesco, 46 n.
Virgil, 46, 91.
virtues, definition of, 84, 98, 100, 102; pagan, 87; Pauline (faith, hope and charity), 60–68; public, 84, 94.
visibilia, 7, 27 n., 89; *see also invisibilia*.
Vitrier, *Life* of Jehan (Erasmus), 12 n., 154.
voluntarism, 55–78.

Walker, D. P., 19 n., 92 n.
war, 7, 86, 143.
Wardman, A. E., 10, 12.
Warham, William, Archbishop of Canterbury, 156.
West, R. H., 123 n.
Wharton, Henry, 23 n., 35 n., 154.
Wilkins, E. G., 71 n.
Whittaker, Thomas, 43 n.
will, and intellect, 56–78, 83, 101, 102, 103 n., 105, 106, 109; as love in Ficino, 57, 82; as opposed to law, 118; Augustinian concept of, 59; correspondence to hope, 60–68; faculty of the, 57, 94–95; freedom of, 42, 73–75, 121; good, 42, 121; right, 97, 98; the divine, 97, 106.
Winchcombe, Abbot of (Kidderminster, Richard), 4 n., 23, 26, 153.
Wind, Edgar, 71 n., 92 n.
Wirsung, Christoph, 32 n., 155.

wisdom, 53, 70–74, 84, 87, 89–91, 94–95, 99–101, 119, 125, 128, 141; and the priesthood, 51, 117; as Mercury, 128–9; as power to distinguish good and evil, 51, 73, 116; as self-knowledge, 115; as Sophia, 131; correspondence to Jupiter, 50; God as, 87, 91, 115; of God, 51, 90, 91, 116.
Wolsey, Cardinal Thomas, 151, 153.
Wood, Anthony à, 14, 15, 25 n., 35 n., 48, 155.
Wordsworth, Christopher, 24 n.
works and faith, 74–75.
world, as creator, 95; end of the, 104; eye of the, 104 n.; visible, 128.
world body, the, 104, 123.
world soul, the, 8, 9, 44, 58, 85, 91, 104, 114, 123–4.
Wylford, Edmund, 22, 25.

Xamolsis, *see* Zalmoxis.

Zalmoxis, 88.
Zautrastes, *see* Zoroaster.
Zeno, 74, 102 n.
Zoroaster, 45, 59, 88.